Reading Riots

For Mary

Reading Riots

Protest and Violence in Late Modernity

Tim Newburn

polity

First published in 2026 by Polity Press Ltd.

Polity Press Ltd.
65 Bridge Street
Cambridge CB2 1UR, UK

Polity Press Ltd.
111 River Street
Hoboken, NJ 07030, USA

ISBN-13: 978-1-5095-7120-8
ISBN-13: 978-1-5095-7121-5(pb)

A catalogue record for this book is available from the British Library.

Library of Congress Control Number: 2025951467

Typeset in 10.5 on 12 pt Plantin MT Pro by
Cheshire Typesetting Ltd, Cuddington, Cheshire
Printed and bound in Great Britain by Ashford Colour Ltd.

For further information on Polity, visit our website:
politybooks.com

Contents

Detailed Contents

Acknowledgements

The material in this book is in part the product of many years teaching, and I am grateful to the cohorts of students that have taken *SP475 Riots, Disorder and Urban Violence* over the course of the past ten years. Their emerging enthusiasm for the subject of what some might see as a somewhat left-field master's option allowed me to feel that riots and protest violence were phenomena worthy of extended examination and discussion. One of the joys of teaching at the LSE has been the fact that my students are drawn not just from my own department (Social Policy) but from across the School, from law, sociology, political science, geography, human rights, philosophy, international relations and much besides. The subject of collective disorder has pretty much bookended my career as a researcher. My very first university job in 1981 was as a research associate on an ESRC (then SSRC) study of collective violence in twentieth-century Britain, and I owe a significant debt to the late Eric Dunning, and to Patrick Murphy and Ivan Waddington, then of Leicester's Sociology Department, for taking a chance on me.

I didn't return to the subject as a researcher for almost 30 years, and then in many respects quite by chance as a consequence of a huge study of the England riots of 2011 that I ended up co-directing with Paul Lewis of the *Guardian* newspaper. It was that study that renewed my engagement with the subject of collective violence and eventually led to my teaching the subject. We took the decision in the *Guardian*/LSE study that we would eschew academic publications (pretty brave, given the Research Excellence Framework and all the other governmental instruments increasingly dominating university life), at least for the first few years, and that we would publish all the findings from the study in the newspaper, on the *Guardian*'s website or in film or other media. After a period of around four years, I did turn to more traditional forms of academic publication, and I would like to thank the editors of a number of journals for permission to quote extensively and otherwise utilize material from the following articles: T. Newburn (2015), 'The 2011 England Riots in Recent Historical Perspective', *British Journal of Criminology* 55(1): 39–64; T. Newburn, R. Diski, K. Cooper, R. Deacon, A. Burch and M. Grant (2018), '"The Biggest Gang"?: Police and People in the 2011 England Riots', *Policing and Society* 28(2): 205–22; T. Newburn, K. Cooper, R. Deacon and R. Diski (2015), 'Shopping for Free? Looting, Consumerism and the 2011 Riots', *British Journal of Criminology* 55(5): 987–1004; T. Newburn (2016), 'Reflections on Why Riots Don't Happen', *Theoretical Criminology* 20(2): 125–44; T. Newburn (2016), 'The 2011 England Riots in European Context: A Framework for Understanding the "Life-Cycle" of Riots', *European Journal of Criminology* 13(5): 540–55; T. Newburn, Rachel Deacon, Beka Diski, Kerris Cooper, Maggie Grant and Alex Burch (2018), '"The Best Three Days of My Life": Pleasure, Power and Alienation in the 2011 Riots', *Crime, Media, Culture* 14(1): 41–59; T. Newburn, T. Jones and J. Blaustein (2018), 'Framing the 2011 England Riots: Understanding the Political and Policy Response', *Howard Journal of Criminal Justice* 57(3): 339–62; T. Newburn (2021), 'The Causes and Consequences of Urban Riot and Unrest', *Annual Review of Criminology* 4: 53–73.

Although by the time I came to write this book publishers no longer had any appetite for a volume that would focus primarily on the 2011 England riots, the scale and originality of that project meant, of course, that I nevertheless drew on it quite heavily in certain sections of this book. In that context, I owe a very sizeable debt to Paul Lewis, the *Guardian* lead on the study and someone who played a key role in every aspect of the research as it proceeded. There are a large number of others connected with that project to whom I'm indebted, including: Matthew Taylor, James Ball, Alex Burch, Kerris Cooper, Rachel Deacon, Rebekah Diski, Maggie Grant, Simon Rogers, Symeon Brown, Paul Owen, the late Eric Allison, Catriona Mcgillivray, Hugh Muir, Ben Ferguson, Alexandra Topping, Amelia Gentleman, Shiv Malik, Fiona Bawdon, Raekha Prasad, Kamara Scott, Suzanne Hyde, Aster Greenhill, Harold Frayman, Yemisi Adegoke, Josh Surtees, Brendan Donegan, Robert Kazandjian, Jamie Mitchell, Alan Morgan, Mags Casey, Helen Clifton, Sam Kelly, Nick Owen, Helen Porter, Anthony Schumacher, Katinka Weber, Sarah Eberhardt, Sarah Hewitt, Aimee Ashton-Freeman,

Rosa Bransky, Sarah O'Connell, Elizabeth Pears, Sonya Thomas, Josephine Metcalf, Daniel Silver, Carol Cooper, Simon Jay, Helen Carter and Paul Cotterill. It is a long list and my sincere apologies to anyone I have left out. I would like to extend my particular thanks to the Joseph Rowntree Foundation and the Open Society Foundations, who funded the study (in double-quick time), and to Alan Rusbridger, the then editor of the *Guardian*, and Professor Judith Rees, the then Interim Director of the LSE, for putting faith in us to run such an unusual, and risky, venture.

Where the book itself is concerned, my biggest debt is to Paul Rock. Paul very kindly read every chapter as I produced it, usually within half a day, and was instrumental in keeping me going and in sharpening my thinking. He has been both good friend and kind mentor for many, many years now. I am grateful to David Garland for his kindness and support, to Sebastian Roché for advice on developments in France, and to Dave Hill from *On London* for advice and support on matters in the capital. For general support, encouragement, thoughtfulness and friendship, my thanks to George Mair, Trevor Jones, Coretta Phillips, David Downes, Niki Lacey, Rod Morgan, Jill Peay, Frances Heidensohn, Andrew Dillon, Alison Goodbrand, Chris Kenn, Liz Gibb, John Williams, David Smith, Robert Reiner, Rod Earle, Adam Crawford, Kieran McEvoy, Mike Levi, Richard Sparks, Lesley McAra, Susan McVie, Michael Tonry, Carolyn Hoyle, Mike Maguire, Ian Loader, Simon Cottle, Lucia Zedner, Miranda Bevan, Emma Louise Blondes, Betsy Stanko, Dick Hobbs, Thomas Guiney, Judith Rumgay, Eugene McLaughlin, Brian Willan, the late 'Tank' Waddington, Kate Williams, the late Andy Ward, Ali Fraser, Luke Billingham, Fern Gillon, Keir Irwin-Rogers, Barry Goldson, Stephanie Hayman, Stuart Lister, David Churchill, Charlie Lloyd, Sharon Grace, Stephen Farrall, Jenni Ward, Dave Wall, David Whyte, Clive Walker, David Dixon, Leo Cheliotis, Alistair Henry, Mary Bosworth, Nigel South, Eamonn Carrabine, Tom Sutton, Richard Martin, Tom Daems, Shadd Maruna, Bernard Walker, Larry Sherman, Heather Strang, Lisa Miller, Michael Welch, Caroline Porter, Gillian Stern, Miranda Nunhofer, Natalie Aguilera, Mark Buckle and Level Crossing Records, Alan Dearling, Rob Canton, Ben Bowling, Mike Levi, Michael Tonry, Alice Sampson, Loïc, Wacquant, Johann Koehler, Lol Burke, Jon Jackson, Elaine Player, Alyce McGovern, Rachel Condry, Jennifer Brown, Ali McGuire, Ben Bradford, Richard Garside, Pat McGovern and Magnus Hörnqvist. My apologies again to anyone I've missed out.

At Polity Press, although he is no longer there, sincere thanks are due to my original editor, Jonathan Skerrett. I had not worked with Polity before and I found him to be a thoughtful and attentive editor. Since his departure, I have had the good fortune to work with Gail Ferguson, Evie Deavall, Karina Jákupsdóttir, Gregory Miller, Julia Davies and Glynis Baguley.

The past couple of years have been something of a roller-coaster ride for me. That I'm here to post acknowledgements is in no small part due to the teams of professionals that have looked after me, initially at St George's Hospital, Tooting, and subsequently at Guy's and St Thomas's Hospital, London. My debt to the UK's National Health Service and to Cancer Research UK is simply vast.

All of which leads me to my family. Here lie the greatest debts and the greatest joy. My love and thanks to all the Newburn–Laisby–Moorhouse clan and partners. A huge hug to my children – Gavin, Robin, Lewis and Owen – and to my grandchildren – Georgia, Freya, Ethan, Bea and Morgan. This book is dedicated to Mary, the person who makes it all possible and worthwhile.

1
Rorschach and Riots

Though artists as far back as Leonardo da Vinci in the fifteenth century were interested in how ink blots could be used to stimulate imagination, it was the early twentieth century before their academic psychological potential began to be exploited. A year before his untimely death in 1922 at the age of 37, the Swiss psychiatrist Hermann Rorschach published the results of an experiment using ten symmetrical ink blots. The blots were the basis for an analysis of the personalities of his respondents. The study compared patients who had a variety of diagnosed mental illnesses with healthy individuals. Asking his respondents, 'What might this be?', Rorschach found, for example, that those with schizophrenia often reported seeing things in the blots that others didn't.

By mid-century, though he was no longer around to see it, Rorschach's eponymous test had become highly popular, in particular in US psychology and psychiatry. At the height of the optimism that surrounded its use, it was variously described as an 'X-ray of the mind' and a 'window on the unconscious'. Under the influence of Freudian psychology and a concern with the unconscious, concentration moved further towards the symbolic nature of interpretation of the blots. Fundamentally, the basis of Rorschach's claims proceeded from an analysis of how his subjects projected meanings onto the blots and what they claimed they saw in them. Though in more recent times the test has become highly controversial, the overall impact is such that Rorschach's blots remain well known, these days more through their association with children's imaginative games than for any widespread psychological application.

I want to suggest here – and I am by no means the first – that many of the claims that are often made about collective gatherings, especially those that become violent, appear little more reliable than the interpretations of ink blots. In everything that follows, I will be at pains to offer a reminder that we must always be careful when assessing what is claimed about riots and protest violence. The reality is that commentators often see in riots the things they want to see. Scholarly approaches to riots and rioters often reflect the standpoint, and perhaps elements of the political preferences, of the authors involved. One of the psychological mechanisms at work here may be *projection*, often a defence mechanism in which an observer uses personal experiences to imbue an ambiguous outside representation with meaning. To some degree, their assumptions, values and prejudices are played out in their interpretations of events. This is not to say their claims are necessarily wrong, or entirely wrong, rather that the claims made are often revealing of the value position of those making them.

As we will see as the book unfolds, this type of projection is perhaps most obviously and straightforwardly seen in the case of politicians who are often asked to respond quickly, if not immediately, to major events such as riots. That the observations of political figures of all stripes regularly reflect their priorities, their preferences and even their prejudices shouldn't surprise us, or necessarily concern us. That politicians make political claims about riots and rioters is not, in principle, a problem. In practice, however, serious consequences can flow from such (mis)interpretations, most obviously in influencing how riots are understood by others, how they are responded to (the actions of the police and courts, for example) and, linked with this, the knock-on effects for both the individuals caught up in the penal system and the wider communities affected. This tendency to read into riots the things we wish to see isn't just a characteristic of politicians' interpretations, it is often true also of academic analysis, and I will briefly illustrate this below and at greater length later. The broad point I wish to make here by way of introduction is a simple one: whenever claims are made about the nature of riots and those who riot, it pays to be sceptical and to question the basis on which any assertions are made.

One way of illustrating this tendency is to begin with the approach of the French psychologist Gustave Le Bon – we will return to him in the next chapter and throughout the book. His ideas about crowds, and about violent crowds more particularly, dominated thinking in the first half of the twentieth century and, though largely discredited now, continue to influence popular conceptions of riots and rioting. As we will see in more detail later, Le Bon, writing in the late nineteenth century, held a largely negative and pessimistic view of crowd power. He considered collective gatherings to be dangerous, their members losing themselves and their individuality and behaving in foreign and uncontrolled ways. In this view, crowd members are easily influenced and in losing their individuality return to a more primitive and animalistic state. As he pithily put it, 'In crowds it is stupidity and not mother-wit that is accumulated' (Le Bon 1952 [1895]: 29).

Le Bon's ideas had many sources. There were other academic arguments on which he drew – indeed, sufficiently so for some to consider him a plagiarist – but, more widely, he and others interested in crowds, their activities and their power were much influenced by the times in which they were writing. In addition to Le Bon, authors such as Hippolyte Taine (a French historian), Gabriel Tarde (a French sociologist) and Scipio Sighele (an Italian psychologist) all reflected the widespread concern that existed in the late nineteenth century about the potential impact of the masses. Le Bon, as we will see, saw the times in which he was writing as the 'era of crowds'. That France should perhaps be the signal source of such claims is largely unsurprising. The success, albeit very brief, of the Paris Commune, the revolutionary government which seized power in 1871 and ushered in the French Third Republic, was anything but stable. The Boulanger crisis – named after the French general and war minister who was accused of plotting to overthrow the state in the late 1880s – was indicative of the Republic's fragility. Not only were these febrile political times but, particularly for those on the right, there were growing concerns about the demoralization of French society. It is against this backdrop, and the troubles that would cast a shadow over Europe until the mid-twentieth century, that Le Bon's and others' largely negative characterization of the masses was conceived. In short, and crudely, much of Le Bon's allegedly scholarly approach to the study of crowds was little more than the dressing up of fairly standard assumptions and late-nineteenth-century fears about mass behaviour (see also Canetti 1962). Much persuaded by Le Bon, in Freud's view the masses were 'lazy and unintelligent', standing outside or beneath civilization (Brantlinger 1983: 167).

As the impact on Freud indicated, Le Bon was extraordinarily influential. One observer suggests that in terms of copies sold, *La Psychologie des Foules* (the original French title of the book) was 'one of the greatest scholarly successes of all times' (Moscovici 1985). Famously, there is evidence that both Mussolini and Hitler were influenced by his work, the Italian claiming to have read all his books and to have received autographed copies from the author. Hitler had a copy of *Psychologie des Foules* in his private library in Vienna, and one author goes so far as to attempt to demonstrate that significant elements of *Mein Kampf* were heavily based on Le Bon's text (Stein 1955). His influence was by no means confined to those on the political right. It is said that Lenin had a heavily annotated copy of at least one of Le Bon's books, and Theodore Roosevelt met Le Bon in Paris in 1914, apparently informing the Frenchman of the importance of his work. That dictators and mass murderers were fans of Le Bon's scholarship naturally contributed to the eventual fall in popularity and influence of his work, not least in academic circles. The backlash was substantial, leading not just to the eventual rejection of the majority of Le Bon's ideas about collective behaviour but, arguably, something of a decline in academic interest in collective behaviour generally.

Slowly but surely, what emerged during the twentieth century was a set of approaches to collective behaviour which increasingly rejected notions of irrationality and loss of individuality, or which saw crowd members as primitive and uncontrolled, and progressively favoured a view which took crowds, including riotous crowds, to be engaged in rational, deliberative conduct. Once again, this reflected intellectual trends more generally, including the influence of the rise of rational choice theory, the emergence of symbolic interactionism as well as changes in the underlying politics of social science. The growth of sociology and a new 'history from below', with its concern with 'the recovery of subjective experience' (Samuel 1981: xviii), both contributed to a burgeoning interest in understanding rather than ignoring or dismissing the lives of those involved in protest violence. In addition to changing academic trends, there were wider social and political changes, not least the American civil rights movement in the 1960s, which pointed towards a more constructive political role for collective crowd conduct. The US urban riots of the same era were then increasingly viewed through such a lens, with rioters treated as having genuine grievances, and the disorders themselves as being, at least in part, articulate forms of protest (Fogelson 1967). The historian George Rudé's work, for example, countered the view that crowds were composed primarily of the criminal and the marginal and challenged the inclination of historians to 'take refuge behind such omnibus and prejudicial . . . labels as "mob"' (Rudé 1964: 195). The prejudices of the late nineteenth century had, by just after the mid-twentieth, largely been shaken off and replaced by a left-wing, in some cases Marxist, historiography, together with the concerns of a more liberal (post-civil rights movement) sociology in which, for example, Howard Becker (1967) was asking 'Whose side are we on?' The aim of both now was to see the world through the eyes of those who had previously been ignored – the members of the crowd – albeit that, so far as critics were concerned, this new outlook was often accompanied by a degree of naivety and romanticism.

I have wanted to make two simple, linked points in this introduction. First, academic fashions have changed and, with them, so too have the ways in which crowd behaviour is broadly understood – and I will look at this in some detail in the coming chapters. But linked to this is the wider point, that claims about crowds, especially political claims about the nature of crowds, often reflect the values and prejudices of the claimant and little more. Put slightly differently, we might simply observe that this is a case where meaning is not fixed, and attempting to privilege one meaning over others is, as Stuart Hall (1997: 228) reminds us, 'the work of a representational practice'. One consistent line of analysis that runs through the remainder of this volume, then, concerns matters of representation. How do we see riots? How do we talk about them? One modern social movement, Occupy Wall Street, was often known by its slogan, 'We are the 99%', something that might be thought of as a 'floating signifier', 'amorphous enough for many different kinds of people to connect with and to see their values within the symbol' (Smucker 2011). Much of my concern therefore is with language and terminology and the implication of the choices that are made. This applies as much to academic debate and discussion as it does to political and public discourses. In all cases, matters of representation tend to involve a struggle, a tussle, a contest over alternatives for, as Rock (1981) reminds us, 'Meaning is rarely established at the beginning of an event – it is more often bestowed retrospectively'. And, importantly (important enough to be repeated regularly in coming chapters), in the midst of an academic trend that emphasizes the rationality and wisdom of crowds, it can often feel 'as if riots cannot be innocent of profound meaning' (Rock 1981). This makes the job of the analyst of collective conduct a tricky one, the aim being to chart a course that avoids the reductionism of early psychological approaches while simultaneously sidestepping the tendency towards over-rationalization found in some contemporary sociological accounts.

My focus in what follows is primarily on the riots that have occurred in the past half-century or so. Many scholars see this period as distinctive, and, for some, it is even resonant of revolutionary Europe of the 1830s and 1840s. According to the French philosopher

Alain Badiou (2012: 41), we currently live in times that bear 'an uncanny resemblance' to the 1815–50 period in France and Europe. The 'rebirth of history', as he terms it, has witnessed the resurgence of mass protest. It heralds a new age of riots. Joshua Clover, the cultural theorist, argues similarly. The title of his (2016) book *Riot, Strike, Riot* gives a sense of how he sees the trajectory of historical change. The first shift was away from riot towards strike. In this vein, Charles Tilly (1983: 464), for example, argued that sometime in the nineteenth century 'the people of most western countries shed the [riotous] collective action repertoire they had been using for two centuries or so'. Although both the riot and the strike continued to be utilized, the strike came to predominate from the mid-nineteenth century, as riots declined in visibility. What has occurred more recently, Clover argues, is the reversal of that trend with now the riot coming once again to the fore. If Badiou and Clover are correct, we are in the new age of riots. Importantly, however, the nature of riots has changed: 'riot after riot begins now not at the granary but at the police station, literally or figuratively, incited by the police murder of a young person with dark skin, or following on the failure of the legal apparatus to hold the police adequately responsible for their violence.' Clover takes the Los Angeles riots of 1992 – riots we will consider in some detail later in the book – to be the paradigmatic example of this modern form of riot. Increasingly, Clover (2016: 11) argues, 'the contemporary riot transpires within a logic of racialization and takes the state rather than the economy as its direct antagonist'.

It is this allegedly new form of riot, and the forms of protest that precede and accompany it, that are my main concern here. In the substantive discussions that follow, I'll examine aspects of the history of riotous protest, the nature and focus of contemporary protest and riots, debates around rationality, the role of emotion in protest and violence, the nature and consequences of policing strategies and conduct, how modern social movements affect protest, and the different legacies of riots and protest violence. In each and all of these, I will argue that matters of representation are central. How we see, discuss, communicate, exemplify and symbolize the actions that make up protest and protest-related violence, together with the beliefs associated with such conduct, lies at the heart of the concerns in this volume.

2
Fear of the Mob

Robert Shoemaker (1987) suggests the term 'the mob' was first used to denote rioters in London in the late 1670s, though there are solid reasons for placing it much earlier (Clement 2016). Certainly, from there it gradually entered common parlance to denote disorderly crowds and, even more generally, to describe a crowd believed or assumed to have disorderly potential, even if there was no evidence of actual violence. Deriving from the Latin *mobile vulgus* (a moveable or excitable crowd), the 'mob' became an established feature of commentary, academic and popular, about life in eighteenth-century Britain and beyond. Thomas Paine, for example, observed that there was 'in all European countries a large class of people of that description, which in England is called the *Mob*' (Paine 1951: 32). From at least the time of the Gordon Riots in London and the fall of the Bastille in Paris in the 1780s, there was widespread worry about the seemingly new-found power of the masses, though concern about the London Apprentice riots can be found as early as the 1590s (see Suzuki 1996), and we can go back at least as far as the time of the Roman emperors to find similar fears about the power of the mob, hence Juvenal's reference to the 'bread and circuses' used to buy them off (Brantlinger 1983). The consequences of industrialization and urbanization focused attention on the activities of the labouring classes and to the incipient danger that was believed to lie within the crowd. Such views coloured historical accounts as well as political discourse, and 'mob' became a barely disguised condemnation of the nature of such collective activity. Stevenson (1979: 10) suggests 'mob' was utilized in two broad ways: specifically as a reference to hired gangs operating on behalf of external bodies, even governments occasionally, to act against political opponents, and, more widely, 'to describe the common people, the multitude or the lower orders generally. It carries implications usually of the "rabble", the lowest sections of society, driven by criminal dispositions and immorality to participate in disturbances.'

Famously associated with the early policing of England's capital, Patrick Colquhoun estimated that up to a tenth of London's population was made up of criminal and associated types. These 'impressionistic estimates' were much criticized, not least by the radical historian E. P. Thompson in his most famous work, *The Making of the English Working Class,* as having been much affected by 'the atmosphere of panic in the aftermath of the French Revolution', an event that coloured pretty much everything in its shadow. That said, Thompson was careful to note that despite the scaremongering about the power of the masses, the fears were by no means without foundation. France had had its violent revolution. 'The British people were noted throughout Europe for their turbulence, and the people of London astonished foreign visitors by their lack of deference' (1968: 66). Nevertheless, what were sometimes presented as careful analyses of popular disturbances in the period were little more than reflections of established prejudices about the working poor, many carrying a clear political message about the status and character of the people involved. This affected even the most sophisticated analyses, including Thompson's occasionally romanticized view of the English working class. The political element in historiography can be illustrated by quoting briefly from the work of Christopher Hibbert, widely described as one of most popular British historians of the twentieth century.[1] Hibbert offered the following descriptions of the anti-Catholic Gordon Riots in 1780, the activities involved, and the nature of some of the rioters:

> Encouraged by troublemakers, prostitutes and runaway apprentices and led by criminals, ordinary, normally quiet and honest people were no longer either willing or able to stand idly watching but felt compelled to join in, forced on by the excitement of violence, the satisfaction of destruction and the chance of loot . . . . In alliance with these criminals and fanatics were the thousands upon thousands of ordinary, poor working men and women and children, flowing out of the slums . . . converging like a sea upon any place where excitement seemed to be offered and there [they] joined with others and became a mob. And thus spontaneously created a mob, they were urged to violence by that sensual, reactive impulse which brings a mob together and which forces it on to devastation, losing their identities in a fusing welter of destruction . . . . They struck out in irrational, unthinking desperation,

> unconsciously hoping to release in their uproar the frustrations and irritations of years of neglect. Any reason for violence would have done. Only the spark was needed. (Hibbert 2004 [1958]: 72, 92)

Here Hibbert, reflecting many contemporary assumptions, presents the crowd as impulsive, reactive, irrational, unthinking, unconscious, intoxicated and often led by the criminal and disreputable. Though more subtle and varied interpretations of the Gordon riots emerged (see, for example, Thompson 1968), it was the criminal, violent and seemingly inchoate nature of crowd conduct that held sway for some considerable time. And while such views have rightly been the subject of extensive criticism, to completely neglect these elements of collective conduct is, as George Rudé (1964: 237) put it, 'hardly more realistic' than presenting them as entirely 'revolutionary'.

The crowd: a study in the popular mind

One figure and one figure alone bestrides discussions of riots and riotous crowds: the French author Gustave Le Bon. His fame is partly the result of his enormous influence on beliefs about crowd behaviour in the first half of the twentieth century and partly a consequence of the almost complete scholarly rejection of his ideas in the second half. Though now largely discredited, his views continue to echo in the statements that politicians and others make in discussions of violent crowds, and they infuse popular understandings and assumptions about the conduct of people en masse. His ideas are now intellectually unpopular, but they retain considerable intuitive attraction. Briefly, Le Bon emphasized what he took to be the primitive, animalistic tendencies of humans in sizeable groups. In essence, his view was that individuals lose their sense of themselves and their normal restraints when acting in a group. In short, in this view crowd conduct, especially violent crowd conduct, is viewed as the product of irrational individuals surrendering to the power of the collective. Such opinions, popular in the early twentieth century, gradually lost their grip as the century wore on, and by the sixties and seventies were being severely challenged by scholars from a range of disciplines who, by contrast, sought to identify and to stress the fundamental rationality of collective behaviour. This divide, this tension, between perspectives that emphasize the apparent senselessness of crowd violence on the one hand, and those that view such conduct as being both meaningful and goal oriented on the other, will form one important backdrop to much of the argument in this book. It is reflected in different academic perspectives, not least in different approaches within psychology but also, albeit to a lesser degree, within history and sociology. But it is important to begin with Le Bon.

Born in 1841, Gustave Le Bon initially qualified as a doctor of medicine, though he never practised except in the military (as did the famous Italian physician and criminologist Cesare Lombroso). He served in the French army during the Franco-Prussian war before spending some years travelling, something that, in part, stimulated or reinforced his interest in anthropology. Writing from his student days, Le Bon was considered something of a polymath and published books on science, on Arab and Indian civilization and culture, and even on the psychology of the horse. Despite an unsuccessful nomination for the Nobel Prize in physics in 1903, within his prodigious output it is his work on the psychology of the crowd for which he is remembered. Van Ginneken (1992: 133) says Le Bon 'closely monitored scientific innovations and often took up new approaches before they had caught on, trying to improve and apply them himself'. He was a scholarly magpie as well as a popularizer of ideas – both something of a remarkable practising scientist as well as a nineteenth-century Malcolm Gladwell.[2]

Among Le Bon's early publications were pieces that compared the skull sizes and shapes of different races and classes, some of which were subsequently quoted by Lombroso. Beyond this emphasis on the physiological, his interests moved increasingly towards matters psychological, leading to his most famous work, *Psychologie des Foules*, which was published in 1895 and was translated into English as *The Crowd: A Study of the Popular Mind.* The book must be placed in context, both in terms of the times and circumstances in which it was published and also against the background of Le Bon's wider body of work. In terms of his own corpus, *Psychologie des Foules* had been preceded the previous year by a volume entitled *Lois Psychologiques de l'Évolution des Peuples*, intended in the main as a summation of much of Le Bon's psychological, historical and anthropological work in the 1880s. It ranged widely, examining what influenced the rise and fall of civilizations, exposing what it took to be the negative role of modern egalitarian ideas (van Ginneken 1992) and outlining the dangers facing the modern world. The dangers of the masses were shadowed in this volume and reflected the generalized pessimism about such collectivities that was common at the time (Spengler 1926).

As widely discussed, a range of historical events had a profound influence on Le Bon's thinking, not least those most intimately linked with France's revolutionary history. The Paris Commune, for example, appears to have made quite a mark, and closer in time the so-called 'Boulanger episode' was similarly influential. A French general, Boulanger was appointed minister of war in the mid-1880s. A divisive figure, he was at the heart of rapidly rising tensions between France and Germany. He was excluded from a newly formed government in 1887, leading to considerable public protest and, eventually, to Boulanger's dismissal from the army for his political activities (which were illegal for a serving officer) and exile to provincial France. In the eyes of some, this cemented his status as hero and martyr. His political career, now formally possible, continued, and returning to the capital he won election in 1889, with tens of thousands taking to the streets in celebration. Fearing his potential accession to high office, his opponents began to organize against him, putting him under constant surveillance, including 'tapping' his phone. Spooked, he left the country. The scale of popular support for Boulanger, however, reinforced fears about the power of crowds and, more particularly, the apparent ease with which they could be (mis)led. Van Ginneken (1992: 160) quotes one analyst as observing that his supporters, the Boulangist League of Patriots, were 'the first of many movements organized not for electoral and parliamentary action, but for the mobilization and manipulation of crowds outside the established structure of parties and parliament, indeed, even against them'. Le Bon, it seems, felt that Boulanger simply lacked sufficient skill or purpose to bring about his objectives, for having become suddenly popular he might 'easily have found a hundred thousand men ready to sacrifice their lives for his cause had he demanded it' (Le Bon 1952 [1895]: 37). Alongside this affair, the growing influence of socialism in France and a developing anti-parliamentarianism all served to focus attention on the potential power of collective action.

It was against this background and a growing scholarly interest in crowds – including influential work by the French sociologist Gabriel Tarde and Italian psychologist Scipio Sighele – that Le Bon's book was published. That there was widespread concern about the fragility of social order no doubt contributed to the quick success of Le Bon's ideas. That said, to what extent these can be entirely portrayed as Le Bon's ideas caused considerable dispute from the outset (van Ginneken 1985). Indeed, Scipio Sighele, a student of Lombroso and Ferri, accused Le Bon of piracy. The book itself begins by placing the crowd at the centre of modern history. According to Le Bon, 'While all our ancient beliefs are tottering and disappearing, while the old pillars of society are giving way one by one, the power of the crowd is the only force that nothing menaces, and of which the prestige is continually on the increase. The age we are about to enter will in truth be the ERA OF CROWDS' (Le Bon 1952 [1895]: 14; emphasis in original).

The era of crowds is a dangerous one, however, for Le Bon felt collective claims increasingly amounted 'to nothing less than a determination to utterly destroy society as it now exists' (1952 [1895]: 15). Though notions of crowds as mad, antisocial and irrational were commonplace, Le Bon's position was more complex. He accepted that criminal crowds undoubtedly existed, for example, but countered that 'virtuous and heroic crowds, and crowds of many other kinds, are also to be met with' (1952 [1895]: 19). To a degree, therefore, he sought to challenge many prevailing orthodoxies, including those that held that crowd members tended to be mentally deranged, criminal or drawn from the very lowest social strata. Nevertheless, he viewed them as dangerous, not least because of the way in which the individual conscious personality could be subsumed by the collective mind. Irrespective of who the individuals were who made up the crowd, the power of this collective mind would make 'them feel, think and act in a manner quite different from that in which each individual of them would feel, think and act were he in a state of isolation' (Le Bon 1952 [1895]: 27).

If they weren't intrinsically criminal or mad, how was it crowds constituted such a threat? For Le Bon and others, it was what happened to individuals as a consequence of becoming part of a crowd. Crowds, in his view, were not simply an amalgam of those that constituted them but, rather, became something different: 'Under certain given circumstances, and only under those circumstances, an agglomeration of men presents new characteristics very different from those of the individuals composing it' (Le Bon 1952 [1895]: 23). In the second half of the nineteenth century, there had been considerable interest in hypnosis and cognate ideas such as hallucinations, mesmerism and somnambulism, concerns which had a degree of influence on Le Bon. Ideas such as hypnotic suggestion and the influence of contagion had a growing impact on work on crowd behaviour in both France and Italy in the years before Le Bon's celebrated treatise was published. The French sociologist Gabriel Tarde, for example, said the following in 1890:

> A *mob* [*foule*] is a strange phenomenon. It is a gathering of heterogeneous elements, unknown to one another; but as soon as a spark of

> passion . . . electrifies this confused mass, there takes place a sort of sudden organization, a spontaneous generation . . . , and these thousands of men crowded together soon form but a single animal, a wild beast without a name, which marches to its goal with an irresistible finality. (Quoted in Borch 2012: 50)

Similarly, in *The Crowd*, the individual is presented as being highly suggestible, with sentiments within crowds being viewed as contagious. This collective interest is reflective of what Le Bon called an organized crowd or, for preference, a 'psychological crowd', expressing in many respects what the French sociologist Emile Durkheim described as 'collective effervescence' (Pizarro et al. 2022). Once formed, this psychological crowd acquires a number of characteristics which, though provisional or temporary, are readily identifiable. Prominent among these, he suggested, were impulsiveness, irritability, an incapacity to reason and an absence of judgement or critical reason. What is crucial in all this for Le Bon is that within the psychological crowd the individuals that compose it are transformed, irrespective of their background, their character or their intelligence. The power of the crowd over the individual, Le Bon argues, 'allows him to yield to instincts which, had he been alone, he would perforce have kept under restraint' (1952 [1895]: 6). As the British prime minister put it when describing the riot in 2011, it involved '[p]eople showing indifference to right and wrong. People with a twisted moral code. People with a complete absence of self-restraint.'[3] Though Le Bon is careful to note, as observed earlier, that crowds can be forces for good as well as for ill, it is the latter that is more typical, not altogether surprisingly given the general characteristics of psychological crowds listed earlier, hence it being stupidity rather than mother-wit that Le Bon believed was accumulated in such groups.

The formation of a psychological crowd, in which individuals take on these new feelings, requires some underpinning mechanism, and it is here that suggestibility and contagion come into play. The idea of contagion is a highly problematic one and is predictably the source of much of the subsequent criticism of Le Bon's arguments. As he himself recognized, 'Contagion is a phenomenon of which it is easy to establish the presence, but that it is not easy to explain . . . . In a crowd every sentiment and act is contagious, and contagious to such a degree that an individual readily sacrifices his personal interest to the collective interest' (Le Bon 1952 [1895]: 30). For Le Bon, the 'psychological law of mental unity' was the source of suggestibility, and it was this that led to contagion, which in turn was the source of the types of conduct associated with crowds. The idea has some power but is not accompanied by evidence. Indeed, there is something circular about the argument. The underlying mechanisms Le Bon relies upon are solely the behaviour each of them is supposed to explain (McPhail 1991). Although claiming that it was always possible for crowds to be better or worse than the individuals comprising them, it was the essentially negative and dangerous character of crowds that was the focus of Le Bon's concern. Crucially:

> by the mere fact that he forms part of an organised crowd, a man descends several rungs in the ladder of civilisation. Isolated, he may be a cultivated individual; in a crowd, he is a barbarian – that is, a creature acting by instinct. He possesses the spontaneity, the violence, the ferocity, and also the enthusiasm and heroism of primitive beings, whom he further tends to resemble by the facility with which he allows himself to be impressed by words and images . . . . An individual in a crowd is a grain of sand amid other grains of sand, which the wind stirs up at will. (Le Bon 1952 [1895]: 32–3)

Crowds in this view are impulsive and mobile – making them intrinsically difficult to govern – and they are dangerous in that they tend to resist and refuse any attempt to come between them and their aims or objectives. Behind his apparently scholarly observations about the crowd, Le Bon had a clear political agenda, and one that was elitist and antisocialist, stressing the importance of maintaining ruling-class authority (van Ginneken 1992). His hope was that his work and that of others would facilitate the control of crowds, and at least in terms of popularity and influence he was hugely successful. He became famous and wealthy, his admirers comparing him favourably to some of the most important thinkers of the time.

From Europe to Chicago

Outside Europe, both Tarde and Le Bon exerted influence on American social science from the late 1890s onwards, initially via Edward A. Ross, a Stanford-based sociologist.[4] Ross wrote widely on issues related to social order and focused on what he referred to as the 'mob mind', to which he attributed a number of features, including irritability, ferocity and criminality. Of even greater influence was the famous Chicago sociologist Robert E. Park. Park, initially a journalist, had spent many of the early years of his academic career in Belgium and also in Germany where he had studied under Georg Simmel. As a student in Germany at the beginning of the century, Park had written a thesis entitled 'The Crowd and the Public'. In it, Park discussed the work of Tarde, Sighele and Le Bon, all of whose influences can be seen in his view 'that the suggestive influence exerted by people on each other constitutes the deciding characteristic of the crowd; and the social epidemic becomes the typical social phenomenon for collective psychology' (quoted in Borch 2012: 142). In his textbook with Ernest Burgess (Park and Burgess 1921: 865), Park defined collective behaviour as that 'of individuals under the influence of an impulse that is common and collective, an impulse, in other words, that is the result of social interaction'. By contrast with some earlier writers, and Le Bon most notably, Park's view of the crowd was generally positive, seeing them as a vehicle for change and potential new social relations. In Park's view, democracy and society were therefore not especially at risk from the crowd, being much more likely to profit from its influence. Where Le Bon had seen crowds as 'the wrecking crews of history' (Leach 1986: 106), Blumer, another Chicago sociologist, saw crowd behaviour as 'a means by which the breakup of the social organization and personal structure is brought about, and at the same time is a potential device for the emergence of new forms of conduct and personality' (Blumer 1969: 77). Though offering a more positive and constructive view of collective behaviour, rather in contrast to the general approach of early Chicago School sociologists, the work of Park and Blumer in this field suffered from an almost complete absence of empirical data in support of the claims made (McPhail 1991).

The beginnings of a change of approach to collective behaviour were arguably first seen in the work of the American psychologist Floyd Allport, simultaneously a critic of Le Bon and someone whose work continued to rely on established ideas. Rather than irrational suggestibility, for Allport collective behaviour was based around the impression of universality, the belief that others share one's views. The mass, however, tends to produce an exaggerated response; as Allport (1933: 295) famously put it, 'The individual in the crowd behaves just as he would behave alone only more so.' At heart, what Le Bon, Park and Allport all shared was the view that crowd behaviour should be understood as primitive and relatively uncontrolled.

A rational mind

The shift towards perspectives that placed greater stress on rationality and sought to avoid the general picture of mindlessness that had dominated scholarship earlier in the century gathered pace with what became known as 'emergent norm theory' (ENT), on the one hand, and rational choice-influenced 'game theoretic' approaches on the other. ENT is most closely associated with the American sociologists Ralph H. Turner and Lewis Killian. Reacting against the idea that crowd behaviour lacked normative standards, and somewhat influenced by the growing popularity of symbolic interactionism, Turner and Killian, as the title of their theory implies, focused on the development of social norms within collective endeavour. People come together for a range of reasons and often do not share clear goals. It is often rumour or other forms of communication that cause people to come together. The focus of ENT was on how essentially leaderless crowds develop new social expectations, ones that are often oppositional, running contrary to broad social expectations or standards. These 'emergent norms' tend to be general guides rather than specific rules and are new definitions of right and wrong developed in situations requiring adaptation. The main question is how do they emerge?

Here, interactionism shows its influence in that members of the crowd in such situations are assumed to be looking for cues as to how to behave. Within this, particularly influential individuals – *keynoters* – are identified as the source of emergent standards. Among multiple options for action, the one that tends to prevail is that which has the greatest latent support within the crowd. Though notions such as 'keynoters' and 'emergent norms' are potentially valuable in thinking about collective conduct, ENT seems less persuasive where very rapid behavioural change is concerned, such as occurs in riots. A second problem concerns what appears to be a somewhat desocialized theory of the crowd, there being little in ENT that places members of the group in their wider social, political and cultural context, still less seeing this as a potentially important element of explanation. ENT points us in an important direction – seeking some means by which to understand shifting standards of conduct – without providing either a solid means of analysing the emergence of norms or placing such crowd activity within its political economic context. Both are important in building up a more coherent picture of crowd behaviour and protest violence.

The mob lives on

Though the mood, tenor and focus of scholarly work in this field have changed dramatically, it remains the case that political discourse has tended to be less influenced by such shifts, continuing to utilize and highlight many of the ideas that derive from late nineteenth-century views of the crowd. In this context, political commentators in particular will often focus their attention on criminal actions, on imputations about the 'mindlessness', 'madness' or amorality of crowd members, or on the failure of crowds to achieve their objectives – thus implying a lack of substance to such protest. In the immediate aftermath of the 2011 riots in England, the then Conservative prime minister simply observed, 'This is criminality, pure and simple, and it has to be confronted and defeated.'[5] Cameron's 'diagnostic frame', characterizing both the acts and the actors as criminal, narrowed the view on offer, assuming other definitions or motivations to be inappropriate or illegitimate. Thirteen years later, in 2024, and once again faced with rioting in England, Labour Prime Minister Keir Starmer said, 'I utterly condemn the far-right thuggery we've seen this weekend', adding , 'This is not protest. It is organised, violent thuggery.'[6] Two waves of rioting more than a decade apart; two prime ministers but from different sides of the political spectrum; one standard message. More recently still, in March 2025 people began taking to the streets of Istanbul after the city's mayor, Ekrem İmamoğlu, was detained on corruption charges. Believed by many to be a tactic to silence a leading opponent of Turkey's president, Recep Erdoğan, there were significant protests several nights in a row. In his response, Erdoğan reached for familiar characterizations of crowds, describing the protest as a 'movement of violence',[7] and those involved as street terrorists; he blamed the main opposition party for inflaming people's passions and said it was 'responsible for our injured police officers, the broken windows of our shopkeepers, and the damaged public property'. The tactics were clear. In each of these cases, Cameron, Starmer and Erdoğan sought, via their claims, to focus attention and, simultaneously, to divert it. Classical psychological conceptualizations of the 'mindless mob' may be academically discredited, but such ideas continue to this day to be a powerful political tool.

3

Not So Primitive Rebels

By the mid-twentieth century, with general fear of the masses having somewhat declined, there began a decisive move away from the classical view of the crowd. Now the desire was to get beyond crude characterizations of the 'mob' and to rescue protesters from what E. P. Thompson in another context famously described as the 'enormous condescension of posterity' (1968: 13). The initial break came in the shape of Turner and Killian's (1957) emergent norm theory, and Neil Smelser's (1963) later proposal that people under strain mobilize to reconstitute the social order in the name of a generalized belief[1] (Smelser 1963: 387), though he was much criticized (see Currie and Skolnick 1970; and Smelser's 1970 rejoinder).

As signalled earlier, the decisive shift away from the early-century emphasis on the fundamental irrationality of the crowd came via two main influences. One was the political and sociological response to the American urban riots of the 1960s. Over a period of approximately eight years, from 1964 to 1972, many hundreds of riots of widely differing intensity occurred in the United States (Hinton 2021).[2] This extraordinary shock to the American body politic led to some reconsideration of its racialized history and, over time, a shift in the official view of such disturbances.[3] In short, far from being irrational mobs, those caught up in the sixties riots were viewed as expressing legitimate grievances deriving from racism. The second crucial influence was the emergence of a new social history, a history from below, or grassroots history (Hobsbawm 1998; Lynd 2014). It focused on the lives of the working classes and sought to treat them with the same seriousness that historians had hitherto tended to reserve for the wealthy and powerful. The seminal figures in this movement were E. P. Thompson, George Rudé and

Eric Hobsbawm. Rudé had led the way[4] (Wilkinson 2009), arguing that 'no historical phenomenon has been so thoroughly neglected by historians as the crowd' (Rudé 1964: 195). Though by no means passing without criticism, Rudé's studies of eighteenth- and nineteenth-century England and France countered the view that crowds were composed primarily of the criminal and the marginal, and he challenged the inclination of historians to 'take refuge behind such omnibus and prejudicial . . . labels as "mob"', illustrating by contrast the part played by rural craftsmen and industrial workers, as well as by women, and that crime and riot, far from being inseparable companions, were only occasional and somewhat uneasy bedfellows (Rudé 1964: 203).

History from below

Hobsbawm and Rudé's (1969) study of the 'Captain Swing' machine-breaking riots of the 1830s in England, for example, found the protesters to be often quite highly organized, their activities characterized by considerable ceremony, and involved in actions marked by much greater symbolic than physical violence. Far from being irrational outbursts, 'behind these multiform activities, the basic aims of the labourers were singularly consistent: to attain a minimum wage and to end rural unemployment. To attain these objects, they resorted to means that varied with the occasion and the opportunities at hand' (Hobsbawm and Rudé 1969: 195). As Hobsbawm observed in his book *Primitive Rebels*, 'The classical mob did not merely riot as a protest, but because it expected to achieve something by its riot. It assumed that the authorities would be sensitive to its movements, and probably also that they would make some sort of immediate concession' (1971: 111).

The new social history produced a picture of working people, especially skilled artisans, particularly printers, as well as shopkeepers and labourers drawn from local communities and integrated into common customs, norms and expectations (Thompson 1993). Rudé (1964), for example, found that of the 160 people brought to trial after the Gordon riots, the vast majority of adult and younger males had settled housing and jobs, and only a tiny number had previous convictions.[5] Further, he observed how remarkable it was that a great many received testimonials of good character from neighbours and employers, something very much in contrast with those who informed against them. Similarly, of the French grain riots of

1775, where much more detailed empirical evidence was available, Rudé (1964: 200) found that of those arrested 'nearly all were local people; few were vagrants, though many . . . lived in lodgings; and only a handful had served previous prison sentences – and only in one instance for an offense that could be described as anything but trivial'.

The next step was for social historians to place such protest activities within the context of their wider political economy. This was done most effectively by Edward Thompson (1971) in his hugely influential study of the food riots in eighteenth-century England, in which he set himself against the 'spasmodic' histories that had dominated thus far. Thompson was critical of Max Beloff,[6] for example, for suggesting of the food riots of the early eighteenth century that 'resentment, when unemployment and high prices combined to make conditions unendurable, vented itself in attacks upon corn-dealers and millers, attacks which often must have degenerated into mere excuses for crime' (1971: 76). From such a standpoint, Thompson argues, Beloff was reducing such protests to 'rebellions of the belly', with little more required for explanation. In fact, such disturbances were underpinned by what he referred to as a *moral economy*. These outbreaks of destruction, rather than being simple, spasmodic reactions to hunger, were almost always underpinned by some underlying, legitimizing notion:

> By the notion of legitimation I mean that the men and women in the crowd were informed by the belief that they were defending traditional rights or customs; and, in general, that they were supported by the wider consensus of the community. On occasion this popular consensus was endorsed by some measure of licence afforded by the authorities. More commonly, the consensus was so strong that it overrode motives of fear or deference. (Thompson 1971: 78)

In this particular case, according to Thompson, the 'central action . . . is not the sack of granaries and the pilfering of grain or flour but the action of "setting the price"' (Thompson 1971: 108). In short, conflict was less a consequence of hunger and more a collective expression of what was believed to be a moral and political right at a time when the practices of a broadly paternalistic pre-industrial society were giving way to the increased influence of laissez-faire industrial capitalism. Far from displaying irrational violence, the actions of the bread rioters showed remarkable discipline. Indeed, it is 'the restraint, rather than the disorder, which is remarkable' (1971: 112), with the protesters' conduct displaying 'a pattern of behaviour of which a Trobriand islander need not have been ashamed'[7] (1971: 131).

Protest and civil rights

At around the same time that Rudé, Thompson and others were presenting a radically different history of popular contention, America was in the midst of the civil rights movement, anti-Vietnam War protests and urban 'ghetto' riots on an unprecedented scale. From Harlem in 1964, to Chicago and Watts in Los Angeles in 1965, to Atlanta, Newark and Detroit in 1967, the scale of the violence and destruction was often vast. Thirty-four people died in the disorder in south-central Los Angeles (Abu-Lughod 2007), 26 died in Newark (Mumford 2007), and 43 died and almost 700 were injured in Detroit (Fine 2007). One estimate suggested that in 1964–8 there was a total of 329 large-scale outbreaks of disorder in 257 cities, with a great many smaller-scale violent disturbances,[8] leading to more than 220 people killed, the majority being Black citizens (Graham 1980). The eventual outcome in the United States was a profound reframing of the ways in which urban violence was understood (Garrow 1978) and would be responded to in the future.

It was the Presidential Commission of Inquiry, chaired by the governor of Illinois, Otto Kerner, and set up by Lyndon Johnson in the midst of the Detroit riot in 1967, that would eventually change the official approach towards and understanding of urban protest. Just two years previously, another public inquiry had reached a much more traditional set of conclusions. In the aftermath of the Watts riot in Los Angeles in 1965, the governor of California, Ronald Reagan, appointed John A. McCone, a former head of the CIA, to lead a commission of inquiry into its background. The inquiry's final report referred to the outbreak of violence in south-central Los Angeles (LA) as a 'spasm', with the rioters 'caught up in an insensate rage of destruction' (McCone Commission 1965: 1), and an 'explosion – a formless, quite senseless, all but hopeless violent protest – engaged in by a few but bringing distress to all' (1965: 4–5). In short, a classic dismissal of the crowd.

McCone was widely criticized for its failure to understand local community experiences and grievances (Blauner 1970; Scoble 1968) or to engage critically with the questions being raised by the civil rights movement. As a consequence, the report came to be seen as 'the apotheosis of the conservative view, or "riff-raff theory"' (Graham 1980: 15) of riots:

> Put bluntly, 'Violence in the City' [the title of the McCone Report] claimed that the rioters were marginal people and the riots meaningless outbursts. The rioters were marginal people, according to the McCone Commission, because they were a small and unrepresentative fraction of the Negro population, namely, the unemployed, ill-educated, juvenile, delinquent, and uprooted. What provoked them to riot were not conditions endemic to Negro ghettos (police harassment and consumer exploitation), but rather problems peculiar to immigrant groups (resentment of police, insufficient skills, and inferior education) and irresponsible agitation by Negro leaders.[9] Also, the riots were meaningless outbursts, according to the McCone Commission, not simply because there was no connection between the Negroes' grievances and their violence, but also because the rioting was unwarranted. (Fogelson 1967: 338–9)

By contrast, for Fogelson (1967: 339) and other critics, 'the rioting, and especially the looting and burning, were articulate protests'. The Los Angeles rioters' selectivity in their choice of targets – the primary focus of their looting and destruction being 'white-owned stores which charged outrageous prices, sold inferior goods, and applied extortionate credit arrangements' (Fogelson 1967: 353; see also Davis 1992; Feagin and Hahn 1973) – carried echoes of the influence of a moral economy. Though the extent of rioters' selectivity could be exaggerated by some commentators, Fogelson (1970: 151) argued that 'in view of the ferocity of the riots, what is remarkable are not the exceptions but the overall pattern and pervasive and intense sense of consumer exploitation underlying it'. Indeed, the patterning that is regularly found in looting within civil disorder is one of the clearer examples of what we will come to recognize as the scripted and dramaturgical dimension of riots. Public protest often has a clear choreography that gives structure to behaviour but remains little analysed (Snow, Zurcher and Peters 1981). It can be seen in things as varied as styles of dress, locations in which protesters meet and the symbols that designate a particular culture of protest (such as the mass burning of cars in French rioting [Fassin 2013]) or that indicate attachment to a cause and solidarity in the face of police violence – such as the yellow umbrellas in the Hong Kong protests in the past decade (Lee and Sing 2019), or the appearance of the *gilets jaunes* on the streets of Paris.

Two societies: one Black, one white

The McCone Commission's report in 1965 proved to be one of the last of its kind. Henceforward, a very different picture of riots and rioters emerged, one in which issues of grievance, inequality and injustice would form a central part. Most important in this was the aforementioned Kerner Commission report which helped establish the dominant narrative about what at the time were generally referred to as urban America's 'ghetto riots'. Three years before its publication, Lyndon Johnson had described the first outbreaks of rioting in much more traditional terms, saying, 'The riots – as well as other criminal and juvenile delinquency problems in our cities – are closely connected', and that each 'riot began with a single incident and was aggravated by hoodlums and habitual lawbreakers' (quoted in Hinton 2021: 4). Kerner took a different view, and his popular report – the paperback became a national bestseller – famously concluded that 'Our nation is moving toward two societies, one black, one white – separate and unequal' (Kerner Commission 1968: 1). White institutionalized racism was identified by Kerner as the primary determinant of the disorder. The picture was rather more complex. Both white and Black upper-income groups were expanding, but there was a sizeable group of Black Americans who were not benefiting from economic gains. The concentration of the poor in city centres was increasing. Those with skills and education, Black and white, had fled from the ghettos (Wilson 1978), leaving populations there that were 'disproportionately, young, uneducated, unskilled and poor' (Sandefur 1988: 50). Underlying the disorder, the Kerner Commission argued, was a 'reservoir of grievances,' varying from city to city, but in general relating to 'prejudice, discrimination, severely disadvantaged living conditions and a general sense of frustration [among African Americans] about their inability to change those conditions' (Kerner Commission 1968: 117). The outbreak of violence was preceded by some precipitating incident or trigger, often minor and of a type that might occur with relative frequency without provoking violence. In the Kerner model, therefore, 'the prior incidents and the reservoir of underlying grievances contributed to a cumulative process of mounting tension that spilled over into violence when the final incident occurred' (Kerner Commission 1968: 118). This form of explanation, and the metaphor of a spark or flashpoint setting light to underlying flammable material usually conceived of as frustration or grievance born of mistreatment in some form, has become the dominant sociological model of riots in the past half-century or more. We will return to it in detail in chapter 5.

The Kerner Report had a huge impact, quickly becoming 'a basic document in the platform of American liberals for social reform, a catalogue and a program of solutions' (Kopkind 1971: 378). Furthermore, the Commission's report 'presented – and legitimized – a specific view of the riots and a particular understanding of America that now constitutes the standard approach to the treatment of social ills' (Kopkind 1971: 379). By the end of the sixties, the established view from Kerner and subsequent reports, such as Jerome Skolnick's to the Violence Commission established the following year (Skolnick 1969), was to present riots 'fundamentally as acts of *political* protest by angry ghetto blacks' (Graham 1980: 16; see also Fogelson 1967). In Skolnick's words:

> [M]ass protest is an essentially political phenomenon engaged in by normal people; that demonstrations are increasingly being employed by a variety of groups, ranging from students and blacks to middle-class professionals, public employees and policemen; that violence, when it occurs, is usually not planned, but arises out of an interaction between protesters and responding authorities; that violence has frequently accompanied the efforts of deprived groups to achieve status in American society; and that recommendations concerning the prevention of violence which do not address the issue of fundamental social and political change are fated to be largely irrelevant and frequently self-defeating. (Skolnick 1969: xix–xx)

The view that riotous collective behaviour was quite highly structured, was attuned to the redress of specific grievances and had targets of violence that were often limited and logical (Currie and Skolnick 1970) slowly became dominant. That such explanations paralleled those utilized by Rudé, Hobsbawm and others in relation to pre-industrial riots was occasionally made explicit. Allan Silver (1967: 1414) suggested the urban disorder of the 1960s appeared 'to be shaping itself into modern equivalents of the traditional forms of riotous protest: a self-conscious drama that substitutes shops, consumer goods, police, and white passers-by for granaries and grain-carts, tax officials, local notables, and townhouses'. In many respects, by the end of the 1960s the general methodology of the new social history and what Silver referred to as the diagnostic sociology of Kerner and other inquiries had formed a dominant, almost hegemonic approach to collective violence that focused on its 'meaningful and patterned character' and laid stress on its 'socially caused, uncollusive character' (Silver 1967: 150). Forty years later, the US-based French sociologist Loïc Wacquant (2008) would ask whether riots such as those in Los Angeles in 1992 or others in France and England subsequently should be understood as 'race riots' or 'bread revolts'. In short, they tended to contain elements of both.

A critical consensus

Little has occurred since to disturb this dominant scholarly viewpoint, one that takes the structural problems facing communities in which riots occur and the grievances such problems give rise to as the primary motivational explanation for the behaviour of rioters. Wacquant (2008: 24), in his analysis of the then recent riots in England, France and America, puts it typically forcefully, arguing that the disorder constituted 'a (socio)logical response to the massive *structural violence* unleashed upon them by a set of mutually reinforcing economic and sociopolitical changes'. It is an approach which posits, more or less straightforwardly, that violence from above begets violence from below. The underlying conditions – inequality, exclusion, racism, state violence and so forth – give rise to tensions and grievances that may, under certain circumstances, explode into collective violence. So apparently entrenched and influential has this broad approach to collective disorder become that one commentator has referred to it as the 'critical consensus' (Waddington 1991). This descriptor was used by Peter Waddington to indicate how those adopting this position set themselves up 'in opposition to the Establishment-conservative view which describes riots as, at best, an irrational and, at worst, a criminal outburst' (1991: 221). He portrayed those taking the alternative approach as adopting the view that riots were generally political in nature and should be seen as a rational attempt to force those in authority to listen. He was not convinced, however, and argued that the problem with linking rioting with inequality and injustice in this way was that there were many, indeed almost certainly the vast majority, who suffered the consequences of such inequality and injustice and yet did not riot. The question, for Peter Waddington, is what is the connection, if any, between injustice and collective action? As he puts it,

> It is one thing to observe that a disorderly or riotous group suffers certain injustices. It is quite another to assert that those injustices are perceived by members of the group in the way they are by the analyst,

> or indeed that they are perceived by members of the group at all. It is yet a further step to assert that it was perceived injustice that caused the disorder. (Waddington 1991: 228)

Consequently, he took the view that in the absence of clear empirical evidence, much contemporary sociology came closer to advocacy than analysis. 'Despite its pretensions to the contrary, the critical consensus might better be seen as justifying or excusing the riots and apportioning blame and responsibility to groups other than the rioters' (1991: 244).[10]

In addition to this general point about the dominant approach to explaining riots, Waddington also took aim at the central metaphor that is deployed in this context: the idea of a 'flashpoint'. Contemporary sociological approaches to understanding riots generally use this notion – flashpoint – as the necessary ingredient that sets alight the underlying tinder. Neil Smelser (1963), writing in the early 1960s, prior to the US riots of that decade, talked of 'precipitating events' as necessary but not sufficient conditions for collective action. As we have seen, the Kerner Commission had identified preceding events, acting essentially as a pool of extant grievances, as the basis of cumulatively mounting tension that resulted in violence when a final incident occurred. In this sense, the entire chain – the grievances, the series of prior tension-heightening incidents and the final incident – was the 'precipitant' of disorder (Kerner Commission 1968: 118). In a similar vein, Lord Scarman in his report into the Brixton riot in south London in 1981 identified one particular arrest made by police officers, similarly, as being the flashpoint. As he put it, 'deeper causes undoubtedly existed, and must be probed; but the immediate cause of Saturday's events was a *spontaneous combustion set off by the spark of one single incident*' (Scarman Report 1981: 3.77; emphasis added). 'The raw material of the explosion was the spirit of angry young men: the spark was their anger at a piece of police action of no great consequence in itself' (Scarman Report 1981: 3.78).

Peter Waddington, the most trenchant of critics, argues that there are two fundamental problems with the notion of a 'flashpoint'. 'First, there is simply too much occurring on any occasion which *might* plausibly explain the presence or absence of disorder for an exhaustive account to be rendered' (Waddington 1991: 231; emphasis in original). 'Second, given that the significance of events lies in how participants interpret them, and this may vary widely, it is impossible to be certain that an event was interpreted in one or other way by those involved. This affords the concept tremendous explanatory elasticity'

(1991: 232). Waddington's crucial criticism here is one that draws on Gary Marx's (1970)[11] observation that scholars have tended to pay insufficient attention to 'issueless riots', i.e., those where protest and grievance play at most a small part in what occurs (and, similarly, see Turner 1969). The danger, to borrow from E. P. Thompson, is to engage in a different form of condescension – one that imputes especial purpose to all collective action, irrespective of the evidence. As Paul Rock (1981) observed, 'Riots are written about by those who attach weight to ideas, intentionality and thoughtfulness, for whom things do not just happen. Riots are seen by them as part of a scheme: vehicles and signifiers of meaning about the world. A riot thus achieves a solemnity which is quite imposing. It is made to say so much.' The danger is that riots when analysed become freighted with a significance they simply cannot carry. We will return in detail in chapter 5 to a discussion of the idea of 'flashpoints'.

In addition to the shifts in history and sociology which increasingly emphasized the fundamental rationality of collective activity, there were also cognate changes within social psychology slightly later in the century. This can now be seen most obviously in the shape of 'social identity' approaches to the crowd, and to what is now referred to by its adherents as the Elaborated Social Identity Model (ESIM). This is without doubt the most persuasive of the social-psychological approaches to collective conduct. With its roots in interactionism and social identity formation, it draws on Turner's (1982) observation that social identity is the fundamental cognitive mechanism underpinning and enabling group behaviour. Based on this, the work of Reicher (inter alia 1984, 1987, 1996) and colleagues offers a thoroughgoing theorization of the social psychology of crowd conduct.

One of the earliest and more comprehensive illustrations of the application of the ESIM is Reicher's analysis of the 1980 riot in the St Paul's district of Bristol, England. Housing Bristol's oldest African-Caribbean community, and characterized by high levels of poverty, racism and exclusion, St Paul's image has generally been poor, and its territorial stigmatization led one set of commentators to describe it as a 'reputational ghetto' (Slater and Anderson 2012). A precursor of the even more serious rioting in Brixton and other parts of England the following year, the Bristol disorder saw the police briefly overwhelmed, controversially abandoning part of the St Paul's area during the height of the violence. Reicher describes the events as being characterized by 'spontaneous social behaviour with the twin characteristics of uniformity across individuals and of clear social limits' (Reicher 1984: 17). These two factors are crucial in illustrating how traditional individualistic interpretations, including more recent approaches such as emergent norm theory, are inadequate forms of explanation. Using a social identity-based psychological perspective, Reicher argues that there was 'a match between the social self-definition used by participants and their actions' (1984: 18). The shape and limits of the actions of those involved in crowd activity illustrate the operation of collective identity. In essence, what you are prepared to do, or not prepared to do, under such circumstances is indicative of underlying shared normative values and sense of identity within the crowd. The behavioural limits in Bristol included an almost exclusive focus on the police as targets – there was not a single attack on an individual citizen, and nor was any private property maliciously damaged. There were also clear geographical limits to action; local citizens did not go beyond the boundaries of the St Paul's community at all and, once the police were forced from the neighbourhood, no one else was stopped from entering the area. Far from descending into anarchy, general order was maintained once the police had left, with locals even managing the traffic flow. Participants saw themselves as part of, and acting as part of, the community in circumstances where this 'notion of community was a real, albeit ideological, creation for participants' (1984: 15).

In line with many other commentators, but from a different vantage point from classical psychologists for example, Reicher argues that such crowds are distinctive in that the circumstances and nature of their actions 'give rise to a sense of power which allows members to express their identity even in the face of outgroup opposition' (Reicher 2001: 196–77). The potential power of the social identity model is evident most obviously in helping explain how the behaviour of collective gatherings can change, and why it might change. Why does the behaviour of crowd members alter or shift? There is no resort here to notions of contagion, suggestion or hypnosis, no question of arguing that individuality is lost or that there is some emergent animalistic tendency within crowds. Rather, Reicher and others argue that it is transformations in social identity during the course of such crowd activity which help us to understand why and how previously non-violent members might come to embrace more aggressive forms of behaviour.

Crucially, social identity is malleable and capable of being plural; we can have multiple social identities. Self-definition involves a process of self-stereotyping, and in terms of a wider categorization provides a framework for action and one which we expect others, sharing this identity, to conform to. Like ENT, for instance, it requires a search for cues for appropriate forms of action. Rather than a loss of identity, it entails a shift to the relevant social identity. Individuals within the crowd are potentially influenced by others they identify with as category members. Within the Bristol riot, for example, Reicher focused on three main elements of the social identity of the crowd members: their attachment to the geographical locality of the neighbourhood; a common adversary in the form of the police; and relatively clear normative boundaries, as illustrated by the arrangement of attacks on property. The patterning of crowd behaviour led Reicher to conclude that rather than a loss of identity, somehow being submerged by participation, it was the nature of their social identity which underpinned and shaped crowd members' behaviour.

In a series of studies that focused on citizen–police interactions (Drury and Reicher 1999; Stott and Reicher 1998) and on riots (Stott, Drury and Reicher 2017), Reicher and colleagues have illustrated the processes lying behind shifting social identities within crowd activity, examining how perceptions of illegitimate and indiscriminate police action 'can be used to explain how a fragmented mass of demonstrators [comes] to form a psychologically homogenous crowd' (Reicher 1996: 130) and one that is more prepared to engage in violence. In these studies, violent conflict tends to emerge as a consequence of gradually escalating and problematic intergroup dynamics (often between the crowd and the police) and may also be precipitated by particular symbolic events, most obviously arrests and other displays of police power, especially where these are seen as particularly inappropriate. As they say of disorder in Tottenham and Hackney in 2011, for example, 'undifferentiated use of force created unity amongst crowd participants, both legitimizing and empowering collective confrontation' (Stott, Drury and Reicher 2017: 978). It is this, leading to shifts in collective identity within the crowd, which lies at the heart of this social-psychological explanation of riot.

Rationality and its discontents

Over time, an approach to riots which stressed the fundamental irrationality of riotous behaviour gave way to something close to its obverse: a viewpoint that focused on the broadly rational nature of collective conduct by placing stress on the underlying grievances expressed via crowd action. The broad thrust has been to jettison outdated assumptions about the 'madness of crowds' and invite closer scrutiny of how we as citizens actually behave collectively. The outcome is an improved understanding of the riotous crowd and, via ESIM in particular, a much more nuanced understanding of shifts within what we might think of as a 'psychological crowd'. We remain in a position, however, that is by no means totally satisfactory. The response to earlier assumptions about the irrationalism of the crowd has arguably involved something of an overreaction. As a consequence, it leaves current analyses too restricted in at least three important ways. First, elements of riotous behaviour that fit uneasily into accounts that privilege rationality, such as spontaneity and emotion – indeed, all conduct that displays few obvious or immediate instrumental characteristics – tend to be avoided or overlooked. No account of collective disorder can be fully realized in their absence. The consequence of the wholesale rejection of Le Bon's work has been the emergence of an unhelpful binary opposition of the rational and irrational in understanding collective conduct with, ultimately, the general expulsion of anything associated with irrationality – most obviously, emotions – from scholarly concern in this field (Borch 2006; Marx 1970).

A second contemporary limitation derives from the centrality of violence in the study of the crowd. While this might seem an unusual observation to make in the context of riots, we should remind ourselves that classical studies in this field, even though now discredited in many ways, were focused on collective behaviour more generally, rather than simply violent crowds narrowly. It is only in the last half-century or so that the study of the peaceful crowd has taken something of a back seat (Holton 1978). Though the new social histories of popular protest were successful in countering Rudé's observation that the study of the crowd had been unfairly neglected, they acted to cement an approach that privileged the violent gathering. At the heart of Rudé's work was an especially narrow view of the crowd which excluded all manner of collective action (see Rudé's own description, 1964: 4), and which Harrison (1988: 11) says made his claim to be studying 'the crowd in history' 'little short of pretentious'. As Harrison (1988: 12) puts it, Rudé may have 'established the "respectability" of the mob, but it was a mob just the same'. The loss of contrast between peaceful and violent crowds may partly help explain the gap between the literatures on riots and social movements, subjects one might reasonably think closely linked.[12] This separation has likely also limited comparative study in this field, in particular restricting potentially instructive comparisons of riotous locations with places that are (relatively) riot free – a subject of great importance but hardly researched (Newburn 2016b; Ray 2014). As classical sociology was only too aware, it is through the study of *order* that we really have the greatest hope of understanding *disorder*.

The final way in which the contemporary study of riots has been unhelpfully narrowed also derives in part from the overriding emphasis on violence, and more particularly from the privileging of questions of aetiology over other concerns. The focus on violence has had its most significantly limiting effect in drawing attention away from what happens in the aftermath or as a result of riots. What are the implications for those involved in the violence as perpetrators and/or victims? What is the impact on the localities affected? If commissions of inquiry are established, what impact do they have on politics and public policy? To take one example, as Sidney Fine, for example, noted in his masterful study of the 1967 Detroit riot, the violence had 'important consequences *for the city . . . the state of Michigan, and the nation*' (Fine 2007: ix; emphasis added). And, importantly, by no means all of these were negative, for, as sociologists from Robert Park onwards were keen to highlight, crowds, including violent ones, may also be vehicles for positive social change. In the final three chapters of this volume, I will examine riots' legacies, focusing on the medium- to long-term impact of systems of punishment, the ways in which riots are constructed and represented as historical phenomena, and the impact this has on social movements themselves and, finally, the public policy impact of protest violence. My next step, however, is to set out the parameters of an approach to the analysis of protest and violence, which takes seriously the need to view the subject both historically and comparatively, and to pay attention to emotion as well as to matters of structure and action.

4
Riots in the Round

In this chapter, I want to outline my approach to protest and protest violence, one which acknowledges the necessity of a broad conceptualization of riots and incorporates questions which are less regularly asked in contemporary work in this field. In moving beyond context and causation, for example, my approach draws attention to what I term the 'life cycle' of riots (Newburn 2016a). The model I outline below recognizes that riots differ not only in what might crudely be thought of as their 'causes' but also in the ways they unfold and spread, in the types and numbers of people involved, their motivations and rationalizations, the forms of violence involved, the ways in which riots are policed, managed and otherwise responded to, and in terms of what occurs in their aftermath and with what consequence. In constructing a model – a necessarily idealized breakdown – it is important to keep hold of the important observation that riots are quite heavily scripted social phenomena. 'Participants' come to them with recipe knowledge about how protest is conducted, how it tends to unfold, what normative expectations about conduct exist and so on. In short, people know how to perform. In the absence of such understandings, such collective conduct would look considerably more like anarchy than tends, in fact, to be the case. It is on the broad patterns of conduct that the analysis presented hereafter is focused.

Most gatherings are peaceful and, where conflict appears likely, most will not actually feature violence. Protest marches, for example, are almost always peaceful. Using German data, Nassauer (2019) suggests that even including the types of protest more likely to feature violence, such as blockades and occupations, only a maximum of one-fifth of such events between 1996 and 2000 became violent, and some estimates were as low as 2%. She reports data suggesting something similar in the United States in the 1960s, where the proportion of protests involving violence was somewhere between 12% and 34%. McAdam (1983) suggests that in only 2% of US protests between 1970 and 2000 were there injuries or property damage. Violence by law-enforcement officers against protesters occurred in between 10% and 25% of protests between 1960 and 1972. Such statistics are, at very best, rough estimates, but it is the broad pattern rather than the detail that is important here, serving to illustrate the 'highly routinized and overwhelmingly peaceful' nature of protest (Nassauer 2019: 24).

Before we turn to the model itself, however, I want to take a step back and look in a little detail at each of the four sets of riots that will form the primary analytical focus in this book. Though riots are by no means limited to these four, they act as specific foci throughout the book. They are: the so-called 'Rodney King' riots that occurred in Los Angeles in 1992; the riots that began in Paris in 2005 and over the course of three weeks spread to much of the rest of France; the England riots of 2011; and the disorder that occurred in Hong Kong in 2019, as well as the other major examples of disorder that preceded it. Though we will return to these examples regularly, others I focus on include the 'uprisings', during what for a time was referred to as the 'Arab Spring', the uprisings (as they are often deliberately or consciously termed) in the United States in the 1960s and in 2020 and beyond after the murder of George Floyd, as well as the riots that began in the north-west of England in August 2024. I am in no way intending to suggest these be seen as exemplary in any respect, and I accept both that other examples might have served just as well and, indeed, might have led to different conclusions from any I might draw here. The point here is simply to illustrate the possibility and utility of comparative analysis in this regard (Tonry 2015).

The 'Rodney King riots', Los Angeles, 1992

The features of the Rodney King affair make this one of the best-known outbreaks of disorder in recent times. At its heart was the videotaped beating of an African-American man, Rodney King, by a group of white Los Angeles (LA) police officers. King, who was on parole and was believed by officers to be under the influence of alcohol (and perhaps other drugs), was chased through downtown LA for a considerable period one night before his car was stopped. The other passengers in the car were quickly arrested, but King's detention was lengthy and violent. There it all might have ended, but the struggle and beating were captured on video camera by a resident who sent it to a local news station. When footage was subsequently broadcast, the scale of the violence led to a public outcry. This was 1991, and it was almost a year later, following the acquittal of four officers accused of assaulting King, that the riots broke out. A number of aspects of the trial were controversial. It had been moved from the city itself to a relatively wealthy suburb and was heard by a jury that contained no African-American members. The initial reaction to the verdicts was one of disbelief, including by the president, George H. W. Bush, with one council woman describing it as 'modern-day lynching'.

Scattered protests began almost immediately, and by night-time south-central LA was on fire. The Police Department (LAPD) looked unprepared, and the initial response by city officials 'was marked by uncertainty, some confusion, and an almost total lack of coordination' (Useem 1997). The disorder spread downtown with protesters attempting to attack the police headquarters, the first fatal shootings occurring in mid-evening. In the following two days, the rioting was so widespread, chaotic and fragmented that any coherent narrative is difficult to achieve. On the first full day of disorder, a 45-square-mile curfew was imposed, many electricity transformers exploded, leaving extended parts of the city in the dark, and for a significant period there were no police present in south-central LA, the epicentre of the violence. The president mobilized the National Guard on 1 May (the verdicts had been handed down on 29 April), and over the course of the next week matters were gradually brought under control, with federal troops eventually pulling out on 9 May, several days after the curfew had been lifted. Over the course of around a week, more than 50 people had been killed, over two thousand injured, over sixteen thousand arrested and the damage incurred estimated as being close to US$1 billion.

Riots in France 2005

The 2005 riots in France began in the Parisian neighbourhood of Clichy-sous-Bois. A group of teenagers who were returning home from playing football ran from a police patrol when they were asked to stop. Like many teenagers of African origin, they were scared of the potential consequences of such a request, not least as they had no identification papers on them at the time. Three of the boys climbed a fence and took refuge in an electricity substation. Their choice of hiding place was predictably disastrous, and when one touched the transformer all three were electrocuted. Only one survived. Rioting ensued later that day, with local citizens blaming the police for the deaths. Of all the responses to the disorder, perhaps the most outspoken and controversial were those by the then interior minister, Nicolas Sarkozy. On the evening that the two boys died, he announced that there would be no special investigation into the conduct of the police (Schneider 2014), having earlier shocked many by saying that he would ensure areas such as Clichy were cleansed of *racailles* ('rabble') and *voyous* ('riff-raff'), comments that many felt inflamed matters.

At the time, Clichy-sous-Bois was the poorest locality in Seine-Saint-Denis, the department with the highest unemployment rate in France (Body-Gendrot and Savitch 2012). The two deaths occurred at a time when tensions between the police and residents of Clichy and other Parisian *banlieues*[1] were already very high. The eventual outcome was some of the most severe rioting in contemporary France – described in American media as 'civil war' (Jobard 2008) – affecting not just Paris but more than 300 locations, at least 85% of which were specifically identified by the French government as 'zones urbaines sensibles' (ZUS)[2] (Jobard 2008), areas characterized by extremely high levels of youth unemployment and a variety of other social problems. During the riots, in excess of 10,000 cars were burned, hundreds of buildings severely damaged, over €200 millions worth of damage caused, more than 4,800 people arrested, over 750 imprisoned (Dikec 2017), and a state of emergency declared by President Chirac.

The England riots 2011

Although British Home Secretary Theresa May cautioned against drawing too direct a link, all major sources appear to agree that the initial 'trigger' for the riots was the fatal shooting of a young mixed-race man, Mark Duggan, in north London on Thursday, 4 August 2011 (see, e.g., Home Affairs Committee 2011; Metropolitan Police Service 2012; Riots, Communities and Victims Panel 2012). Two days later, family, friends and others marched on the local police station in Tottenham to protest about the shooting and about the claims that had been made about Duggan in the aftermath. The false claims, which eventually brought an apology from the Independent Police Complaints Commission, included that Duggan had been armed and had fired at police officers (in fact, the firearm was found approximately four and a half metres from Duggan's body and had not been fired) and that a police officer had been hit by a bullet fired by Duggan (the bullet, which lodged in an officer's radio, had actually come from a police firearm).[3]

Tempers were further inflamed both by the very poor communication between the Metropolitan Police Service (MPS) in London and Duggan's family, and by the subsequent mishandling of the Saturday evening protest. Initially, it was the perceived failure of the MPS to put forward an officer of sufficient seniority to signal that they were taking the protest seriously which upset many outside the police station. Subsequently, what appeared to some present to be the rough handling of one young female protester by the police also contributed to the deteriorating mood. By early evening, two police vehicles had been set on fire and, with the police service seemingly reluctant to intervene, the disorder spiralled, with further serious outbreaks resulting in more than 400 recorded criminal offences, more than 200 arrests and the eventual deployment of 3,500 police officers (Metropolitan Police Service 2012).

Over the next three days, the rioting spread, initially across London (including 21 of its 32 boroughs) and subsequently to other cities, including Birmingham, Manchester, Salford and Liverpool. In all, five people lost their lives during the riots, an estimated 15,000 people were involved in the disorder, more than 4,000 arrests were made and approximately 1,300 people received custodial sentences averaging 17 months each (Ministry of Justice 2012). British insurers expected to pay out something in the region of £200 million as a consequence of the violence (Association of British Insurers 2012). The English riots of 2011 can consequently lay claim to being the biggest civil disorder in a generation (Newburn 2015).

Hong Kong disorder 2019

According to one estimate, in the year ending May 2020 there were more than one thousand separate protest events involving in excess of 14 million protesters in Hong Kong. Central to this was Hong Kong's controversial Extradition Law Amendment Bill (ELAB), which enabled the deportation of people accused of crimes in Hong Kong to mainland China for trial. It all culminated on 12 June in clashes in which the police fired hundreds of tear-gas canisters and bean-bag rounds to quell the protest,[4] followed four days later by almost two million people taking to the streets of Hong Kong in further protests, though on this occasion peacefully. More demonstrations occurred in late June, including one which involved an attack on the governmental offices of the Legislative Council (LegCo). In early July, the first protests took place in the New Territories and continued, in different areas, all the way through to mid-August, ending with several deaths and a six-day siege at Hong Kong Polytechnic University. One of the reasons for including the Hong Kong disturbances as one of the key examples here is the spread of time over which they occurred. First, and like the riots in France in 2005, the 2019 Hong Kong protests lasted many weeks, also moving geographically over time. Second, with some similarity to the other main examples here, they were preceded by many years of protest and violence; indeed, they cannot really be understood outside of such a historical perspective (Newburn 2020).

When thinking about 'events' in the pre-history of 2019's protests, the question is where to start. Though any choice has a degree of arbitrariness about it, one might reasonably begin with the protests that preceded Hong Kong's anticolonial riots of 1967, in which one person died, 26 were injured and almost 1,500 arrested. The events exposed serious political and social fault lines in Hong Kong and helped stimulate elements of the civic activism that were to be especially visible in the 1967 riots (Scott 2017). The 1967 riots arose out of a strike that began in the Hong Kong Artificial Flower Works, and resulted in eight months of struggle during which 51 died and over 800 were injured. During this period, there were more than 1,200 bomb incidents and a further 8,000 devices dealt with by bomb disposal squads (Wong 2017). These riots are widely seen as a watershed moment. Indeed, the deputy colonial secretary at the time said, 'Before 1967, there was no real channel of contact between the government and the people. I don't think there would have been any reform at all [without the riots]' (Wong 2017: 99). More particularly, as Cheung (2017: 69) observes, 'the 1967 riots aroused "Hong Kong consciousness" and a sense of belonging to the city amongst the young generation'. From this point, the signal 'events' continued with the post-Tiananmen Square rally on 4 June 1989 – which prompted very significant changes in stance by the British colonial government towards Beijing and which influenced much in the political sphere in the period up to the handover in 1997 – and the 1 July 2003 rally against a proposed national security law.

Young people, especially of high-school age, became increasingly visible in protest movements and campaigns in the second decade of the twenty-first century, initially via the emergence of the Scholarism movement in 2011 and student protests against the proposed introduction of a new school curriculum. The withdrawal of the new curriculum plan in September 2012 was too little too late, as the leaders of the Scholarism movement were by then fully engaged in the swiftly mutating protests in what became known as the Umbrella Movement (UM – or Umbrella Revolution, characterized by the highly stylized use of yellow umbrellas), and in founding Demosisto, a new political party, in 2016 (Wong 2020). The period from 2013 onward saw a series of escalating protests, including Occupy Central (focusing on Hong Kong's business district), and the Mong Kok riot on Chinese New Year 2016, all leading towards 2019's concentrated period of protest and violence.

The life cycle of riots

In the model below (Table 1), I focus on the *context*, *dynamics* and *nature* of and the *reaction* or *response* to riots. *Context* most obviously refers to the structural, political and cultural circumstances in which violence occurs. What are the relationships between social groups, between social groups and political systems, and so forth, that set the stage for the breakdown of order? Crowd *dynamics* refers not just to those matters that appear to be the more immediate origins of rioting but also the features that influence how disorder matures and spreads and how extensive it is temporally, including details of the local recipe knowledges that guide and shape such conduct. *Nature* focuses on issues of participation and motivation (who and how many people are involved in the rioting, how they experience their involvement, and the reasons and rationales for their participation), the ways in which the disorder is policed and otherwise managed and people ordered and controlled and, finally, what forms violence takes, together with some consideration of the question of if and how violence mutates. Finally, there are issues of *response*, *reaction* and *impact*. Again, as with the three other broad themes, I have separated these into three further subdivisions: the political, public and media responses that frame violent events; the response of the penal state; and, finally, the economic, political and cultural policy responses. In each of these cases, the questions that face us concern not simply the nature of the responses to violence but the immediate, medium-term and long-term consequences of such reactions. The model is essentially didactic, setting out the broad parameters for analysis and attempting

Table 1 The life cycle of riots

	Structural context	Political/ideological context	Cultural context
Context	The material and social circumstances of the society and the cities and neighbourhoods in which riots occur The nature of the relationships between different social groups and the state The ways such structural matters relate to the breakdown in order	The nature of political systems – national and local – and their impact on different social groups The relationships between different social groups, especially dissenting groups, and a range of political and ideological institutions, including the police and other agencies of social control	The ways in which different social groups understand the social world and their place in it The nature and organization of national, local and other media The cultural understandings by communities of themselves and of the history of conflict
	Setting and precipitating events	**Diffusion and development**	**Extent and ending**
Dynamics	The spatial and communicative context, together with what is often thought of as the flashpoint or triggering event(s), in combination with linked developments that may act to stoke or mitigate tensions	How rioting spreads from one place to another and what happens to the nature of disorder during that process The factors that work to limit the diffusion of disorder	The temporal and geographic extent of the riot event The factors that contribute to the ending of disorder
	Participation and motivation	**Policing and control**	**What is involved**
Nature	The identity of the individuals, groups and communities that are involved in the rioting Their alleged/perceived motivation Their feelings and emotions	The ways in which the police and other agencies of control respond to the disorder The ways in which the role/tactics of control agencies change as the rioting unfolds, and their impacts	The nature of the different forms of violence involved, e.g., physical violence, arson, damage and looting Which forms, if any, predominate How the balance between different forms changes over time
	Political/public opinion and media response	**Penal response**	**Public policy response**
Response/ reaction	How political leaders, other opinion formers and the public understand and react to the riots, including the forms of language and rhetoric used How the riots are reported and constructed in the mainstream and social media	How the state, through the police, the courts and other institutions, deals with the rioting both during the disorder and in the aftermath The consequences of this for all those involved	The ways in which the state – both nationally and locally – reacts to the riots in broader public policy terms In the short term, whether an official inquiry was instituted In both the short and medium terms, how the state reacts economically, industrially, culturally, and socially to the groups involved and the problems identified
Impact	The long-term impacts of the ways in which the state, and all its institutions (as well as the private sector and civil society), understand, frame and respond to civil disorder		

Source: Newburn (2021)

to ensure that such social phenomena are understood 'in the round' and as having, as 'life cycle' implies, an extended existence.

The context of riots

The discussion in the opening chapters of the book already gives a sense of what extant scholarship has to say about the context within which riots occur. As the table above outlines, I identify three broad contextual categories: the *structural*, the *political/ideological* and the *cultural*.[5] It shouldn't need saying but, in order to avoid any misinterpretation, the proposal of these categories is in no way a suggestion that they are somehow comprehensive – covering all contextual possibilities – or mutually exclusive in some way: as will become clear, there is no simple barrier or set of distinctions to separate the categories. In this context, the Presidential Commission established by Lyndon Johnson in 1967, generally referred to as the Kerner Commission, observed that 'the causes of recent racial disorders are imbedded in a massive tangle of issues and circumstances – social, economic, political and psychological .... These factors are both complex and interacting' (Kerner Commission 1968: 203). In these following sections, by way of continuity, I will refer primarily to the evidence from the Kerner Commission as a means of illustrating different elements of the life cycle of riots.

Structural context

This refers to the broad social and economic circumstances in the neighbourhoods, regions and societies within which civil violence occurs. It includes other factors such as the nature and history of relationships between the state, state representatives and various social groups, particularly those involved in protest, and how these relate to breakdowns in social order. The Kerner Commission drew particular attention to three forces – pervasive discrimination and segregation; Black migration and white exodus; and Black ghettos – which 'converged on the inner city in recent years and on the people who inhabit it' (Kerner Commission 1968: 204) and which were central to understanding the circumstances in which the disorders emerged. In Kerner's view, such matters, fundamental though they appeared, did not cause the disorder. It was other, more immediate factors, such as those linked with policing. All this talk of 'context', and reference to structural features which come to influence the array of conduct that interests us here, ideally requires some unpicking. Those matters referred to as 'factors' must also be regarded as resources which may or may not be recognized, chosen, treated or invoked in rather different ways as having causal efficacy. They are forms of interaction that typically involve choices about courses of action, adhering, or not, to general and local behavioural norms. They are, as it were, in part the materials available to be chosen and deployed as vocabularies of motive, rather than simply being inexorable and fateful pressures that the terminology might be taken to imply.

Political/ideological context

This concerns formal and informal political systems and currencies, the ways in which political decisions are made, who they favour and why, and how different social groups relate to systems of decision making and resource allocation. In this context, the Kerner Commission focused particularly on 'powerlessness'. Many Black Americans, it said,

> have come to believe that they are being exploited politically and economically by the white 'power structure'. . . . The frustrations of powerlessness have led some to the conviction that there is no effective alternative to violence as a means of expression and redress . . . . More generally, the result is alienation and hostility toward the institutions of law and government and the white society which controls them. (Kerner Commission 1968: 205)

In many of the cities studied by Kerner, political responsibility and accountability was found to be fragmented, and Black Americans to be relatively poorly represented politically. Grievance procedures, where they existed, were sometimes moribund, often ineffective and in many cases, especially where the police were concerned, subject to very considerable distrust.

Cultural context

This focuses more on the ways in which citizens, or particular groupings of citizens, understand their social world, their place in it and how they relate to the systems that surround them. It includes the nature and organization of different forms of media, mass and social, together with some sense of the differing cultural understandings of particular communities and how they relate to others and to the social order more generally. In relation to such matters, Kerner drew attention to, among other things, two further catalysing ingredients: frustrated hopes and the legitimation of violence. Of the former, it said that the 'expectations aroused by the great judicial and legislative victories of the civil rights movement have led to frustration, hostility and cynicism in the face of the persistent gap between promise and fulfillment' (Kerner Commission 1968: 204). Of the latter, it suggested that 'white terrorism directed against nonviolent protest' had spawned a climate that tended 'toward the approval and encouragement of violence as a form of protest' (Kerner Commission 1968: 204–5). In this context, there was some empirical evidence found to support the so-called 'revolution of rising expectations' thesis (Chandra and Foster 2005). The Kerner Commission Report had attributed the disorders to rising expectations among Black urban populations, in turn suggesting that these rising expectations owed much to the legal successes of the National Association for the Advancement of Colored People (NAACP) on such issues as the abolition of school segregation. Chandra and Foster's (2005) model of 'relative deprivation', for example, points to the important conclusion that where many studies employ a simple notion of inequality as differences between two groups, the reality was more closely measured by focusing on the more subtle discrepancy between *value expectation* (the material and social condition that individuals think they should achieve) and *value capability* (the material and social condition that individuals think they will achieve). The conclusion drawn by President Johnson from the analysis of the Kerner Commission was that:

> The only genuine, long-range solution for what has happened lies in an attack – mounted at every level – upon the conditions that breed despair and violence. All of us know what those conditions are: ignorance, discrimination, slums, poverty, disease, not enough jobs. We should attack these conditions – not because we are frightened by conflict, but because we are fired by conscience. We should attack them because there is simply no other way to achieve a decent and orderly society in America. (Quoted in Kerner Commission 1968: xv)

The dynamics of riots

This element of analysis focuses on how rioting spreads (if it does) temporally and geographically, what happens to the disorder as it spreads (do the forms of violence change, for example, or do the activities of control agencies change, or both?) and what influences the patterns that are observed. Finally, it also considers what brings the violence to an end. How long does the violence last? What contributes to its diminution and eventual termination, including everything from concerted state action via the police and/or the military through to more prosaic matters, such as changes in the weather. Kerner observed that there was no civil disorder that could be considered to be 'typical'. The disorders varied markedly, not least in terms of levels of violence and damage. Some involved quite extreme levels of violence, whereas the majority were far less significant. Four-fifths of the deaths and one half of the injuries occurred in two cities alone (Newark and Detroit) in a period in which there had been several hundred large-scale riots (Hinton 2021). Kerner found that, of the riots the Commission studied, the tendency was for them to occur with increasing frequency during the approach to summer and in the summer months. Although big cities were a common site for disorder, about one-fifth of riots occurred in relatively small communities. Despite considerable variation, Kerner felt it was possible to identify a broad 'riot process'. The Commission suggested that this involved: a reservoir of deeply held grievances which were widely shared within African-American communities, followed by 'in virtually every case a single "triggering" or "precipitating" incident', often misunderstood, then developing violence ([i]n differing ways) and, finally, a control effort involving both formal and informal approaches. We will return to this broad pattern once again in the next chapter.

Once violence was underway, Kerner suggested, levels were observed to increase to their peak quite rapidly and thereafter to decline more slowly. Rioting often began with less serious forms of violence (rock and bottle throwing and window breaking), though once shop windows were broken looting tended to follow and was more common in the midst of riots than at the outset, as were gunfire and sniping. In relation to the latter, these are peculiarly American forms of violent disorder, reflecting the unusual access to arms that distinguishes that nation from the bulk of liberal democracies (Garland 2025a). In terms of how riots end, Kerner is not untypical in concentrating mainly on control efforts – in particular focusing on the work of the police and other agencies in restoring order. In this context, Kerner, however, also drew attention to what it referred to as 'counter rioters', primarily African-American private citizens who 'were active on the streets attempting to restore order primarily by means of persuasion' (Kerner Commission 1968: 127). Some of these were officially sanctioned, others acted informally and independently of official control channels. How effective they were was difficult to assess, Kerner concluded, but their role in shaping civil disorder is potentially important and often ignored, and is one to which we will return.

The nature of riots

Riots typically engender considerable speculation, not just about major questions of causation but also about who was involved, what their motivation may have been and what claims they make about their involvement. As we have noted, the Kerner Commission dismissed ideas associated with 'riff-raff' theory comprehensively, saying that, characteristically, 'the typical rioter was not a hoodlum, habitual criminal or riff-raff; nor was he a recent migrant, a member of an uneducated underclass or a person lacking broad social and political concerns' (Kerner Commission 1968: 111). Kerner had used eyewitness testimony, interview data and arrest records to draw a picture of participants in the sixties urban riots. A 'typical' rioter (a necessarily crude model), Kerner said, was African-American, aged between 15 and 24, born locally (within the state) and generally a lifelong resident of the city in which the riot took place, an important point given standard claims about 'outsiders'. The Commission noted that 'typical' rioters were moderately well educated, were likely to be working in a menial or poorly paid job and had experienced unemployment. They believed strongly they deserved something better and felt that the barriers they faced were not the result of 'lack of training, ability, or ambition, but because of discrimination by employers' (Kerner Commission 1968: 128). They were better informed than their peers, who had not been involved in the rioting (something noted in relation to the 2011 riots in England also), were likely to be actively involved in civil rights efforts but were 'extremely distrustful of the political system and of political leaders' (Kerner Commission 1968: 129).

Additionally, there is the question of the nature of violence itself. Broadly speaking, this can be divided into violence against people on the one hand and property on the other. The former can be subdivided into violence against official control organizations and that focused on other citizen groups. Violence against property primarily includes stone and bottle throwing, arson, criminal damage and theft/looting. The levels of violence and the balance between different forms of violence are important elements in understanding the nature of rioting, and I return to this subject in chapter 7. Appropriately, one area of inquiry that is central to an understanding of riots generally, and to their shape more particularly, is the nature of policing and the activities of other control organizations. The questions raised in chapter 8 range quite widely from what role, if any, policing has in the generation or incitement of violence all the way through to what role the police and other control organizations play in the mitigation and prevention of violence.

The response to riots

Fundamental to my argument here, and as outlined previously, is that any full understanding of riots must move beyond a fixation with violence. More particularly, a rounded understanding of such social phenomena ought to incorporate some analysis of what happens once the violence has ceased. Although half a century or more ago scholars evinced an interest in the consequences of protest for communities (Gamson 1975; Kelly and Snyder 1980; Turner 1969) and for the individuals involved (Johnson 1972; Mann 1974),[6] this has tended to cease as the preoccupation with violence has grown. While accepting that some of these features may begin in the midst of the violence, I divide post-riot matters into three broad groups. The first concerns the political, public and media responses. How are riots framed? Indeed, first of all, is the term 'riot' used and, if so, by whom? How is collective violence talked about, defined, defended and attacked by politicians, pundits and the public? Such issues deeply affect popular conceptions of disorder and are matters that vary considerably by time and place or, if one prefers, historically and comparatively. In this regard, the impact of what politicians, journalists and others have to say often continues long beyond the period of rioting itself, affecting the ways such events are perceived and how they are responded to. Typically, and perhaps not surprisingly, given the challenge to social and political order presented by riots, political leaders of all stripes often reach for simple prescriptions, focusing on the surface criminality of the actions of participants rather than seeking any underlying meaning. Notwithstanding the more nuanced and more liberal tones of his riots commission, President Johnson's view was that each riot 'began with a single incident and was aggravated by hoodlums and habitual lawbreakers', dismissing looting, arson and sniping simply as 'crime'. Occasionally, governments will appoint inquiries in the aftermath of major disorder, and their findings tend, for obvious reasons, to become the official narrative attached to understandings of the disorder, its causes and implications. Relatively little is known about the impact of official inquiries. Although the Kerner Commission stimulated considerable debate at the time (Fogelson, Black and Lipsky 1969) and as a response to its fiftieth anniversary (Gooden and Myers 2018), riot inquiries are not typically the subject of sustained academic analysis, despite their importance and their potential consequentiality (although see Benyon 1984; Campbell 1970; Platt 1971).

In addition to the immediate and subsequent reaction of political leaders in this context, media framing may also have a very significant impact on public images of protest, establishing understandings that are both pervasive and durable (Halloran, Elliott and Murdock 1970; Newburn, Jones and Blaustein 2018; Snow, Vliegenthart and Corrigall-Brown 2007). Political framing can affect almost everything, including both the penal and public policy responses. The Kerner Commission, despite finding that newspapers, radio and television 'made a real effort to give a balanced, factual account of the . . . disorders' (Kerner Commission 1968: 363), felt they ended up proffering a picture that exaggerated both the extent of violence and of the general mood, not least in overplaying the degree of interracial conflict. In terms of how reporting was received and understood, reactions were highly racialized, and Kerner argued that most Black people saw the newspapers as the mouthpieces of the 'power structure' (Kerner Commission 1968: 374). This is not untypical, with the residents of riot-affected communities often feeling beleaguered and misrepresented by both politicians and journalists.

The second area of response is what I refer to as the reaction of the 'penal state'. In short, this is the important issue of how the police and other control agencies and penal systems respond to disorder, the levels of police violence involved, the ways in which the courts are utilized to bring offenders 'to justice' and the scale of the sentences imposed on those found guilty. Staying with the example of the riots in the United States in the sixties, some scholars, foremost among them the historian Elizabeth Hinton, have argued that the riots had huge consequences for American policing and, in turn, for the shape of the American penal system. She puts it thus:

> The enduring impact of the violence of the 1960s and 1970s has been felt more regularly, and more acutely, by Black people in American cities who faced new policing practices that emerged under the banner of the War on Crime: the routine stop and frisks that attacked people's dignity, the breaking up of community gatherings, the presence of

> armed, uniformed officers in the hallways of under-resourced public schools, and more. While such strategies helped repress mass violence as a regular phenomenon, they ironically made further 'riots' inevitable . . . . Mass incarceration is one consequence of the draconian police ethos born in the 1960s and 1970s in response to mass violence. (Hinton 2021: 3)

That the police violence that is used in response to collective disorder may itself foment further disorder can be seen in many other examples, not least in the case of the Hong Kong disorder outlined earlier (though on how de-escalation can work see Halloran, Elliott and Murdock 1970; Stott, Scothern and Gorringe 2013; Waddington 1994). The recent history of Hong Kong has seen several significant public protests involving, among others, the Occupy movement (Graeber and Hui 2014), student demonstrations against attempts to introduce a new school curriculum (Wong 2020), the Umbrella Movement (Lee and Sing 2019; Pang 2020), resistance to the Legislative Council's attempts to reform the extradition law (Pang 2020) and, most recently, to the new Beijing-imposed security law. As suggested earlier, there is a strong case to be made that these successive waves of protest, from at least 2012, were influenced by the handling of earlier events and, in the anti-extradition case, strong evidence that the policing response was a driving force in the growing scale of the protest and its changing tactics and focus (Ng and Wong 2017; Wong 2019). The historical evidence on violence seems of undeniable social scientific importance (Newburn 2020).

The third and final area of reaction is the public policy response to riots. This includes formal acts of government, encompassing economic, political and cultural policy responses relating to the communities affected, to the social, religious or ethnic groups involved, and to other issues raised by the conflict. Again, such responses arguably contain lessons for our understanding of the society within which such disorder occurs, as well as forming an important element of any fully fledged understanding of the life cycle of riots. As observed earlier, when riots break out, there is almost inevitably a rush to offer judgement on the nature of violence and how it is to be understood and explained. The ascription of labels, claims and diagnoses has potentially significant consequences, including influencing the opening and closing of 'policy windows' and, consequently, influencing the likelihood of governments and others following particular courses of action.

The legacy of riots and protest violence

So far as the medium- to longer-term social and economic consequences of collective violence are concerned, arguably they are more likely to become a focus of attention where there appears to be some coherent political narrative or set of claims attached to the protest or riot. The scale of the American urban riots of the 1960s would have provoked considerable political and public concern and attention regardless, but the proximity of the civil rights movement undoubtedly helped keep the issues raised by the riots on the public agenda. This is far from always the case, however, and the attention stimulated by riot, once described by Martin Luther King Jr as the 'language of the unheard', is often quickly silenced. For the communities involved, the consequences of riots linger long after the violence has ceased, the riot police have left, the streets have been cleaned and politicians and much of the public have turned their attention elsewhere. Disasters and riots, both forms of social crisis, are often treated similarly in some academic literature, but it has been argued that an important reason for thinking of these social phenomena separately is that riots 'seem to leave more of a residue than disasters' (Quarantelli 1993: 71). Although in arguing this Quarantelli was focusing primarily on the psychological and mental health consequences of such phenomena, a parallel argument can be made that the ongoing economic (Collins et al. 2004; Collins and Margo 2007) and social (Casey and Hardy 2018; Gillham and Marx 2018; Stoesz 1993) consequences of urban riots are often profound and are no less important a subject of study than the confluence of factors that might have led to violence in the first place.

The Economic Policy Institute (EPI), a non-profit, non-partisan think tank, released a report in 2018 examining the American landscape 50 years after Kerner (Gooden and Myers 2018). The report offers an insight into a half-century's social and political change: quite radical and far-reaching in many ways, but rather limited, indeed deeply disappointing from another perspective. According to the EPI's assessment, 'the year 1968 was a watershed in American history and black America's fight for equality', drawing attention to the signing of the Civil Rights Act and the assassination of Martin Luther King Jr. Looking back over half a century, its headline findings were that African Americans were now far better educated than had been the case in 1968 – for example, they were almost twice as likely to have graduated high school – but despite significant improvements they continued to lag behind whites in terms of college graduation rates. Such educational progress would be expected to translate into improvements in employment and income and, to a degree, this appears to be so, though African Americans still earn less than whites and are significantly more likely to live in poverty. The Black unemployment rate had increased over the period and, roughly speaking, was twice that of whites, though, as William Julius Wilson (1978) controversially but influentially argued, the fate of poor Black American families was consequent not simply on labour-market changes and discrimination but on the relative improvement in the lot of the American Black middle class. More broadly, home ownership was low and virtually unchanged since 1968. The report concludes by considering incarceration, acknowledging that there had been a tripling of African Americans in prison or jail[7] between 1968 (604 of every 100,000 in the total population) and 2016 (1,730 per 100,000). It is true that the overall prison population has expanded, and thus the number of whites incarcerated also increased markedly, but from a lower baseline. African Americans are now well over six times as likely as whites to be incarcerated. As we will explore in greater detail in chapter 11, beyond these crude life chances, it is the wider impact of penal intervention on individuals and communities that is really what is at stake here.

The urban riots or 'uprisings' of the sixties and seventies represented the most extraordinary disruption. Peter Levy (2018) estimates that something close to one-third of the population of the whole nation lived in communities that were affected by the violence, and tens of millions more were indirectly affected. Traditional explanations were firmly rebutted and rejected, and a new diagnostic consensus emerged, one with racism at its heart. Kerner's view was that there was much that could be achieved via public policy in the fields of housing, education and employment to improve life chances, reduce inequalities and, it was hoped, thereby to reduce the likelihood of future similar violence. Indeed, nothing on the scale of the sixties riots *has* occurred since, including the widespread protest violence that arose after the murder of George Floyd in 2020. And yet it would be hard to claim that the relative absence of riot is a consequence of progressive policy making. The EPI report's summary of the situation 50 years after Kerner is that 'While African Americans are in many ways better off in absolute terms than they were in 1968, they are still disadvantaged in important ways relative to whites. In several important respects, African Americans have actually lost ground relative to whites, and, in a few cases, even relative to African Americans in 1968.'[8] A stark assessment indeed.

5
Tinder and Spark

From Kerner onwards, the dominant sociological, and to an extent historical and psychological, model of riots had at its core the metaphor of a 'flashpoint' or a 'spark'. In this, riots require two ingredients: the *tinder*, the raw material which, under the right conditions, can be set alight, and the *spark* or flashpoint which transforms this raw material into a fully fledged outbreak. In practice, classical approaches that focus on the 'madness' of the mob and revisionist work that stresses the rationality of collective conduct both still regularly reach for the 'flashpoint' metaphor when seeking to explain how disorder begins.

To repeat, Kerner had said of the sixties ghetto riots that in the Commission's view 'the prior incidents and the reservoir of underlying grievances contributed to a cumulative process of mounting tension that spilled over into violence when the *final incident* occurred. In this sense the entire chain – the grievances, the series of prior tension-heightening incidents, and the final incident – was the "precipitant" of disorder' (Kerner Commission 1968: 118; emphasis added). A little over a decade later, in his report into the Brixton riot in south London in 1981, Lord Justice Scarman said something very similar. Focusing on the main day of rioting, he identified one particular arrest made by police officers as being the 'spark' leading to the disorder. 'Deeper causes undoubtedly existed,' he said, 'and must be probed, but the immediate cause of [the] events was a *spontaneous combustion set off by the spark of one single incident*' (Scarman 1981: 37, para. 3.77; emphasis added). Here, Scarman's broad model parallels Kerner's: grievances, tension-raising incidents and a spark which led to the eventual disorder. But Scarman's account also contained an added allusion that was not so explicit in Kerner's reading of the riots – the idea that there was something *spontaneous* about the violence. Though it is a commonly made observation, it is hard to know precisely what Scarman meant by this, but I take it to refer to the suddenness of the emergence of crowd violence, and its unanticipated and apparently extemporaneous or unrehearsed nature. The shift from a situation in which things are perhaps tense but relatively peaceful to one where violent, perhaps extraordinarily violent, incidents occur often appears to happen remarkably quickly and with little apparent warning. Yet, as both Kerner's and Scarman's verdicts reflected, riots were often understood as having lengthy antecedents, most often described as long-held grievances and frustrations, which provide the basis from which violence potentially emanated.[1] The important question that then necessarily arises is what caused this shift, and it is here that the metaphor of a flashpoint or spark comes into play and terms like 'spontaneity' are often utilized. Such incidents, the sparks or flashpoints, often relatively minor in character and, as mentioned, quite fleeting in nature, provide the link between the lengthy antecedents of riots and the violence itself while also accounting simultaneously for the apparent suddenness and extemporaneity of riots. As we have seen, the 'flashpoint' metaphor is now so well established and embedded, both academically and within public discourse around riots, that one commentator has described it as forming the basis of a 'critical consensus', created in opposition to 'establishment-conservative' views that see riots 'as, at best, an irrational and, at worst, a criminal outburst' (Waddington 1991: 221). To explore the 'flashpoint' metaphor in more detail, we can begin by using the four main illustrative examples as the basis for comparative analysis. Though there is much to recommend the general 'tinder and spark' approach, the idea of a flashpoint has been significantly under-theorized, something I endeavour to begin to rectify at the end of this chapter.

Flashpoints in four riots

The riots in Los Angeles in 1992 occurred not in the aftermath of the beating of Rodney King, after whom the riots often take their name,[2] but a year later and immediately after the verdicts in the prosecution cases brought against four of the officers involved. This raises a number of questions. Why did the riots not occur in the immediate aftermath of the broadcasting of King's beating? Why were there no riots when the beating was aired on television, whereas extraordinary scenes of disorder followed almost immediately on the verdicts over a year later? Why was one a flashpoint but not the other? Indeed, if 'flashpoint' often implies spontaneity, then this looks especially peculiar. Prior to the riots, there had been widespread speculation about the possibility of disorder and, indeed, when the violence did break out, the Police Department was criticized for its alleged failure to be better prepared. The implication was that they should have anticipated disorder. All this rather undermines the idea that there was anything especially 'spontaneous' about the violence itself. The intriguing issue in France, in 2005, also concerns timing, and the fact that almost three weeks separated some of the riots from the initial outbreak of violence and, therefore, any initial flashpoint. I return to this below.

The shooting of Mark Duggan was a focal point for the anger of many involved in the rioting in London in 2011 (Lewis, Newburn, et al. 2011; Waddington 2012). However, the two-day delay before rioting occurred once again raises questions about what is meant or believed by a spark or flashpoint. In fact, the initial violence occurred when tempers became inflamed during a protest by Duggan's family and others outside the local police station the weekend after the shooting. Both Duggan's death and what many believed to be false claims being made by the police about Duggan's behaviour and character contributed to the anger felt by protesters. In fact, it seems plausible that it was an incident in the handling of the demonstration that was the flashpoint in this case (Stott, Scothern and Gorringe 2013). This raises the possibility of the existence of two or even more flashpoints, though to use it in this manner means losing some explanatory power. A better approach is to see Duggan's shooting as a condensation symbol, something which acted to focus wider feelings and emotions linked to long-standing distrust of and enmity towards the police that were later further provoked by what occurred outside Tottenham Police Station – the latter being the flashpoint. In social-psychological terms, both the shooting (which didn't lead directly to rioting) and the incident outside the police station (which did) arguably provoked shifts in collective identity. The shooting was important in bringing people out onto the streets to protest – in Tottenham and much more widely – but on the Saturday evening it was a much more specific set of events that acted as a flashpoint to collective violence. Shifts in protesters' collective identity and the changing patterns of behaviour they displayed were, it might be argued, guided by emergent norms and promulgated via 'keynoters' within the crowd.

The final example, that of Hong Kong's disorder in 2019, is extremely complex, involving a lengthy series of protests, some violent, over a period of a number of years. These preceding events undoubtedly contributed significantly to the tensions visible in 2019 and to the eventual violence. Once again, given their distance in time, such preceding events can hardly be thought of as flashpoints in any traditional sense, though they were undoubtedly, to use Kerner's terminology, tension-raising incidents. If one or more flashpoints existed in 2019, they were surely to be found in a much more proximate location. A distinction is often drawn between *necessary* and *sufficient* conditions for events; the former, possibly one of several conditions, that must be present in order for the events to occur, and the latter being that which produces the event concerned. Riots, in this sense, may be preceded by many events we might broadly characterize as *necessary* or proximate, as well as (possibly) one or more matters which might be *sufficient* to tip matters into violence. The necessary or proximate causes of riots are quite well established. Notwithstanding considerable work on flashpoints, establishing what might be considered the sufficient conditions for riots has proven much trickier.

It is really only the work of the British sociologist David Waddington and a number of colleagues (see, for example, King and Waddington 2005; Waddington, Jones and Critcher 1989) that offers any sustained analysis of the idea of a flashpoint. Waddington and colleagues (1989) argue that the metaphor has explanatory utility, and they develop a model through which to explore this further. Their 'flashpoints model' is somewhat more complex than the basic idea of tinder and spark, though they acknowledge that, despite its immediate attractiveness, a flashpoint remains a somewhat elusive notion (Waddington, Jones and Critcher 1989: 2). Their model places the idea of a flashpoint in a number of widening contexts. The underlying assumption is that a flashpoint should be viewed as 'a dramatic break in a pattern of *interaction* which might itself help to explain why and where disorder broke out' (Waddington, Jones and Critcher 1989: 21; emphasis in original). The original model had six levels of analysis, set out as concentric circles ranging from the macro to the micro, and including political, cultural and other contextual elements forming the backdrop to violence.

Waddington (2008) acknowledges that it is not just immediate factors that may act as the source of grievance and frustration but longer-term historical experiences and folklore which may inform and shape such matters as relations with the police. In this regard, he quotes Keith's (1993: 169) observation that 'Trigger events are not epiphenomenal or incidental to the development of violence. They provide a key element in the signification of action, the meaning of the *riot* set against its spatial and social context.' This sentence is of considerable significance to our understanding of the notion of a 'flashpoint', 'spark' or 'trigger'. As Keith highlights, these incidents are by no means secondary or of marginal importance to any model of the emergence of violence we may develop, but central to it. They are central, in part, because of their ability to condense the different meanings and motivations that participants bring to the action, all within its wider social, economic and cultural context. At heart, Waddington and colleagues' flashpoints model is a didactic one, designed to focus attention on those social, political, cultural, economic and more immediate situational features that influence the nature and shape of collective disorder, and pointing to the interactional level where flashpoints themselves are to be found.

Flashpoints in France

Moran and Waddington (2016) offer a full application of the flashpoints model to the 2005 French riots. Where the 'tinder' was concerned, they examine the structural, cultural, political and institutional factors that are conducive to violence. Among the structural factors, they point to the progressive economic and social exclusion that had affected the French *banlieues* (the stigmatized urban suburbs, and the French equivalent of 'ghettos')[3] and their relationship with mainstream French society. *Banlieues* were characterized by high unemployment, sociocultural exclusion of the immigrants who increasingly lived in these poor suburban estates, poor to non-existent public transport and increasingly dilapidated living conditions, together with endemic racial and ethnic discrimination (see also Dikec 2017; Wacquant 2008). Moran and Waddington identify high levels of crime and delinquency which dominated public and political attitudes towards the *banlieues*, together with a generalized absence of any substantive stake in French society among the residents of these areas, as the more prominent cultural factors. Young people, they argue, adapted by adopting confrontational subcultural styles and developing a street culture which emphasized 'respect' and which was organized around crime and drug dealing.[4] The parallel 'political/ideological factors' reflected the sense of exclusion experienced in the *banlieues*, a rejection of many of the mainstream political parties and their leaders – with particular enmity reserved for Nicolas Sarkozy, interior minister at the time of the riots and later president of France, and for his dismissive view of the estates and their residents. Many of the *banlieues* were viewed as places where some residents displayed an increasing degree of attraction to elements of Islamic fundamentalism. All of the above, perhaps predictably, had led to (and no doubt been partly created by) increasingly confrontational and repressive policing and a move away from proactive and preventative styles. Chirac's right-of-centre government had promised 'zero tolerance' and promoted a series of repressive measures, including the circulation of flash-ball guns to the *police de proximité* (Dikec 2017: 112).

These varied features were there long before the riots broke out and, indeed, continued to exist thereafter. The violence therefore requires a trigger or spark. Initially, Moran and Waddington claim that there can be no doubt that 'the highly emotive and symbolically significant incident involving the electrocution of the two youths from Clichy-sous-Bois and the immediate outrage it generated [was] the initial "flashpoint"' (2016: 58). Before long, a two-hour 'rampage' involving local youths was underway, with Sarkozy's intervention further unifying and antagonizing local citizens. A temporary period of peace ended when police officers fired a gas grenade into the entrance of a mosque, which in Moran and Waddington's view effectively acted as a *further* flashpoint and, certainly, there are those that describe events in Clichy as occurring in two phases over a six-day period (Dikec 2017: 98).

The picture that Moran and Waddington develop is one in which the deaths of 17-year-old Zyed Benna and 15-year-old Bouna Traoré provide the spark which set fire to the deeply embedded grievances and frustrations and the widespread sense of injustice held by many residents of Clichy-sous-Bois and, indeed, more widely subsequently in many other of France's *banlieues*. The background factors – structural, political/ideological, cultural, institutional, situational and communicational – found in Clichy are very typical of such communities and help explain in part why the riots became so widespread. Moran and Waddington's analysis of the spread of the riots focuses primarily on the political, communicational and institutional factors at play: provocative official statements and actions, such as the imposition of a curfew, together with the weaknesses, or perceived weaknesses, displayed by the French police. These collectively created a situation that was conducive to violence. Their account, like most others, sees the deaths of the two teenagers as the 'incident that opened the metaphorical floodgates, unleashing the anger of the suburbs and causing a situation that had long been in an extremely volatile state to explode' (Moran and Waddington 2016: 61). The subsequent police operation that resulted in an attack on a mosque acts as a second flashpoint, reinforcing earlier tension-raising processes. The question that then arises where the riots beyond Clichy are concerned, particularly those at some temporal or geographical remove, is whether the initial flashpoints are sufficient for us, alongside the other communicational and institutional features, to explain the breakdown of order. An account of the rioting that occurred in other locations, and times, would in principle also require a more particular look at the interactional level in order to unpack the ways in which order broke down and violence began.

Spread and contagion

One of the questions raised by the French example, and which continues to require explanation, is how do riots spread? As we have seen, a great many accounts assume spread is through what as shorthand is often thought of as *contagion* – spread via close contact between people. As a notion, contagion comes across in a slightly mystical manner, often implying something invisible and *spontaneous*. In its crudest forms, associated with classical psychology, the individual loses themselves in the crowd, and becomes highly suggestible. Reduced to a more primitive state, and prey to their worst instincts, these individuals form what is most usually a dangerous and violent crowd. Though the bulk of Le Bon's psychology has been firmly rejected, the broad idea of *contagion* is another example of continuing influence. Beyond possible exposure to common stimuli or forms of contact, including the impact of 'mutual gaze' (a powerful form of non-verbal communication), what is *actually* happening is generally left unexplained. What are the processes involved? In this context, terms like 'inspiration' and 'spontaneity' are often adopted but do little to unpack the practices involved in the spread of perceptions and conduct.

A somewhat more grounded manner of approaching such matters involves a form of social learning as people come into contact with others. Again, this occurs either through something approximating rational learning models or some other form of inspiration. A mix of proximate influence – more or less guided by some form of bounded rationality – is where the main authors using the language of contagion tend to focus. As Baudains, Johnson and Braithwaite (2013: 212) put it, 'large-scale outbreaks of disorder may be consequences of underlying tensions and grievances within a widely distributed population. If news of an initial riot at a given location spreads, then others who share similar grievances, regardless of where they are, may be inspired to behave similarly in an effort to address their grievances.' In this model, which is underpinned by rational choice theory and sees decision making as essentially reducible to self-interest, the word 'inspired' is once again made to do a lot of heavy lifting. News of riots spreads, and those in other areas may be inspired or provoked to respond to their common grievances (poverty, inequality, racism, injustice). What is missing in such an explanation is an identifiable 'spark' setting fire to such shared grievances. A similar argument is made by Aidt and colleagues' (2022) study of the distribution of the Captain Swing riots in 1830–1, in which careful empirical analysis of systems of communication between villages in England offers a nuanced picture of the spread of disorder and the key role of information diffusion without, unfortunately, being able to answer the question of why some people choose to act on the basis of this information while others remain peaceful.

A different, and theoretically more subtle, approach to the spread of riots comes from the work of the social psychologists working in the collective identity tradition. Using data from my study of the 2011 riots, Drury and colleagues' (2019) examination of the spread of rioting in south London, for example, identifies two 'pathways' of influence in the diffusion of riots. The first they call a 'cognitive pathway', and in this 'influence is a function of knowing who "we" are and hence inferring what "we" should do' (2019: 649). In short, they suggest that a shared social identity with others involved in, say, anti-police rioting (which is how they characterize the London riots) provides the normative basis for similar action elsewhere. Moreover, if they are part of a sizeable group intent on confronting the police, this shared social identity may also empower those involved. The second, the 'strategic pathway', is focused on the 'perceived vulnerability of a shared out-group' (the police in this case), a perception which enables action that would in other circumstances be repressed. As we will see in more detail in chapter 8, the riots in London and elsewhere in 2011 produced a situation in which there was, albeit briefly, a reversal of roles between the police and young people on the streets, with the latter temporarily in control and the police perceived to be 'on the run'. Drury and colleagues' (2019) 'strategic pathway' provides a guide to understanding not only why riots might spread in particular directions – because of the perceived vulnerability of the police in this case – but also the social-psychological mechanisms involved. They conclude that 'the evidence . . . is consistent with the idea that rioting spread from Tottenham [where it began] to a place where there was a critical mass of people who shared a social identity with those in the initial riot location and to places where there was a critical mass of people who shared a common enemy' (2019: 657–8). In a follow-up article, Drury and colleagues (2022) add a further, third, pathway – 'the "police pathway" – one in which 'it is possible that the occurrence of rioting leads the police in other cities to act in ways which inadvertently produce (or at least accelerate) rioting'. This third pathway involves a self-fulfilling prophecy, one in which police anxieties about the threats they face, given what has happened elsewhere, lead to increasingly repressive measures that produce changes in the social identity of the groups being policed – uniting them against the police and, in turn, generating precisely the forms of crowd behaviour that the police first feared.

Where does all this leave us? As I've argued, the strength of David Waddington's flashpoints model appears to lie in its didactic power, setting out in considerable detail ways in which the background factors to riots may usefully be considered and analysed. In short, it sets out a range of ways in which the first element of a *tinder and spark* model might be understood. It is, at its most convincing as a macro- or meso-sociological model, helping identify and, to a degree, separate the economic, political, cultural, institutional and situational antecedents of public disorder. While recognizing much beyond this, not least the centrality of symbolic and substantive interaction and communicative conduct in unpicking why certain events become violent, it is on much weaker ground here. Though acknowledging the importance of the micro-sociological and social-psychological elements of explanation, it is far less detailed and less convincing in articulating them. Ironically, it is the very nature of the 'flashpoint' itself that is the least well specified element of Waddington and colleagues' model. What is required is greater clarity around the interactional level of riot development. The aim must be to unpick the micro-sociology of violence and, more particularly, the precipitating events. To aid this process, I draw on three bodies of work that I take to be broadly mutually compatible: Stephen Reicher's (1984, 1996) social psychology of collective identity and, in particular, his previously discussed Elaborated Social Identity Model; Randall Collins's (2008) path-breaking work on the micro-sociology of violence; and, finally, linked with Collins's work, Anne Nassauer's (2019) empirical analysis of what she refers to as 'situational breakdowns'. Collectively and iteratively, these additions allow us greater critical insight into the *interactional* level of the flashpoints model and, crucially, into the very idea of the mechanism of the flashpoint itself.

Analysing flashpoints

As we know, the matters we later label 'flashpoints' can be trivial in themselves. What makes them a flashpoint, according to Waddington, Jones and Critcher, is that they are amenable to interpretation and can therefore set in motion a chain of response and counter-response, both behaviourally and emotionally. They are signs which 'connote an underlying set of assumptions about each group's perception of the other' (1989: 166). What transforms an incident into a flashpoint is not so much its inherent characteristics as the way the incident is interpreted in the moment. This is a plausible argument, but we're teetering on the precipice of tautology at the same time: a place where flashpoints can come dangerously close to simply being matters defined by those present as catalysts for changing behaviour. I have argued that flashpoints tend to occur at the interactional level. Naturally, what influences the interaction within a flashpoint is the context within which it occurs, the cultural predispositions of the participants, the political circumstances, and what those involved stand to win or lose. Yet, for all the work that has been done in exploration, application and clarification, the question of what constitutes a flashpoint remains unresolved. It continues to look opaque. It remains at heart the 'black box' in the explanation of riots and protest violence. How might resolution be achieved?

Ostensibly, the most obvious meaning of 'flashpoint' is an incident that marks the escalation of a previously largely peaceful situation into one that is violent. And this is the way that the term, of course, is most often used. It is occasionally deployed to describe events that might plausibly have led to violence but, for particular reasons, did not (see, for example, Waddington, Jones and Critcher 1989: 115). Indeed, more recently, Moran and Waddington (2016) have suggested that a 'failure to ignite' is one of the potential outcomes of a flashpoint. In my view, little is gained, and much is potentially lost, through such an extension in meaning. Finding a link between preceding, apparently precipitating, incidents and subsequent violence becomes even more challenging if the core analytical term – 'flashpoint' – is stretched to include matters that *might have been* a precipitant but did not result in violence. Nevertheless, there remains important potential comparative analysis here between incidents that lead, directly or indirectly, to significant disorder (flashpoints) and cognate events that had the potential to become a flashpoint but where such violence was not the outcome. Why might an arrest in one circumstance appear to be a catalyst or tipping point but another, in close to identical circumstances, not be so? Notwithstanding the important comparative analysis that might be stimulated in this context, referring to both types of incident as 'flashpoints' is decidedly unhelpful.

More nuanced comparative analysis of flashpoints can begin by utilizing the social-psychological ESIM. Centrally, as implied by its title, it focuses on social identity, seeing this as fundamental to group conduct. Where traditional psychological approaches posit a loss of identity as occurring within violent crowds, ESIM sees changing conduct as a consequence of shifts in social identity. Crowd members are influenced both by other members of the crowd and by the actions of outsiders with whom they interact, not least, for example, the police. Understandably, where collective violence is concerned, many of the most fateful or consequential interactions are between crowd members and the police. Work utilizing ESIM helps demonstrate the ways in which police action – often experienced and interpreted as illegitimate or inappropriate police action – affects the way crowd members see themselves. Some start out as peaceful, as non-violent, but may, having witnessed fellow crowd members being mistreated or, through being mistreated themselves, slowly come to identify with those in conflict with the police, thus increasingly seeing resistance, and perhaps even violence, as legitimate and appropriate.

The Kerner Commission suggested that around 40% of the sixties urban riots were preceded by allegedly abusive or discriminatory police actions. Most of these incidents began routinely and tended to centre on a response to a small number of people rather than a large group. Thinking of flashpoints as 'signifiers' is, in essence, where the ESIM begins to show its value. The flashpoint, from this social-psychological perspective, is a symbolic moment and one that works to solidify social identities and, more particularly, to create oppositional social identities. As Waddington and colleagues acknowledge, though without direct reference to the psychology of social identities, there is often

> a breaking point, at which the *treatment of the crowd*, the *treatment of the police*, or the *treatment of targets*, is seen to breach the agreed norms of interaction, justifying retaliation in kind. One mark of this breakdown is the shift of insults from routinized general jeering to highly personalized

> abuse. Physical or verbal, such exchanges are interpreted symbolically as indicative of how each group actually feels about the other. (Waddington, Jones and Critcher 1989: 166)

Social identities shift, and consequently behaviour may do so also. As identities become more oppositional, violence – though far from inevitable – becomes more likely.

Emotions and flashpoints

One word that has barely appeared thus far, but which lies below the surface of everything discussed, is 'emotion'. I have argued that flashpoints, whatever the word is taken to mean, occur at the interactional level. Shifts in collective identity involve the subjective interpretation of events by contesting groups and the emotional reactions of these groups to what they perceive to be happening and how they feel they are being treated. One further means of exploring these processes lies in Randall Collins's (2008) micro-sociology of violence and, in particular, what he calls 'forward panic'. He acknowledges that meso- and macro-level conditions are important in theorizing violence (as we have seen when thinking about the 'tinder') but suggests that 'the key stumbling blocks and turning points are at the micro level' (2008: 34). His work, therefore, focuses very much on the interactional territory that we have established requires greater explication. In an antagonistic interaction, people experience what Collins calls 'confrontational tension', and at its higher levels this can transform into fear. This is an internal fear rather than fear of the other, and 'forward panic' – the gradually increasing tension in the lead-up to violence – is one of the main pathways through which confrontational tension and fear are overcome. This is a two-stage process. The first involves the build-up of tension, the second a shift in which a previously passive opponent suddenly achieves a degree of dominance, giving their conduct an 'out of proportion' appearance.

Notwithstanding the terminology, Collins's argument isn't really focused on panic as we ordinarily understand it. The sequence of actions he focuses upon, which is often quite drawn out, involves ongoing frustration more than particular danger or anything approaching panic. Rather, tension builds up and frustrations develop, which provoke a set of emotional responses, all building towards something climactic. The end result can be quite dramatic, leading to actions that would not normally occur. Most instances of police misconduct that lead to public scandals have the character of a forward panic, Collins argues, and he gives the example of the Rodney King beating. What occurred in that situation was a prolonged car chase during which police officers experienced extended frustration in carrying out routine duties, all set in the context of high tension and, potentially, fear. The outcome is well known. The film of King's assault at the hands of four LAPD officers[5] illustrates well the rage and fury that tend to typify the end point of a forward panic. The same general patterns can be identified in the context of crowd violence. Some of the violence seen during riots is often quite extreme and, in parallel, generally occurs after an extensive build-up of tension and, possibly, of frustration and fear, often on both sides – both protesters and police. In addition to these emotions, research shows that a mood of elation may be present during and after the violence, with hysterical laughter also characteristic of such situations. We will see examples of such emotions among protesters in the next chapter and among the police later in the book. Importantly, these are also collective emotions; they are shared and emerge from the group experience of the interaction.

We discussed earlier the temporal delay that sometimes occurs between events labelled as 'flashpoints' and subsequent outbreaks of violence. Similarly, Collins (2008: 115) notes that the forward panic associated with crowd violence is often characterized by a lull appearing before the eventual storm. The lull, which lasts at most two days, is often an ominous one where the dominant emotion is tension, a tension born of fear of the enemy and of concern about what may be about to happen. The eventual release of tension that accompanies the outbreak of violence is often accompanied by a sense of exhilaration – what Collins (2012) refers to as 'going down the tunnel'. Violence tends not to break out quickly but, once it does, 'it attains a self-perpetuating, escalatory dynamic' (Bramsen 2023: 92). In this sense, violence becomes an interaction ritual, or set of rituals, in its own right, 'with its own rhythm and momentum that can be difficult to stop' (2023: 103). Interaction rituals transform emotions. Collins (2004: 105) notes that 'rituals [such as protest] begin with emotional ingredients (which may be emotions of all sorts); they intensify emotions into the shared excitement that Durkheim called "collective effervescence"; and they produce other sorts of emotions as outcomes (especially moral solidarity, but also sometimes aggressive emotions such as anger).' This might serve to reinforce the picture I have been building of what occurred in London in 2011. In that case, a young man was shot by police and, as outlined earlier, in the immediate aftermath rumour and counter-rumour circulated and tensions rose. Such miscommunication is often an important contributor to the outbreak of collective violence (Nassauer 2019). There was little doubt that tensions would rise, in part thanks to the fact that Mark Duggan lived on a well-known local estate, Broadwater Farm, which had a history both of previous serious rioting and of poor relations with the police. Around 48 hours later, protesters had gathered outside a symbolic location, Tottenham Police Station, making demands of the police, demands it was felt not only fell on deaf ears but were responded to with disrespect, providing almost perfect conditions for 'forward panic'. This 'disrespect' included a young woman allegedly being pushed violently to the ground by a police officer, an incident that led directly to the first signs of violence. For their part, the police had endured two days of threatened violence and conditions which required high levels of self-control and collective restraint. Once violence was underway, the release of tension would have been substantial, though the police remained relatively constrained by lack of numbers. What happened subsequently was much influenced by police preparedness or, in reality, its relative absence. Though Collins (2008: 121) is clear that rationality is far from absent, in a forward panic 'the emotional impulses are overwhelming, above all because they are shared by everyone: by one's supporters and fellow attackers, and in a reciprocal way, by the passive victims'. Finally, forward panics, he argues, are 'typical in situations where a group has overwhelming local superiority in numbers and strength, following a situation in which a confrontation among organized crowds has built up tension' (2008: 128).

Further detail can be added both to the emotional dynamics that Collins outlines in his micro-sociological approach, and more generally to our understanding of the immediately preceding events leading up to violence, by drawing on the work of the German sociologist, Anne Nassauer (2019), who examines the interactional patterns over a somewhat longer time frame. Nassauer focuses on what she calls 'situational breakdowns', where ordinary, expected routines and surprising outcomes – in our case, collective violence – emerge. She identifies five sets of interactions which, when found in certain combinations, encourage violence. These pathways contribute to increased police–protester tension. She calls them: *spatial incursions*; *police mismanagement*; *escalation signs*; *property damage*; and *communication problems*. Spatial incursions occur where one side invades the other's associated or negotiated territory, and it is these that she argues have the most dramatic impact on the eruption of violence.[6]

In her study, Nassauer found that spatial incursions were 'a necessary condition for violent outbreaks in peaceful public protest marches' (2019: 54), paralleling Castells's (1983: 71) argument that the contestation of 'definitions of urban space' was at the heart of much urban unrest. They were a necessary but not sufficient condition for violence; they couldn't cause violence, but were present in every case where there was violence. In short, therefore, flashpoints will tend to involve the perception that one or both sides in an emergent conflict has strayed into the other's actual or symbolic territory. Following Collins, Nassauer similarly argues that violence requires a form of domination, in this case where one side in a conflict perceives itself to be under attack or about to be under attack.[7]

Police mismanagement refers to situations where those in operational command lack an overview of the situation they face, have no clear plan of action for how to proceed, or experience some form of communication breakdown during the operation. Of all the riots we've considered here, it is perhaps in the 1992 Los Angeles riots that such mismanagement has been most clearly and carefully documented (Cannon 1999; Katz 2016; Useem 1997). Useem (1997: 373), for example, describes the LAPD as having 'drifted through the first half dozen hours of the disturbance', as remaining unprepared despite considerable warning and, very specifically at the so-called flashpoint at the Florence and Normandie intersection, as having displayed a range of problems of 'command', including location, level (insufficient seniority) and unity. Beyond this, of course, there may also be wider *communication problems* between police and protesters. *Property damage* is an important factor, not least because of its symbolic effect in leading the police who witness it to anticipate further problems, most obviously physical violence. Finally, there are other *escalation signs* defined as conduct 'perceived as foreboding harmful actions' (Nassauer 2019: 75). These may be as varied as the clothes that participants wear ('black bloc' clothing, hoodies and masks worn by protesters, riot gear by the police), the slogans they shout and the materials/objects they carry (from stones or bricks to CS gas and other munitions).

Combinations of these various factors lead Nassauer to identify three primary pathways towards violence. In the first – what she refers to as the *losing control* pathway – a combination of police mismanagement and spatial incursions lead to a situational breakdown. Neither police mismanagement nor spatial incursions, she argues, can produce violence on their own, but in combination they are sufficient. Protests, at heart, involve conflicts over space, and negotiation over where protesters are allowed, and when, is a crucial element of public order policing (it is fundamental to everyday policing also; Newburn 2022). Similarly, local residents – in places such as Clichy-sous-Bois, south-central LA, and Broadwater Farm in north London – will often have strong feelings about the integrity of their neighbourhoods and consequently about police incursion into such areas. Territory, to draw a link with social-psychological theory, may form one basis for collective identity. Spatial incursions don't necessarily involve physical proximity but refer more straightforwardly to the violation of spatial norms. 'In short,' Nassauer (2019: 56) observes, 'spatial incursions drastically disrupt peaceful protest routines and contribute to changing emotional dynamics.' While this doesn't lead to violence on its own, if it coincides with, or is driven by, police mismanagement, officers will often feel themselves losing control of the situation and, naturally enough, fear the consequences. The fact that officers will often feel relatively powerless in such situations causes further difficulty. Setting out elements of this 'pathway' offers insight into one form of flashpoint. This is a case, academics such as Reicher and others would argue, where changes in collective identity are likely to occur among protesters and police. The resulting heightening of tension and emotions leads, or can lead, to the eruption of violence through the removal of the barriers Collins identifies, particularly where one group identifies some emotional or other substantive weakness (see Bramsen 2018b) in their opponent and sees an opportunity to regain some control. What then follows is an interaction ritual characterized by violence. In Collins's model, this tends to be portrayed as an asymmetrical relationship, with one side dominating the other. Bramsen (2017: 9) argues, importantly, that violence need not always emanate in this fashion, for it can 'be observed *both* as an asymmetrical domination ritual and as a symmetrical conflict ritual, depending on whether or not the victim is too dominated to fight back'.

The second pathway Nassauer describes as the *offence path*. In this case, the spatial incursions are combined with escalation signs and property damage, leading to increased tension and fear and 'to violence when individuals or small groups establish emotional dominance' (2019: 71). Police (and protesters) may often expect the worst. Escalation signs are insufficient to lead to violence on their own, for such negative expectations don't create a self-fulfilling prophecy. Nevertheless, where one side, or both, perceives actions as foreshadowing harmful behaviour, then that is likely to increase tension and fear. As already suggested, both police and protesters are likely to lay claim to particular territories and see incursions into them as challenging, threatening and potentially dangerous, increasing the likelihood of escalation. In this context, property damage has a similar impact. It raises tension among the police, who are faced with having to make decisions about how to respond and having to assess and anticipate what reaction any response might provoke. Officers will tend to see protesters who engage in damage – let's say either looting or arson – as more generally 'violent' and to react to them in this manner. Protesters are aware of the threat their behaviour carries and of the dilemmas facing the police. Their engagement in activities that contain escalation signs forms part of the scripted nature of riotous activity. These are well-practised and rehearsed strategies. They are ritualized forms of interaction. Activities such as arson and looting are communicative forms of conduct, and this is one reason they are regularly observed during such disorder. As Nassauer (2019: 84–5) puts it, where 'property damage occurs in the offense path, it provides actors with evidence that dangers perceived through escalation signs and spatial incursions are real'. Again, returning to the Elaborated Social Identity Model, it is not difficult to see the impact police incursion in symbolic territory, and their repression of acts such as arson and looting, might have on protesters' sense of collective identity.

The third route to collective violence Nassauer calls the *missing information path*, and once again involves spatial incursions and escalation signs, on this occasion with communication problems. It produces situations in which 'people are confused, fearful, and overwhelmed' (2019: 87). In the first two pathways, it was perceptions of a loss of control on the one hand and an offence on the other that led to escalating tension and fear. In the third, it is missing information or lack of knowledge about what the other intends, in the context of spatial incursions and escalation signs, which unsettles police and/or protesters and produces increased tension and fear. In such a situation, one side's interpretation of the likely actions of the other may change, rumours can easily spread, and anticipated routines break down, all of which brings us back to emotions. Following Collins, Nassauer argues that though anger is often present, it is tension and fear that are most closely linked with the breakdown of order. The next stage is for tension to be released through emotional dominance over a weak victim, or a victim perceived to be weak, with this acting as the basis for the eruption of or increase in violence.

These micro-sociological approaches add a great deal of necessary detail to the more macro-sociological analyses so often applied to rioting, and indeed even to social-psychological approaches, such as the social identity model. We nevertheless still find ourselves back in a situation in which some form of trigger or turning point has to be identified. A combination of ESIM, forward panic and situational breakdowns offers a means of analysing those small-scale interactions that produce violence. But the question of *which* interactions still hangs over such analysis. What will be clear from the tenor of the discussion in this and preceding chapters is that there is no straightforward or consistent answer to that question. But it appears some broad patterns do appear. During protests, Nassauer says, there are a number of 'triggering moments' that evidence suggests can promote emotional dominance and protest violence. These include the break-up of police–protester lines. Police often adopt straight lines when confronting protesters, and the integrity of these lines appears important to the likelihood or otherwise of violence. However, if lines break up, 'individuals can establish emotional dominance and attack the situationally weaker opponent' (Nassauer 2019: 101). The visible, relative or perceived absence of formal controls acts as an invitational edge to violence. Similarly, 'falling down can trigger violence'. In her empirical analyses of filmed footage of violent confrontations, Nassauer (2019: 101) found that 'when a protester falls down or struggles to regain footing, one officer – usually the one closest to the protester – hits the person who has fallen. Right after the first attack, other officers start hitting that person as well, usually much harder' (this can also happen the other way round, of course). These and other triggering moments are dangerous in situations where tension has built up, and they encourage violence because of the opportunity they offer for emotional dominance to be established. Perceived powerlessness is an important contributor to the escalation of violence. Often, initial outbreaks will relatively quickly be brought under control. However, the perception that the police are incapable of restoring order – as was the case in both Los Angeles in 1992 and London in 2011 – leads swiftly to widespread and significant violence. All this tends to happen remarkably quickly – hence the invocation of terms like *spontaneity* – and relies upon the ways in which those involved interpret the situation and the actions and dispositions of others. Crucially, 'Without perceived danger, and the perception that routine interactions cannot be relied on anymore, tension and danger would not increase' (Nassauer 2019: 104). Relatedly, Nassauer argues that the extent or degree of emotional dominance felt by participants helps to explain the intensity of violence that is involved. To this nuanced picture, Isabel Bramsen adds a further important insight. Collins's theory, and much of Nassauer's work in its wake, posits that emotional domination or lack of direct confrontation are conditions for violence and that violence, therefore, goes against the grain of typical social interaction. While accepting this, as we saw earlier, Bramsen argues that there are occasions when violence can be an interaction ritual in its own right, where parties fall into each other's rhythms and where emotional dominance becomes less important. A game of cat and mouse – an action/reaction sequence – evolves. Importantly, 'once violence occurs it can likewise be *driven* (rather than inhibited) by emotional entrainment and the tendency to fall into the rhythms of the opponent' (Bramsen 2017: 9).

A necessary micro-sociology of precipitating events

In his now classic work on collective behaviour, Neil Smelser identified 'precipitating events' as important – necessary but insufficient – bases for future collective action. Herbert Blumer wrote of 'exciting events' which catch the attention and arouse the interest of crowd members and help give 'common orientation' to their activities. 'The precipitating factor confirms the existence, sharpens the definition, or exaggerates the effect' of pre-existing matters such as structural strain (Smelser 1963: 249). Flashpoints, as we have been referring to them here, are another way of conceptualizing precipitating events.

The basic metaphor of 'tinder and spark' continues to dominate political and public discussions of riots. Indeed, whether explicit or sotto voce, academic analysis tends to organize itself around the same basic idea. Despite this we don't have a convincing theory of flashpoints, and I have argued that greater specification of what may be occurring within such events is required. There is nothing intrinsic to the social phenomena we label flashpoints that sets them apart. Most frequently they arise out of interactions between the police and protesters. Significant or trivial, what is important is that they are capable of being seen or perceived as potentially transformative; that is to say, to carry the potential to increase tension and indeed increase the likelihood of violence. In short, flashpoints are potentially important symbolic and communicative moments which signal a shift in mood and a potential shift in collective identity. They are, as I put it earlier, 'signifiers' of symbolic moments where collective identities shift and solidify, albeit temporarily. In Bramsen and Poder's (2018: 8) terms, these situations of 'conflictual interaction' are ones that generate negative emotional energy, binding 'opponents to each other in hatred'. Flashpoints, then, are micro-sociological turning points, in which there are emotional shifts, leading to the gradual dominance of one 'side' over another, however briefly.[8]

It is in the analysis of micro-sociological turning points that I have suggested that Reicher and colleagues' Elaborated Social Identity Model has an important role to play. In its focus, for example, on exchanges between protesters and police, the model illustrates how problematic dynamics may lead to shifts in social identification, how such shifts in social identity polarize protesters and police and, in turn, create an increased (or decreased) willingness to embrace more confrontational forms of conduct. In addition to greater utilization of the ESIM at the interactional level of riot development, I have argued that insights from both Randall Collins's (2008) micro-sociology of violence and, relatedly but more particularly, Anne Nassauer's (2019) analysis of 'situational breakdowns' offer additional benefits in this regard.

Collins's value lies initially in his vitally important observation that we're not very good at violence. There are very significant emotional barriers of 'confrontational tension/fear' that have to be overcome before violence can take place, at least on any scale. The broad background circumstances that conduce towards collective violence, the economic, social, cultural, political and institutional factors that make up the 'tinder' underpinning any collective violence, are often both easy to identify and an everyday presence. But significant barriers to *actual* violence tend to remain, and these 'key stumbling blocks and turning points are at the micro level' (Collins 2008: 34). One of the ways in which such stumbling blocks are overcome is via the process we have previously seen referred to as 'forward panic', and Collins convincingly uses the Rodney King beating as an example of the process in action. In this model, violence tends to be preceded by perpetrator domination (police or protester, for example); violence in effect is a form of ritualized domination, albeit a relatively brief one. In looking to extend this analysis, I have argued that Nassauer's analysis of 'situational breakdowns' offers a further possible step forward. She identifies three primary pathways where combinations of events lead to heightened tensions, declining trust and a greater likelihood of violence. One of these, the 'offence path', involves what she calls 'escalation signs', combined with 'spatial incursions' and property damage. The breakdown of order outside Tottenham Police Station in August 2011, which was the beginning of what turned out to be four days of the most serious rioting seen in post-war England, involved spatial incursions by both police and protesters (inflaming tensions on both sides), symbolic property damage (in particular, when police cars started to be torched and when the police station itself was threatened), and a vital escalation sign when a young woman was pushed to the ground by the police (see Stott, Drury and Reicher 2017). A situational breakdown such as this further heightens tensions and potentially provokes shifts in group social identification. To take a second brief example, Nassauer's 'missing information' pathway involves both 'spatial incursions' and 'escalation signs' once again, together with 'communication problems'. A clear illustration of such a development can be found in the spread and growth of the 1992 Los Angeles riots. In particular, as noted earlier, the spatial incursion that occurred at the intersection of Florence and Normandie, where the televised beating of Reginald Denny took place, was in the context of a more general series of managerial and tactical failures (Useem 1997). Not least of these was the abandonment of the intersection by the LAPD (Miller 2001). This 'event' featured a series of escalation signs, among which were instances of apparently unpoliced and unrestrained violence. Of these, the most egregious was Denny's beating itself, involving young people enjoying an 'epiphany of invisibility' (Katz 2016), seemingly unconcerned by the presence of cameras and apparently acting with impunity. The Denny beating is a further example of Collins's 'forward panic', with the outstanding nature of the violence in this incident acting once again as the basis for shifts in social identity.

Our understanding of riots and protest violence requires a marriage of macro- and meso-level factors representing the underpinning frustrations and grievances that are expressed by those engaging in protest, together with a micro-sociological account of the precipitants involved. In earlier chapters, I set out a broad means of considering the structural features of riots and rioting – in effect, how we might approach an understanding of the underlying 'tinder' found in connection with major riots. There is much here that is agreed upon. The missing element in social scientific analysis, however, is a more detailed breakdown of the other element in the metaphor: the 'spark' or 'flashpoint'. To deal with this, I have proposed the utilization of three main approaches as the basis of a more detailed and nuanced analysis of the micro-sociology of the breakdown of order. These three elements are: first, Reicher and colleagues' 1995 social-psychological Elaborated Social Identity Model. This helps us chart the shifting of social identities in the interactions between protesters and others, notably the police, and allows an understanding of how the condensation symbols and flashpoints identified in the lead-up to disorder underpin changes in social identity and the shifting legitimacy that attaches as a consequence of protest. To this picture we add aspects of Randall Collins's micro-sociology of violence and, more particularly, his theory of 'forward panic'. This focuses on the way that tension builds up over time, providing the basis for what often appear to be extreme levels of violence in small groups – say, the officers involved in the beating of Rodney King – or much larger events that we tend retrospectively to describe as riots. Riot is often preceded by considerable increases in pressure, anxiety and tension, and it is these, when pressure finds release, that lie behind the tremendous levels of violence sometimes found in the early stages of disorder. Third, and finally, I have argued that the type of empirical work undertaken by Anne Nassauer in her studies of 'situational breakdowns' offers a further important development in the analysis of riot. In short, she identifies a series of particular micro-sociological circumstances in which routines break down, tensions are raised, normative boundaries are breached and conflict ensues. No doubt further empirical work adopting this type of approach will reveal a range of pathways beyond the three primary routes to situational breakdown that she has thus far revealed but, allied to the other conceptual tools outlined above, this offers, collectively, by far the most nuanced approach to date to those precipitating events we have come to think of as 'flashpoints'.

6
The Quest for Excitement and Beyond

One of the great lacunae in criminology, Jack Katz[1] says, is 'evidence of what it means, feels, sounds, tastes, or looks like to commit a particular crime' (1988: 3). A growing body of criminological work has recognized the shortcomings of extant approaches, arguing for the importance of taking 'more serious account of the *affective* dimensions of criminal behaviour; something that requires a more active engagement with – and in – the sociology of emotions' (de Haan and Loader 2002: 245). Why, one might ask, is such a corrective necessary? Why, if it is true, have social scientists so often avoided engaging with emotions when considering matters of criminal conduct and, in turn, protest and riots? What are the main 'resistances' (Calhoun 2001) to deeper sociological engagement with emotions? The answer, I believe, lies primarily in the association of emotions with irrationality.[2] The historian William Sewell (1996: 865) argues similarly, saying social scientists 'seem to fear that if they take emotion seriously as an object of study, they will be tainted by the irrationality, volatility, subjectivity, and ineffability that we associate with the term – that their own lucidity and scientific objectivity will be brought into question'. As Goodwin, Jasper and Polletta (2004: 415) put it, emotions 'have been considered too personal, too idiosyncratic, too inchoate, or too irrational to be modeled or measured properly'. Arguably, it is with Max Weber that the distinction between 'rational action' and all other forms of conduct begins, and the origins of the continuing discomfort with emotions and affective behaviour are to be found in the classical early representations of the crowd.[3] It is not just social scientists, however.

As Katz (2002: 260–1) correctly observes, 'Close description of what happens when people laugh, cry, get angry, or get ashamed will show that emotions are not, as they have almost always been understood, in tension with thought, reason, or strategic self-examination. Just the reverse: emotions are lived as metamorphoses toward thought, as movements from an unself-conscious being-in-the-world to relatively more self-reflective postures.' Or, as Jasper (2018: 21) puts it, 'Cognition and feeling are parts of the same universe, not opposites' (see also Turner 1964; Turner and Killian 1957). Even the 'cultural turn' has left such assumptions largely undisturbed, with cognition continuing to be the primary focus of the social sciences, rather than feelings (Goodwin, Jasper and Polletta 2001). Around a quarter of a century ago, Goodwin and colleagues made the following observation:

> Emotions are perhaps the ultimate Rorschach test for sociologists, revealing their basic theoretical assumptions about social life .... Once at the center of the study of protest, emotions have led a shadow existence for the last three decades, with no place in the rationalistic, structural, and organizational models that dominate academic political analysis. In these models, humans are portrayed as rational and instrumental, traits which are oddly assumed to preclude any emotions. Even the recent rediscovery of culture has taken a cognitive form .... Somehow, observers have managed to ignore the swirl of passions all around them in political life. (Goodwin, Jasper and Polletta 2000: 65)[4]

Emotion and protest violence

Michael Keith, in his thoughtful analysis of the significant urban disorder of the early 1980s, argued that extant accounts were incomplete. What was required and was so often missing was

> a conception of *rioting* which captures the impromptu nature of events without reducing the actions of individuals to the behaviourist response to an array of environmental stimuli. Such a description demands a notion of *spontaneity* that does not devalue the rationality of individuals yet at the same time conveys a notion of the social context in which such actions are situated. (Keith 1993: 94; emphasis added)

Importantly, Keith's observation reminds us that a concern with feelings and emotions is a matter of macro-sociology as well as micro-sociology; it is part and parcel of collective behaviour just as much as individual reactions to circumstances.

The tendency to elide emotion with irrationality is quite mistaken for, as Norbert Elias (1982: 230–1) observed, the social dynamic 'is neither "rational" – if by "rational" we mean that it has resulted intentionally from the purposive deliberation of individual people; nor "irrational" – if by "irrational" we mean that it has arisen in an incomprehensible way'. The consequence is that approaches focusing only on 'the consciousness of men [*sic*], their "reason" or "ideas", while disregarding the structure of drives, the direction and form of human affects and passions, can be from the outset of only limited value' (Elias 1982: 284). This takes us full circle back to Jack Katz (2002: 260), who reminds us that 'Any social act, from making love to making war, must be constructed if it is to exist. Seen from the outside both sex and violence may appear to be a lot of wild thrashing about, but from the inside they have coherent interactional meanings and are recognizable as a distinctive type of activity because they develop along non-random lines.' This observation applies just as much to protest and riots as it does to any other social phenomenon. If we accept this, as we surely must, then the inevitable conclusion is that the conduct of protesters, including when protest turns violent, must be understood as a set of constructed social acts containing many potential levels of meaning.

Gary Marx wanted to direct attention away from the assumption that riotous conduct necessarily has some form of (political) ambition or aim. He sought to offer a corrective against those approaches that treat riots as 'if they were internally homogeneous phenomena' with consensually approved goals (1970: 26). Rather, both the degree of internal coherence and the nature of legitimating beliefs (including whether or not they are present) ought to be treated as criteria for distinguishing different forms of riot or protest violence.

Banal though it may at first seem, Marx's initial important observation is that riots vary in nature. They vary by the characteristics of the participants, in the aims and objectives of those participants (so far as they exist and can be known), in the means that are used to bring about any such objectives, by the intensity of the events, the violence in particular, and by the reactions of state authorities, among others. In all this, Marx urges us not to lose sight of the fact that there are riots that have little in the way of instrumental goals beyond perhaps securing free goods or experiencing fleeting excitement, of which more below. Marx's second point is that 'pronounced strain' is not a necessary condition for rioting. In 'issueless riots', he argues, it can be 'difficult to identify sources of strain, such as racial discrimination or competition, low salaries and job insecurity, colonial domination and the like – though, as the riot develop[s], people experiencing an array of strains may become involved' (1970: 32). Linked with these points is the reminder that it is perfectly possible, indeed arguably typical, for *ex post facto* motives to be formulated and applied. In this manner, recognizing forms of disorder beyond the stereotypical pictures of riots driven by ideology and protest, he argued, would deepen our analysis and understanding. The contrast between protests that are driven by political ambitions and claims and those where such factors are relatively absent is a potentially illuminating one. This message is one that was seemingly lost on many social scientists in the following decades. As a final observation, we must also remind ourselves that everyone experiences emotions. Although in the analysis of conflict between groups it is most often rioters' emotions that are the focus, as we will explore later in the book, there is also much to be said about the emotional experiences of police officers faced with a potentially violent crowd.

Excitement

Jasper reminds us that there are positive as well as more obviously negative forms of emotion. The reminder is important because studies of protest and conflict are dominated by a focus on negative emotions (Bramsen and Poder 2018). If anger is largely a negative emotion, then joy, or what Jasper refers to as *thrill*, is more obviously positive (though it may have negative undertones). Collins's work on interaction chains begins with such thrills: 'human bodies moving into the same place starts off the ritual process. There is a buzz, and excitement, or at least a wariness when human bodies are near each other' (Jasper 2018: 50–1). Discussions of rioting can easily overlook just how exciting the initial activity can feel. For reasons that are perhaps understandable, just how much fun rioters actually appear to be having, at least in the early stages of a riot, is rarely foregrounded in scholarly discussion. One slight exception, though he was adopting a particularly critical stance towards riots, came from the American sociologist Edward Banfield (1970), who asked to what extent the urban riots in sixties America should be seen as having been 'mainly for fun and profit', an argument we'll return to in the next chapter.

My own interest in this emotional dimension originated in research on the England riots of 2011. My research team conducted a total of 270 interviews with 'rioters' – people who had been on the streets during the four days of disorder and had engaged, to varying degrees, in various forms of violence. This, we believe, is a uniquely large body of data, and it forms the basis for much of the argument in this chapter. These 270 interviews were fully transcribed and then analysed using standard social scientific qualitative thematic techniques. In preparation for writing this book I once again read all these interviews. In doing so, one confronts the range of emotions experienced and expressed during riot. What is immediately striking is how close the expression of emotions is to the surface, and what comes shining through is the sheer amount of fun many people said they were having. It was enjoyable for them, or at least elements of it were. A 21-year-old man from Manchester described a situation in which 'Everyone obviously had had a few drinks. You know, smoking spliffs. Everyone was happy, like throwing stones at the police 'n that. Ha ha, yes it was a party atmosphere like, it was a carnival atmosphere.' In many ways, his experience reflects the 'collective effervescence' (see also Le Roy Ladurie 1980), which 'acts as an exceptionally powerful stimulant . . . [underpinned by] a sort of electricity . . . which quickly transports them to an extraordinary degree of exaltation'. It potentially leads to the crowd member being 'carried away by some sort of an external power which makes him think and act differently than in normal times . . . . It seems to him that he has become a new being' (Durkheim 1964 [1912]: 215–16, 218).

Many who become involved in a riot do not set out with instrumental aims. Often, they are part of a peaceful crowd which subsequently finds itself – and therefore themselves – embroiled in violence. Or, alternatively and very commonly, people hear about violence taking place, perhaps via television or other media, and decide to go and see what is happening. Often at this stage there is no particular aim, according to their accounts, other than satisfying curiosity. In the England riots of 2011, such views were commonplace. A 21-year-old female from Clapham described going to the site of the disturbances, having seen what was happening on television. 'I was just curious. Because you see it on telly. In Tottenham and other places . . . So I was just there. Basically to see for myself what was going on.' For some who heard about outbreaks of violence, there was something beyond curiosity, a desire to get involved in some manner. In particular, having seen or heard about what was going on, there were those who were concerned about missing out. There was something attractive about the prospect of involvement, at least at the margins of the disorder: 'there's just so many people doing it. You just think you're missing out as opposed to anything else', said a 21-year-old male from south London. What they were missing out on some found difficult to describe, but in reading their accounts it is hard to avoid the impression that it was primarily 'the buzz' associated with the disorder. Without wishing to draw too strong a parallel, anyone who has heard a shout 'fight, fight' go up in a school playground will likely understand the initial thrill associated with it, as well as the attraction of seeing what is going on. Riots, similarly, draw spectators. This is inevitable. Those drawn to the disorder in London and elsewhere in 2011 were not disappointed, it appears, for many vividly described how once they were there, a 'massive adrenaline rush' took hold, meaning that 'once you'd started you just couldn't be bothered stopping' (18-year-old white male, Manchester). For one 19-year-old man in London, 'it was a buzz, it was like a drug that you couldn't say no to'. Such accounts speak directly to the drama of riots and rioting. Those involved were not simply excited, they were aware of others' excitement and that they were part of a visual display, a performance – indeed a performance in front of an audience. That audience comprised at least three groups: other 'rioters'; others out on the streets (non-combatants, who witnessed such events but weren't involved directly in the violence); and the police. The police were a highly significant audience, there as witnesses to the anger directed towards them and others, and to the theft and destruction of police cars and torching of police buildings, as well as being rendered passive witnesses to theft, arson and violence. The police and indeed some of the 'non-combatants' found what they witnessed deeply disturbing. Though we have noted the tacit support rioters sometimes received within the community, many within the neighbourhoods most affected also found much riotous conduct repellent.

Riots occur in circumstances where the normal rules of everyday life have, at least in part, broken down. There consequently exists a sense of freedom, albeit a limited and temporary one, that can be enjoyed and exploited. There is the fleeting possibility of experiencing something highly unusual, to do things that would otherwise be impossible. This involves, however briefly, an upending of social norms and, crucially, offers the possibility of thrills in a context of lives that lack many legitimate opportunities for excitement and are characterized by relatively little freedom. For some, therefore, riots offer the opportunity for a 'moral holiday', one not to be missed, whatever risks that might involve. The term, coined by the philosopher William James (2000 [1905]), connotes the necessity of occasional breaks from the potentially stifling influence of social mores and norms[5] and has been used in studies of collective behaviour to aid reflection on those circumstances where normal social constraints falter or are absent. During a moral holiday, Collins (2008: 243) observes, 'the crowd as a whole is galvanized into a collective consciousness in opposition to [conventional] restraints . . . . [A moral holiday] comprises a free zone in time and space, an occasion and a place where the feeling prevails that everyday restraints are off; individuals feel protected by the crowd, and are encouraged in normally forbidden acts'. This broad description somewhat masks the earlier point, however. This is not *any* crowd. Generally, riots involve the poor, the disenfranchised, the excluded.[6] Their lives are, for economic and social reasons, relatively speaking, limited and constrained. In such circumstances, consequently, there is something particularly attractive about the opportunity offered by a temporary suspension of everyday social restrictions. A moral holiday is an especially seductive possibility for this segment of the population, and it is one that is often gleefully exploited.

Carnival atmosphere

Earlier I quoted a young man from Manchester in 2011 talking about the 'carnival atmosphere' that pervaded elements of his experience of the riots. Similarly, one 50-year-old female described the rioting in north London as like being at 'Tottenham Carnival . . . seeing people that you hadn't seen for ages . . . during the year, it was like, "Oh, hi" [laughing]. Honestly it was . . . it was really like that. It was quite enjoyable. It was really enjoyable actually.' Presdee (2000) noted that carnival is a much used and abused term but is nonetheless often an appropriate way of addressing 'excitement and transgression' in human conduct. Carnival 'can be both violent and break the law'. The *Oxford English Dictionary* defines 'carnival' as: 'Any occasion or period of celebration or festivity characterized as indulgent, unrestrained, or licentious. Hence: anything likened to a carnival in being lavish, exuberant, or chaotic; an extravagant, ostentatious, or unruly display *of* something.' The Russian literary critic, Mikhail Bakhtin, one of the more influential scholars of popular culture in the first half of the twentieth century, suggested that carnival 'embodies a popular, folk-based culture which is defined by its irreverent antipathy to the official and hierarchical structures of everyday, noncarnival life' (Stevens 2007: 1). The carnivalesque is a form of release from established orders in which hierarchies of privilege and power are at least partly suspended. In many respects, therefore, it fits neatly with what we observe during a riot, especially during a riot's early stages.[7]

Such a perspective is useful to us, Ferrell argues, because it counters orthodox social sciences' 'reduction of crime to a rational, instrumental undertaking, while also situating an understanding of emotionally charged criminality within a contemporary context of alienated work, commercialization, consumerism, and control' (2010: 314). There are resonances here with elements of Norbert Elias's application of his theory of the civilizing process to the arenas of sport and leisure. Elias suggests that in a world that is increasingly routinized and is characterized by a relative absence of risk, it becomes necessary to find alternatives in the 'quest for excitement'. In this context, sport and leisure can be seen as forms of 'mimetic activity' that offer 'a social enclave where excitement can be enjoyed without its socially and personally dangerous implications' (Elias and Dunning 1986: 90). Though he makes no direct reference to Elias, Presdee (2000) similarly suggests that the emotions once articulated via carnival are matters that now find alternative forms of authorized expression.

Many of those involved in riots are undoubtedly stimulated by, and then carried away by, the excitement and thrill of the possibilities opened up by the breakdown of order. However, as I have already argued, the extent to which they set out with such an intention is more doubtful. Rather, the 'quest for excitement' is in some ways less a journey towards a particular goal (excitement or ecstasy) than an unfolding set of experiences in which an initial buzz, or a sense of an opportunity for such thrills, opens up territory in which continued involvement is possible but by no means guaranteed. For some of the rioters, rather like those in Presdee's account of the big joyriding-related disturbances in early 1990s England, their activities involved a symbolic retaking of territory (what, following Nassauer, we will refer to as 'spatial incursions') in a way that involved a form of street performance, games of 'cat and mouse' with the police and the construction of 'an identity of excitement and opposition' (Presdee 2000: 51) that many experienced more as 'carnival' than 'criminal' or, at least, experienced as *both* 'carnival' and 'criminal'. Participation in riotous situations involves contrasting feelings: the excitement and fun already described, together with an appreciation that it is a high-risk activity, in terms of both the threats of violence and the potential consequences of arrest, prosecution and punishment. Indeed, it is partly the risks that make such involvement or proximity exciting.

Anger, fear and disappointment

A focus on the 'quest for excitement' could easily lead to the assumption that the disorder is otherwise purposeless; that the only, or at least the overriding, concern is thrill-seeking. In the 2011 England riots, for example, although the carnivalesque excitement of 'riot' was a powerfully expressed element of the experience by a large number involved, it was far from the only emotion discussed. Alongside the excitement engendered by a moral holiday, the overwhelming impression gained from reading the lengthy interviews with the rioters is one of anger – directed, in particular, towards the police: 'basically my time to show, like to show my anger. That's why I went there' (18-year-old female, London). A strong view, expressed by many, was that much of what occurred in the riots was a means of expressing a deep, often visceral, hostility towards the police (we return to this in chapter 8), and this was articulated by respondents in all the main cities in England that the research covered. Such anger extended to others, particularly those in power who, it was felt, often misused their positions and were rarely if ever held to account. Such anger came from respondents of all ages. In part, the anger towards the police stemmed from the shooting that preceded the rioting in 2011, and a sense that this was another injustice that would never be righted:

> Murdering scum, it's like, you fucking, you think you can do what youse want. Get away with anything. You can fucking run around killing people. I was there, I know from the past, from a relative, who got shot, innocently, in East London, and that's when I, that's when I was standing with the police fucking giving them verbal abuse. 'You think you's can run around' .... I know all the injustices that they police do, it's like, horrendous, like, and they can just stand there with their ignorance, and get away with anything they bloody well want and nothing's done about it. (42-year-old male, London)

The antagonism towards the police brought many of the 'rioters' out onto the streets, as well as underpinning many of the other emotions they experienced during the disorder. For a proportion of those involved, the initial excitement and enthusiasm that surrounded the experience of the disorder began to give way to a mixture of fear – for themselves and for others – and disappointment at the perceived displacement of the focus of the original protest by other types of activity. In part, fear was one of several emotions felt simultaneously – fear and excitement being quite closely related (Rosenberg 1990)

– as the disorder intensified. Indeed, fear is considered a central emotional driver of conflict (Bramsen and Poder 2018). In the early stages of the disorder, when police numbers were relatively low, many rioters experienced a huge rush of enthusiasm at the possibilities that confronted them. Once the potential consequences of their actions became more evident, some at least became significantly more concerned: 'because at that time there was like no police so I weren't scared. But then when all the police were around I was like, "Oh my god, what have I done?"' (15-year-old female, London). For others, it was fear that came to the fore as the scale of the destruction and violence became evident, as demonstrated by the change in attitude of a 15-year-old in Birmingham, who had originally felt that 'yeah this is sick [crazy, awesome]' but over time realized that 'everything was just out of control and then anything could happen, you could easily get stabbed or anything'. A realization that some rioters had little regard for the lives of others was also another understandable cause of anxiety: 'It was scary because people were just throwing anything like bins, they were just throwing them, it was scary in case you got hit because they didn't care, they was just throwing them, if you were there you were going to get hit' (17-year-old female, Liverpool).

For others, the feeling that emerged as the riots progressed was a sense of sadness and regret. A number of respondents spoke of their disappointment as they saw rioters turn on their own communities. For others, the sense of disappointment stemmed from a realization that the riots no longer reflected what they imagined were their original ideals or intentions and instead had been 'overtaken' by something else. One 23-year-old male in London described how his initial feelings quickly gave way to despair as he felt the riots change character, losing an initial sense of rebellion, and quickly turning to burning down the houses of 'innocent people'. This, he said, made him 'sick to my stomach'. This disappointment was most closely felt in Tottenham, the start of it all in 2011, where a number of observers expressed feelings of regret that the riots had been 'misused' and, critically, that the cause of the original protest had been forgotten. Some felt this occurred quite quickly, and they could detect a change of mood out on the streets by the end of the first night of rioting. As the following respondent described it:

> When I first saw [the rioting] I thought obviously people was doing it for the right reasons, that a young man has been killed in Tottenham, there's not . . . no one's had any answers and . . . then it seemed to go

> from that to let's do whatever we want and as soon as it got to that point I decided I weren't gonna go out onto the street because I felt that it was too dangerous . . . , When you get to eight o'clock in the morning now you're starting to see the actions of opportunists. (23-year-old male, London)

As implied in the quote above, and as has been noted in connection with many riots, many respondents focused their criticism on the looting, viewing it as unjustified and as a distraction, observing, arguably somewhat naively, 'cos I don't think Mark [Duggan] would have wanted that. The family didn't want that' (41-year-old male, north London).

This view was perhaps captured most succinctly by the respondent who said that, in his opinion, after the initial protest 'everyone started forgetting why they were doing it and just started doing it for fun and stuff' (17-year-old male, London) – for 'fun and profit', as Edward Banfield put it. While there is undoubtedly something in this, there are also at least two interrelated difficulties with such a perspective. First, across those involved as a whole, there was undoubtedly a range of motivations and emotions on display. Second, individuals themselves also held and displayed multiple motivations and experienced the riots in a variety of ways.[8] As Bramsen (2023: 100 quoting Collins) observes, 'motivations for conducting violence are often dynamic and tend to emerge as the conflict heats up'. Not only must we be wary of reducing the 'nature' of the riots to any single, overriding factor, we should also avoid assuming that the conduct and beliefs of individuals can be reduced to a single or simple stimulus. The final observation we might make about individuals' seemingly shifting views on the legitimacy of different courses of activity, and what the riots were allegedly *about*, is that there is no doubt a significant element of post hoc rationalization, of neutralization techniques, on display here also. Rioters' accounts of their conduct, attitudes and values need to be approached with a healthy degree of scepticism.

A sense of control

The issue of 'control' is often significant within many rioters' narratives. In this context, 'control' refers to feelings of power, how relations with others were experienced and how it was imagined they would play out. Many involved in the riots felt at heart a sense of empowerment, at least initially, and this was most directly experienced in connection with actual or symbolic relations with the police. It was illustrated in two broad ways. The first was the way rioters talked about physical territory and, in relation to the police, how they competed for territory. As an 18-year-old man from Birmingham described it, this was experienced by some as an opportunity to take advantage, albeit briefly, of a turning of the tables, a brief sense of being the ones in control of, in this case, the locale:

> [The police are] pinpointing the main areas like Handsworth, Aston, most of the black communities, you don't see 'em pointing out any white communities in Birmingham, you get me, so, I was getting back at the police for that. For everything ain't it . . . it was an opportunity, we was the ones in power, so, we was showing our authority. By throwing stuff and running them off, you know what.

The second way in which empowerment is discussed is more obviously existential in character and is described as a feeling of experiencing greater control in their lives.

There is a lengthy sociological literature illustrating how police officers focus considerable attention on obtaining knowledge about the areas they patrol or otherwise police, and use this consciously as a source of domination (see, inter alia, Bittner 1967; Van Maanen 1973). The policed are very aware of such dynamics and clearly respond to them. As one 16-year-old from Birmingham put it, 'What I really noticed that day was that we had control. It felt great. We could do what we wanted to do. We could do as much damage as we can, and we could not be stopped' (Clifton 2011). This sense of empowerment was personally expressed as a feeling of relative impunity, of freedom of action and of power that, for some, bordered on invulnerability. As Katz (2016: 238) puts it, this is partly about numbers, as 'would-be participants understand that the more visible they will be as a mass, the less vulnerable they will be to punishment as individuals'. Central to this feeling of invincibility, then, was a sense of power over the police. Not only did those involved quickly realize that the police were often ill-equipped to deal with the scale of the disorder facing them, but they talked about it being the first time that they had experienced the possibility of imposing on the police the same feelings of fear and dread that they regularly experienced themselves: 'For once it felt like you had so much power . . . it was the sense of power that shocked me. I've never seen police so scared before' (15-year-old female, south London).

Not only did this feeling of control in the face of the police bring a sense of power, but for some rioters it also evoked a sense of achievement, with one 19-year-old female in Croydon, south London, commenting that this 'battle' felt 'good' as at last 'we could actually show them that we are capable of taking action if we don't get a right to speak, if we don't get a right to put our ideas forward'. Once again, we are in the territory of carnival and Saturnalia, places within which role reversal is intrinsic, those typically controlled becoming, however briefly, the controllers, and vice versa. The feeling of personal achievement, however briefly experienced, was reinforced for many involved by a sense of watching or being part of something that was of significant and lasting importance. It was new and being there, whether on the sidelines or directly in front of police lines, was momentous. For some, the perception of being part of history had been one of the drives that provoked their involvement.

'The best three days of my life'

I've highlighted the initial excitement of involvement during a riot, the freedom from constraint that the carnivalesque character of the disorder offers, the anger that motivates some rioters, the fear that emerged (for some) as the disorder unfolded, and the disappointment experienced by those for whom the protest element was felt to be gradually drowned out by other activities and actions. Above, I outlined the sense of empowerment, the temporary feeling of control over events and others, that added to the excitement and exhilaration of the experience of disorder. In his analysis of 'edgework', Lyng (1990: 860) argues that the participants he studied claimed to have experienced a sense of 'self-realization', 'self-actualization' or 'self-determination'. By that he meant that the activities he studied (such things as skydiving, rock climbing and downhill skiing) led to a heightened, or as he put it, 'purified and magnified', sense of self. Phrases like 'I felt really alive' abound. The sequence of emotions in such activity, he says, begins with fear and moves to exhilaration and omnipotence. Participants in edgework, he argues, develop a pronounced sense of their own competence as a consequence of an illusory sense that they are able to control the fateful aspects of the activity. Importantly, Lyng goes on to argue that this enhanced self-conception 'is the direct antithesis of that under conditions of alienation and reification' (1990: 878).

This observation, and more particularly it seems to me Lyng's invocation of the notion of alienation, is of considerable utility in understanding some rioters' accounts of their motivations, their actions and their emotional experiences during the disorder. To this extent, there are some parallels here also with Elijah Anderson's (1999) use of alienation in explaining the nature of 'the code of the street'. For Anderson, the code of the street is a form of cultural adaptation, most particularly to a lack of faith in the police and the penal system, and more generally it reflects profound alienation from society and its institutions. Lyng utilizes an understanding of alienation that takes the traditional Marxist focus on the limitations of the experience of work under conditions of capitalism and broadens it to include the absence of opportunities for 'creative, skillful, self-determining action' beyond the workplace (Lyng 1990: 877). Contemporary conceptualizations of alienation have become increasingly variegated, encompassing at least powerlessness, meaninglessness, normlessness, cultural estrangement, self-estrangement, and social isolation (Seeman 1975). To this point, rioters' accounts have suggested elements of both 'powerlessness' (the disorder offering a fleeting experience of power and control in lives in which these are felt to be absent or rare) and 'normlessness' (riots enabling some participants the experience of momentary pleasures as a result of the breakdown of everyday regulatory controls). There is more to it than this, and rioters' accounts of their experiences and emotions suggest that their participation sometimes brings a form of meaningfulness, almost purposefulness and, however ironically, a quality of life rarely experienced in their everyday worlds. Involvement in the disorder offers a temporary release from problems of self-estrangement and social isolation.

'Social isolation' as referred to here is, at base, what Durkheim (1947 [1893]) referred to as the under-integration of the individual in wider social structures and institutions. The England rioters, to take one example, talked about lives in which they had limited resources, no jobs, antagonistic relations with police and felt generally powerless and frustrated, with the consequence that participating in disorder was an easy choice to make. Importantly, rarely did this involve any attempt at rationalization or self-justification, with many talking openly about their violence, destruction and absence of regret. There was only occasional deployment of techniques of neutralization or other means of retrospective self-defence. Indeed, rather than expressing any remorse, they were much more likely to talk of their enjoyment: 'I ain't bothered, it was done, I actually enjoyed the bits that I was there, and the regrets, yeah I could have got arrested . . . . You do your best to try and not get arrested but if you get arrested you get arrested but what does it matter' (46-year-old male, Salford).

Strikingly, a number of respondents, when reflecting back, talked excitedly about how important an event the riots had been for them. Rather than concern for others, or much emotional empathy, what they expressed was a sense that the disorder was one of the most significant things they had been involved in. In short, beyond the fun and excitement that was to be had, the experience took on the quality of something of major personal significance. As the following young man[9] from Merseyside put it – and here we're back to some of the dramaturgical elements of riots discussed earlier:

> I was having a laugh I swear to God. It was like a dream, it was like a game. Do you know what I mean? It was better than a game. I was actually doing it. I felt alive there's no word to explain it. It was like that first day it happened will always be the best day of my life forever ever I swear to God.

It is this final phrase – 'the best day of my life forever' – on which I will conclude. One young man, whom I'll call Daniel, offered a revealing glimpse into the complex emotional and psychological world that underpinned his experiences.[10] Daniel's story, though very much at the extreme in some respects, nevertheless captures many aspects of the emotional side of the riots. At the time of the outbreak of disorder, Daniel was on holiday. Watching the images of the disorder on television, he was excited and felt an overwhelming desire to get involved. This was 'fear of missing out' on a grand scale. He continued:

> Soon as I saw [film of the riots] I was happy . . . . This chance may never come again . . . . Now was the opportunity to get revenge. It wasn't just the police, just the whole government like. Everything they do. They make things harder for us. Like, they make it hard for us to get jobs. Even like when we do get benefits they cut it down . . . . I knew if we get back to England and we actually damage, like do a lot of damage to the point where, forget all the benefits they cut off, they'll have to pay like twenty times worse than that. So it was just our way of getting revenge.

Daniel's initial account talked of the excitement of the chance that presented itself, his worry about the possibility of missing the opportunity and his sense that he wished to take 'revenge' on the authorities – the police and the government – who 'make it hard for us'. Having returned from his holidays to join in the rioting, he became involved in some of the destruction of property: 'I saw McDonald's get set on fire, and then it was completely set alight, and I've petrol-bombed it, even though it was set alight. And I felt good.' His account then goes on to describe his involvement in the violence and rioting and, like a number of other respondents, he compared the drama and ritual of riots to the playing of computer games. His account in many respects is not a deeply felt emotional one but again one generally lacking in empathy and sympathy:

> When we first got there we saw police. They had their shields up, running.[11] So we thought, OK like, they're on the defensive. So we just sort of started picking up bricks and bottles and threw it at them. It felt good. It felt like *Call of Duty*.[12] It made me feel cold as well. I knew when I was doing it that that was someone's Mum or Dad, but I just didn't care about that. I just thought it was a chance to get revenge and I took it with both hands. It was a war, and for the first time we was in control. We had the police scared, innit. There was no more us being scared of the police. We actually had a choice of letting officers off the hook or seriously injuring them. Like, I threw a brick at a policewoman. I saw her drop. I could easily have bricked her again. I didn't because it was a woman . . . . I wasn't there for the robbin'. I was there for revenge.

Daniel was one of many who made reference to computer/video games, with *Call of Duty* and *Grand Theft Auto* among those regularly mentioned. For many, the only yardstick they had from with which to compare or assess the drama of the riots was what they had seen on screen. There are parallels here with the Dutch historian Johan Huizinga's (1949: 9) observations about play, which, he said, 'presents itself to us in the first instance: as an intermezzo, an *interlude* in our daily lives'. It is characterized by 'fun', though this '[a]s a concept . . . cannot be reduced to any other mental category' (1949: 3). It does, however, tend to be highly ritualized. In parallel with the games the rioters cited, their experience of involvement in the street disorder was 'scripted': there were roles to be played, expectations about performance, and an audience in front of whom to perform.

Back to Daniel's story. He had been extensively involved in the rioting, in several locations, and had been engaged in some of the more extreme violence and destruction over the course of more than one day. When asked to look back on the experience, to talk about how he now felt about it, his lack of empathy with others, and his absence of remorse, continued. In fact, and reflecting what a number of rioters had to say, Daniel's sense was that this marked a special, almost magical moment for him. It was something to look back on, and consequently stood in very significant contrast with much of the rest of his life. In a powerful end to his account of his involvement in the riots, Daniel said, 'I'll always remember the day that we had the police and the government scared. For once they were living on the edge, they like felt how we felt. They felt threatened by us. *That was the best three days of my life*' (emphasis added).

His account – with his sense of detachment from others and his sense at one stage of standing outside himself while he engaged in some of the very worst of the violence – speaks strongly of 'social isolation' and 'self-estrangement'. There are strong resonances here, once again, of Collins's (2008) observation that, in practice, violence is far from straightforward. Many barriers must be overcome. There is now a lengthy history of work that suggests that it is often those who are structurally isolated, and who carry a subjective sense of powerlessness and disengagement, that are regularly to be found involved in significant social disorder (see, for example, Ransford 1968). This does not in itself explain riots, but it does help to make sense of the attraction some participants feel towards the opportunities offered by the breakdown of order, and what maintains their involvement, if only for a relatively short time. Many of the elements of what occurred on the streets of London and other English cities in August 2011 had strong parallels with the other urban riots of the past half-century. There is good reason to think that the particular dimension of the 2011 riots discussed here, that is to say, their psychological and emotional characteristics, is likely to be found in cognate form in the majority of other disturbances. These would include the ghetto or urban riots of the 1960s, and more recently in the United States, the riots in France and Hong Kong, as well as the protest movements in Tunisia, Egypt and elsewhere during what was known for some time as the 'Arab Spring'. No account of such disturbances could maintain any claim to comprehensiveness in the absence of consideration of this emotional dimension.

7
The Nature of Violence

What do riots involve? Are there patterns to the violence associated with protest and what, if anything, can we learn from such patterning? As I have argued, the choice of terminology surrounding collective violence often reveals much about the ideological position of the author. There are many cases where an outbreak of violence will come officially to be known as a riot, but others will use other terms, such as 'revolt', 'rebellion' or 'uprising'. The choice of terminology tends to indicate both variations in the nature of the protest and where the observer stands in relation to that protest. To take one controversial example, the events of 6 January 2021, when protesters attacked the US Capitol Building in Washington, DC, have been described in highly contrasting ways. Some saw it as a legitimate protest, others as a riot or even an insurrection. The descriptions of its participants varied from patriots and heroes at one end to traitors at the other. The storming of the Capitol illustrates perfectly that the word *riot* is polysemic and that there is much about riots that is unsettled and contested and involves a struggle over the narrative with, in this particular case, potentially profound implications for the politics of the nation.[1]

Discussions of what constitutes a riot often begin with legal definitions. The British Riot Act 1714, which was required to be read publicly, defined a riot as twelve or more people disturbing the public peace for a common purpose. Once the proclamation had been read, such groups were required to disperse and, failing that, those in authority were able to call on military forces (there was little else) to intervene. The English common law at the time defined a riot as an unlawful assembly of three or more people (Wilkinson 2009). The primary problem with such definitions is immediately obvious. First, most commonly held views would tend to see riots as events involving larger numbers, probably far larger numbers, than indicated by legal definitions. Second, both context and purpose are important. Relatively small groups of people disturbing the peace at a football match or in a pub or club on a Saturday night would meet few people's idea of what constitutes a riot. Implicitly, therefore, we clearly tend to think of riots as being more serious matters and as involving quite substantial numbers, with perhaps some aim or objective beyond the violence itself, or at least some underpinning concern or source of anger. Social scientists and historians have pointed to groups of 30–50 or more as being the minimum involved in a riot (Rudé 1964; Spilerman 1976). The objectives of those involved in the violence – the so-called 'common purpose' – are both difficult to ascertain and only a partial way of distinguishing one form of collective violence from others. Why people are involved in disorder is anyway difficult to discern – how do we discover it? – and, as we have seen, it is rarely consistent or settled. A disorderly crowd may contain people with a range of motivations and, indeed, individuals themselves may have multiple and malleable apparent motivations. Little of this helps us distinguish riots from other forms of group violence, and this perhaps explains why even work that focuses directly on riots rarely endeavours to define its object of study (see Moran and Waddington 2016).

Riots vary markedly. The Kerner Commission, for example, distinguished between what it referred to as 'major', 'serious' and 'minor' disorders. By their estimation, major disorders accounted for about 5% of the total, the serious disorders in the sixties a further 20%, and more minor disorders the remaining three-quarters.[2] Riots vary as to the numbers of people involved, the nature of the violence used by those engaged in 'rioting', the aims, ambitions or purposes attributed to the actions being taken, and the time over which violent activity extends. These are just four important ways in which riots vary – all four in some ways being interrelated. My concern in this book is primarily with what Kerner would have considered major disorders, and to this end we return once again to the four primary examples: LA 1992, France 2005, England 2011 and Hong Kong 2018–19. There is by now a very considerable literature on the nature of 'violence' and what constitutes it (see, for example, Collins 2008; de Haan 2008; Galtung 1990). Exploring these definitional debates is not my concern here. Rather, my focus is on those broad categories of conduct usually referenced under the rubric of 'violence', albeit those that take place in the context of collective disorder.

Violence in Los Angeles, France, England and Hong Kong

In all, 54 people died in the Los Angeles riots of 1992.[3] Official data suggest that 2,499 people were hurt, of whom 249 were critically injured. The number of fatalities in the US riots generally far outstrips those elsewhere, no doubt in large part because of the uniquely widespread gun ownership in America (Garland 2025a). All of those killed were citizens; no law-enforcement personnel died in the riots. Similarly, all but one of those who suffered life-threatening injuries were citizens (the exception was an LA fire officer who died when a wall collapsed).[4] Of the 2,250 people suffering non-critical injuries, 2,077 (92%) were citizens. A total of 101 LAPD officers were injured, as were 58 fire officers, 11 National Guard and three non-LA police officers (DiPasquale and Glaeser 1998). Notwithstanding these large numbers, violence against property still predominated. Approximately 16,000 crimes were reported, of which just under 10,000 were categorized as serious. Approximately 1,120 buildings were badly damaged, of which 377 were completely destroyed and a further 222 were very seriously damaged, and estimated damage costs stood at more than US$446 million. The bulk of property damage (94%) was to commercial buildings, of which 76% were retail stores (DiPasquale and Glaeser 1998). The scale of the violence between 30 April and 9 May 1992 is also indicated by the fact that a total of just over 7,000 people were arrested – twice the number arrested during the Watts riot in 1965 (Petersilia and Abrahamse 1994).

The shape of rioting in France was, of course, quite different, as were aspects of the nature of the violence. There were 21 nights of unrest in all, compared with four in LA, which affected at least 300 neighbourhoods across approximately 200 cities. According to Lagrange (2008), so far as serious violence was concerned, there was almost no use of firearms[5] and, beyond the deaths of the two young men in the electricity substation (where a third sustained serious injuries), the only fatality during the disorder was that of a man assaulted by rioters after being robbed, and a near fatality involving a disabled woman who became trapped in a burning bus and who was rescued by the bus driver. In all, around 11,500 police officers and gendarmes were mobilized, and 217 were injured during the rioting, but most of their injuries were minor. There was no official count of injuries to rioters, but public hospitals reported no particular spike in admissions. It all leads Mucchielli to describe the toll in terms of human life as '*particularly moderate*' (2009: 733; emphasis added).

By contrast, Mucchielli (2009: 733) describes the material toll as being considerably greater. In all, over 10,300 vehicles were burnt during the disturbances (Body-Gendrot 2007), including more than 4,200 in the Paris region (Lapeyronnie 2009). The overall damage sustained was estimated by insurance companies at €200 million. Over 4,400 people were kept in custody and 750 imprisoned. In terms of the targets of property-related violence, Jobard (2009) suggests that there was no obvious racial patterning – unlike, for example, the targeting of Korean-owned shops in the Los Angeles riots in 1992, or the focus on white-owned premises in the English city of Bradford in 1995 (Bagguley and Hussain 2008). In France, 'the early attacks were focused on institutions: the cars set on fire belonged to the municipality and the post office, the buildings attacked included schools, a postal distribution centre and the town hall' (Dikec 2017: 97). Among the public buildings, the Ministry of National Education noted more than 250 attacks on its property, especially secondary schools (Lapeyronnie 2009), with other targets including town halls, sports facilities, police stations and internal revenue offices (Mucchielli 2009).

During the four days of rioting in England in 2011, five people lost their lives. Three Asian men aged between 21 and 31, who had intervened to try to protect local businesses in Birmingham from looting and damage, died after being run over by a car. In addition, a 68-year-old man was punched by a teenager as he was trying to put out a fire in Ealing in west London. He hit his head when falling, suffering brain damage, and died three days later from his injuries. The fifth victim was a 26-year-old man who became involved in a dispute with some looters, and was subsequently shot in his car in Croydon, south London. Although the number may seem small compared with Los Angeles 1992, these five fatalities equalled the total number of riot-related deaths in all other riots in England in the period since 1945: Kevin Gateley at Red Lion Square in 1974; Blair Peach as a result of being hit by a police officer at Southall in 1974; David Moore at Toxteth, Liverpool in 1984; PC Keith Blakelock at Broadwater Farm in 1985; and Isaiah Young-Sam, stabbed during the 2005 Birmingham riots. In none of these cases were guns used.

In all, the police recorded more than five thousand criminal offences related to the riots between 6 and 11 August 2011, two-thirds of which were in London. In terms of violence, there were close to 500 cases of robbery (though it is not clear how much interpersonal violence was involved), around 200 incidents involving violence with injury, a further hundred or so cases of other violence against the person, and approximately 150 cases of violent/other disorder. Some of these cases of disorderly conduct will have resulted from the throwing of missiles at the police – 'pelting the enemy', as Collins (2008: 246) puts it – which tends to form a standard part of rioting, and whose attraction lies partly in its dramatic quality, being something that is easy to engage in, being full of smashing sounds, leaving visible signs such as broken glass and so on, and yet being far less extreme than serious violence against the person. It also has the advantage of avoiding physical proximity, one of the key barriers to engaging in violence. There were approximately 1,600 cases of burglary and a further 1,600 of criminal damage. To these, one can add around 200 cases of theft, around 300 of arson and a small number of handling stolen goods. Many thousands of shops were damaged – there were over 3,800 claims under the Riot Damages Act in London alone, with the final 'bill' for damages, loss of trade and policing estimated at £250–£500 million (Riots Communities and Victims Panel 2011). Data on prosecutions show one half of all offences to be burglary/robbery or theft, just over a third (36%) arson/criminal damage, and only 7% violent offences.

Tang's (2022) analysis of the protest repertoires utilized during the 2019 protests in Hong Kong found that beyond public assemblies and blockades, it was damage to property and graffiti that was used most frequently. There was very considerable criminal damage, with 86 mass transit and 68 light-railway stations badly affected, 740 sets of traffic lights destroyed, 53 km of street railings, and nearly 22,000 square metres of paving blocks damaged (Shek 2020). As with other examples given above, arson was also quite frequent. By contrast, physical attacks by protesters were much less frequently recorded. There was significant violence throughout the protests, increasing in intensity during the year. It is difficult, however, to offer an accurate picture of what occurred as few reliable indicators exist, and official accounts have been the subject of considerable criticism. It is known that two people were killed: a 70-year-old street cleaner died, having been hit on the head by a brick thrown by a protester during clashes between the authorities and pro-democracy groups; and a 22-year-old university student died after falling from a multistorey car park during a police operation. In terms of criminal charges, the vast majority appear to have been for non-violent crimes, though it is not always easy to determine from the nature of some charges whether violence was involved. Thus around 17% were charges of assault on a police officer. Otherwise, the main charges were 'unlawful assembly' (essentially breach of the peace – 25%), 'possession of offensive weapons' (23%), 'criminal damage' (18%) and 'possession with intention to destroy/damage property' (16%) (Chan, Lai and Kellogg 2023). The official narrative – governmental and police – nevertheless played very strongly on the existence and threat of violence.

Broad patterns of violence

One can take a number of fairly straightforward and consistent messages from the brief overview of violent protest repertoires in our four regular examples. An obvious point, but nonetheless one that it is important to repeat, is that riots vary markedly in intensity. Studies of riot intensity are, however, relatively rare and, where they exist, fairly crude in execution (Wanderer 1969). Research suggests that fatalities are rare, and the duration of physical violence is generally very short, often lasting only a few seconds, reinforcing Collins's (2008; see also Nassauer 2016) observations concerning the barriers to interpersonal violence. Indeed, Collins correctly observes that fighting within a riot tends to become 'very spread out, and most of what one sees during continuous observation of disorder is people standing around, some running across open spaces, plus usually more stationary or slowly moving formations of security forces. Moments of violence in a riot are scattered in time and space' (Collins 2008: 413). Most of those present are not violent. Rather, the 'action' involves a lot of shouting, some milling about, running back and forth and throwing insults and occasionally missiles or other ammunition. Within a crowd, it is only a small minority that will throw missiles; the others are witnesses, providing support and helping set the atmosphere. As Collins (2008: 418) puts it, their presence 'is emotionally necessary so that some can be the few who are violent'. There are likely to be choreographed stand-offs between 'rioters' and the police which, very occasionally, will lead to sufficiently close physical proximity to allow the 'violent few' to engage in direct physical confrontation. Although there are occasions where there is some premeditation, and weapons – bricks, milk bottles and so forth – have been stockpiled, more often rioters will use whatever comes to hand. Bramsen (2024: 98), for example, in her research in Tunisia, reports asking protesters why they threw stones. The answer, one respondent said, was 'because we had no guns'.

Where collective violence is concerned, damage to property tends to far outstrip violence against the person at almost all stages. Certainly, property destruction and damage appear to be the dominant forms of violence in most stages of rioting. As the Kerner Commission observed of the sixties riots, the disorder 'generally began with rock and bottle throwing and window breaking. Once store windows were broken, looting usually followed' (Kerner Commission 1968: 6). Such activities tend to precede attacks on persons, both by rioters and by the authorities. In some respects, it is attacks on property, the dangers that these bring on the one hand and the signals that such activities send on the other, that act to foment interpersonal violence. That is to say, attacks on buildings, arson and looting work to stimulate some in the crowd to engage in other forms of physical violence and, by serving as indicators of what may happen if unchecked, also push the police to intervene more forcefully. As the Tillys observed, 'most collective violence . . . grows out of actions which are not intrinsically violent' (Tilly 1978: 177). In reality, and without wishing in any way to underestimate its extent or its impact, in the vast majority of cases violence against the person is a relatively small part of overall riotous conduct. Importantly, though it may seem an odd observation, there is much about riots that is characterized by restraint (see, for example, Thompson 1971 on restraint in eighteenth-century bread riots). Collins (2008: 252) gives the parallel example of sexual conduct. In circumstances where normal social rules appear to have been suspended, where a 'moral holiday' is underway, 'One might expect that . . . individuals would take whatever selfish pleasures they could; and in chaotic crowds, many strangers would be encountered who could be sexually victimized with impunity'. But this tends not to be the case.

Not only is violence against the person far outstripped by violence against property in riots, where it does occur, much of the violence against the person is relatively minor. Though there are exceptions, indeed some frightening exceptions, fatalities are rare. A few, varied illustrations: the most serious riots in contemporary American history occurred in the 1960s and early 1970s. Depending on how such disorder is identified, somewhere between 750 and 2,000 outbreaks of disorder occurred, affecting more than 500 cities. Within this, one can point to a number of occasions where the scale of the violence was particularly significant. The Watts riot in 1965, for example, was one of the most serious outbreaks of civil violence, lasting a week, resulting in 34 fatalities and over a thousand injured. Two waves of disorder, which occurred in summer 1967 and in the week following the assassination of Martin Luther King Jr, led to 125 deaths and over 7,000 injuries (Levy 2018). Finally, the Detroit riot, one of the largest and most serious of the period, had an eventual death toll of 43. These, thankfully, are outliers. As Kerner observed, of the 75 disorders that were the particular focus of analysis by a Senate subcommittee, 83 deaths were reported, or an average of slightly over one per riot – and US riots, as we have seen, in terms of fatalities and serious injuries far outstrip the majority of their counterparts in other jurisdictions where access to firearms is much more limited. Overall, in 1967 four-fifths of the deaths recorded and over half of the injuries occurred in just two riots: those in Newark and Detroit. To repeat, within riots, critical injuries are far outweighed by injuries of a less serious nature, and in most riots fatalities are rare to non-existent.

If one accepts Max Weber's broad observations about the monopolization of legitimate violence in modern nation-states, then it comes as little surprise to find that whichever form of physical violence against the person we are considering here – fatalities, critical injuries or minor injuries – it is protesters or local citizens rather than police officers or other professionals who are most frequently the victims. Bergesen (1982), in his study of the Detroit and Newark riots in 1967, examines in some detail the nature of victimization in each. Across the two riots, in all but eight cases the perpetrators were police, National Guard or federal troops. In only two cases – one police officer and one fire officer who it was claimed were shot by snipers – were the victims officials. Of the 42 fatalities in Detroit,[6] Bergesen classifies seven as having been a result of 'accident' (for example, where civilians were hit by fire engines or other emergency vehicles) and six where the perpetrator was also a civilian. The remaining 29 fatalities were the result of shootings by police (19), National Guard (9) or federal troops (1). Of the 29, 18 were said to be looters; the others were killed when shots were fired into crowds, cars or apartments. The pattern was broadly similar in the Newark riot. There, of the 21 fatalities, he classifies two as accidents, two as the result of civilian activity, and the remaining 17 as deaths caused by either police officers (14) or National Guard (3). Only four were looters, whereas six died when police fired into crowds or cars. 'The civilian and accidental violence seems to largely precede official violence and the official violence becomes more indiscriminate, random, and personal as the riot unfolds. Further, this escalation of official violence occurs in the virtual absence of any corresponding civilian violence' (Bergesen 1982: 269). These patterns are long established. In the Watts riot of 1965, as noted earlier, slightly more than a thousand people were injured. Among these were 90 LA police officers, 136 firemen, 10 National Guardsmen and 23 people from other agencies. By contrast, 773 were civilians. We should note once again that such patterns are most likely to be the result of the availability of firearms, the scale of serious violence against the person appearing significantly greater in the United States than in many other jurisdictions. Outliers – egregious examples from elsewhere – can be found, including the Tiananmen Square protests in 1989, which are alleged to have resulted in more than ten thousand deaths,[7] and the more than 700 people shot in the protests that have occurred in Myanmar in the past decade, reflecting the differences between various states' licences to use extreme violence (see Schoon 2014).[8]

Sniping

One of the features of commentary about a number of the more significant outbreaks of disorder in America concerned the alleged role of 'snipers'. Sniping is a form of violence that takes advantage of one of the situational conditions that enables the perpetrator to avoid direct confrontation; it is, by its nature, violence *from afar*.[9] Janowitz (1968) argues that civilians shooting at police in particular was a distinctive characteristic of US riots in the 1960s (see also Masotti and Corsi 1969). In the main, Janowitz suggests, snipers acted alone or, very occasionally, in groups of two or three. In the larger riots of the period, there were regular reports of snipers being active and of some of the fatalities being a result of their actions. In fact, there is little evidence that sniping was especially common. Hinton (2021: n. 96) suggests the term 'sniping' became 'shorthand for the shooting that very often provided the soundtrack for rebellion', with the targets being precinct stations, fire stations and other symbols of state power. As a consequence, it became a focus of considerable official concern.

The police in Detroit and in Newark were particularly exercised by such dangers, and confusion about the source of gunfire – snipers or possibly even the police firing at each other – appears to have been common. The confusion is reminiscent of Clausewitz's (1984 [1832]) observation that 'War is the realm of uncertainty; three quarters of the factors on which action in war is based are wrapped in a fog of greater or lesser uncertainty'.[10] Certainly, a number of reports, including Kerner, were doubtful about some of the claims that had been made. In Detroit, for example, where there was more sniper fire reported than in all the other riots combined, the police suggested that four had been killed by snipers. Fine (2007), however, says only one fits the description and can definitely be attributed to a sniper. Reinforcing this, Brown (1975: 231–2) observes that 'Highly publicized media accounts of rioters sniping at police, troops, and firemen seem, in retrospect, to have been wildly exaggerated . . . , and the mistaken impression (understandable in the confusion of the riot) of the riot-control forces led to an overreaction on their part'. According to Fine, only 57 of the alleged sniping incidents were confirmed by the police (Fine 2007: 300).

Hinton places the controversies surrounding 'sniping' in the wider context of Black self-defence that had been developing throughout the 1960s. Increasingly, reports of snipers in the four to five years after the Detroit and Newark riots paralleled, she argues, increasing lawlessness among the police. The murders of the leaders of the Black Panthers, Mark Clark and Fred Hampton, in Chicago in 1969 brought fears of retaliation, and a cycle of increased violence seemed inevitable: 'The belief that sniping, or simply Black self-defence, was part of a larger revolutionary conspiracy or an expression of community pathology prevented those in power from imagining alternatives to further escalation of the crime war' (Hinton 2021: 120). Fears of the actions of snipers always outstripped the reality of such activity, whether it be the likely numbers involved or the consequences of their actions. W. I. Thomas's dictum (see chapter 5, n. 1) bears reintroducing here, for however misplaced official assumptions were, the fact that they were believed led to very real, and sometimes fatal, consequences.

Overall, we are left with the wider question of how to explain the apparent dissonance between what appears to be the violent, often extremely violent, intent of riotous crowds on the one hand and the somewhat lower levels of serious or critical injuries that tend to be sustained on the other. What I mean by this is that, huge as the numbers of violent offences may have been in some riots, they do not match the potential of large crowds that are presented as being 'out of control' for days on end. It appears, in fact, that a great many crowd members, arguably the vast majority, are neither intent on nor become significantly involved in physical attacks on others. Indeed, a great deal of what takes place appears symbolic in nature. As outlined in the previous chapter, for at least some participants involvement in rioting is an opportunity for pleasure, excitement and fun – for acting out in various ways, displaying what we might think of as 'defiance' (Sherman 2010). Much behaviour within a riot, including violent behaviour, is ritualized. There are aspects of many riots which are highly structured and patterned, where participants are involved in a game of cat and mouse, and where taunting, physical threat, the throwing of missiles and attacks on property dominate. The extent to which inflicting injury is the aim also varies. Buckley and Kenney's (1995) study of riots in Northern Ireland during the Troubles illustrates precisely these forms of ritualized disorder in which, for example, young people learned to launch stones and bottles up into the air in order to give the police time to raise their shields and protect themselves. Research by historians on riots in Europe in the seventeenth and eighteenth centuries found that in a great many, if not most, of these events, there was much about the collective activities that was 'ceremonial'. Indeed, the designation 'riot' would be hard to apply in the absence of such ceremonial characteristics. Research by Hobsbawm, Rudé and others found threats of violence to be commonplace, but these were rarely matched by actual physical violence. Indeed, among the landlords, farmers, parsons and others on the receiving end of riotous violence, they record not a single fatality.

Violence against property

Broadly speaking, we may divide violence against property into three groups: physical damage, arson and looting. We have noted that it is often the case that some or all of these will precede any physical violence against the person and, indeed, may act as a stimulant, a provocation or an incitement to physical violence – an 'escalation sign' (Nassauer 2019). Research shows many examples of selectiveness of targets: which shops, buildings or occupants/owners of shops/buildings are the focus of such violence? Violence against property is far from always targeted though; equally, it is neither random nor without structure or pattern. Returning to Rudé's research on seventeenth- and eighteenth-century riots, we find that much of the violence was, as he notes, 'strictly discriminating and was directed against carefully selected targets' (Rudé 1964: 60). Moving forward in time, Greenberg, in her 1992 study of the Harlem riot of 1935, argues that protesters targeted only those white-owned stores that had been the focus of an earlier failed boycott in an attempt to push store owners to hire Black workers, though her evidence for this is sometimes slim (Rosenfeld 1997). The Kerner Commission, in its overview of the 1960s 'ghetto riots' (1968: 116), suggested that 'White-owned businesses are widely believed to have been damaged much more frequently than those owned by Negroes. In at least nine of the cities studied, the damage seems to have been, at least in part, the result of deliberate attacks on white-owned businesses characterized in the Negro community as unfair or disrespectful toward Negroes' (Kerner Commission 1968: 116). Jump forward a quarter-century to the Rodney King riots in 1992, and it was Korean-American-owned stores in south-central LA that bore the brunt of the victimization. A failure to abide by certain normative expectations makes certain groups the target of violence.

Such selectiveness is often used by scholars as the basis for reading intention and purpose into rioting or, relatedly, as a means of understanding the expression of collective identity by protesters. Reicher (1984), in his analysis of the riot in the St Paul's area of Bristol in 1980, argues that much of what occurred during the riot was 'marked by uniform behaviour showing distinct social limits', and that 'the content of crowd action can be related to social definitions of themselves and their social world' (1984: 10).[11] Thus, for example, in addition to the police, who were a consistent target, the only victims of intentional violence were photographers or camera operators. Furthermore, when the looting began, and spread, it did so within particular boundaries, essentially those of the St Paul's area itself. One of the most striking findings, he noted, was 'the correspondence between the limits of behaviour and the definition of "community" in terms of which participants described themselves' (1984: 17), both geographically (St Paul's) and oppositionally (against the police). From one perspective, therefore, violence against property can be seen as a form of claims-making (Tilly and Tarrow 2006), without denying that 'fun and profit' (Banfield 1970) are also often present.[12]

Understanding 'looting'

The literature on riots has relatively little to say about criminal damage or arson,[13] and scholarly interest in the violent crowd is, at heart, a preoccupation with violence *against the person*. However, looting and arson are deserving of more concentrated attention. Academic discussion of looting, to the extent it occurs, has generally been confined to studies in the context of (civil) war. Though arguably with longer historical origins, the modern usage of the term 'looting' has military roots (Dynes and Quarantelli 1968), appearing in the early nineteenth century and generally being used to refer to the taking of property by force by invading armies, usually in circumstances where the 'owners' were unable or unwilling to defend it. It tends to be used loosely to refer to a 'wide range of activities that differ markedly in terms of the degree of organization, societal level of operation, scale and object' (Mac Ginty 2004). Nevertheless, a series of core characteristics can be identified. Most obviously, looting involves the *appropriation* of goods but is differentiated from straightforward theft by the *particular circumstances* in which it occurs, generally ones in which there is a major challenge to the rule of law via civil emergencies/disasters, (civil) war, and riot or disorder. Each of these cases involves significant disruption to daily life and, consequently, enormous challenges to the police and other emergency services. It is within such a breakdown in control that theft tends to become defined as 'looting'.

Looting, as opposed to theft in other circumstances, is a *collective* activity. By and large, it is something undertaken by groups of people, not isolated individuals, and has its own organizational forms. Often, looting has 'leaders', those at the forefront of breaking into stores, making such activities possible for the much larger numbers that tend to follow. Many in the latter will only become involved once barriers – physical and psychological – have been removed, and entry to and exit from stores can be quickly accomplished (Hannerz 1969). In addition, looting tends to be *widespread*, particularly during riots and disasters, though less so in the latter case, where it attracts less popular support (Quarantelli 1994). This in turn leads to another characteristic, which is that looting is *public*.[14] Indeed, looting is often done in a remarkably open and public manner – almost as an act of display in conditions in which participants are acting under the 'epiphany of invisibility' (Katz 2016). Definitionally, looting can be taken to be 'the widespread appropriation of goods in the context of wider civil disorder, undertaken by sizeable numbers of people, often in a highly public manner' (Newburn et al. 2015).

In the major urban disorders in 1960s United States, looting was so regular an occurrence that one group of scholars argued that it should be seen as having the status of an established 'group response pattern' (Quarantelli and Dynes 1970: 178) and as being 'semi-institutionalised' (Quarantelli and Dynes 1970: 169). Of the nearly 200 major incidents of disorder (by one count) that occurred between 1964 and 1969 in the United States, a significant element of looting featured in at least 122, and over 60,000 people were arrested for such activity. In the 1967 Detroit riot, according to the American Insurance Association, 2,509 stores were looted, burned or destroyed. These included more than 600 supermarkets and grocery stores, more than 500 dry cleaners and laundries, more than 300 clothing stores, 285 liquor stores, 240 drug stores and 198 furniture stores. In his analysis, Fine (2007: 292) suggested that 'looters tended to seize just about anything'. 'Although some black-owned stores with "Soul Brother" signs were conspicuously spared, there is abundant evidence from black and white sources alike that, at least after the early hours of the riot, looters and arsonists did not, for the most part, bypass black-owned or -operated establishments' (Fine 2007: 292). By contrast, Kerner argued that there was strong patterning to the looting in many of the sixties 'ghetto riots'. As noted earlier, Fogelson suggested the main target of the Los Angeles rioters was 'white-owned stores' perceived as selling poor products at extremely high prices (Fogelson 1967: 353; see also Davis 1992; Feagin and Hahn 1973). Indeed, Fogelson suggested that 'in view of the ferocity of the riots, what is remarkable are not the exceptions but the overall pattern and pervasive and intense sense of consumer exploitation underlying it' (1970: 151). During the 1981 Brixton riot in south London, it was estimated that nearly 150 premises were damaged, 28 of them by fire, many during looting. Once again, the targets were far from randomly chosen: 'Predictably, suppliers of consumer durables (particularly clothes, shoe and electrical equipment shops) and off-licenses proved favourites. However, shops owned by popular local figures in Railton Road escaped unscathed' (Keith 1993: 101). Though some commentators will always tend to present riots as fundamentally anarchic, looting's targets are a further illustration of its often structured, patterned and organized character.

There are practical influences over what can be shoplifted, of course, and routine activities theory has some utility in this regard, not least the emphasis on opportunism (see Cromwell et al. 1995; Gaherity and Birch 2022). With more than an echo of some of the reports from other riots, including those in London and elsewhere in 2011, a local newspaper reported a police log at the time of the Handsworth riot in Birmingham in 1985 saying, 'An air of excitement is noticeable among the looters – one man pushing a trolley-load of stolen property shouts: "I'm shopping early for Christmas".'[15] 'Christmas come early' is a further reminder of the dangers of over-reading conduct, assuming in this case that some form of political or quasi-political motivation characterizes all looting. It reminds us also of the emotional dimension of rioting and of the importance of emotions to our understanding of protest violence. Edward Banfield was perhaps the most trenchant critic of the view that dominated from the sixties onwards that racism and social disadvantage were the primary precipitating factors in rioting, 'rebellion' or 'uprising'. This view, Banfield argued, avoided seeing much rioting for what it was – an 'outbreak of animal . . . spirits' or an event in which the 'motive is theft' (Banfield 1970: 187–9; and for a more recent, but cognate, critique of contemporary ethnographic practice, see Katz 2019[16]). He divided riots into four broad ideal types, suggesting, in practice, that particular instances were always an amalgam of two or more such ideal types. The four were the *rampage* (the excitement and animal spirits as above), a *foray for pillage*, where the primary motive was theft, an *outburst of righteous indignation*, which was largely a leaderless spontaneous outburst in response to perceived injustice and, finally, a *demonstration*, with more obviously political motivation often involving greater planning. Banfield was himself subject to no little criticism, arguably some a consequence of the title of the chapter of his book dealing with this issue – 'Rioting Mainly for Fun and Profit' – rather than the detail of what he argued in it. Notwithstanding Banfield's acceptance that matters beyond fun and profit were important, his arguments generally minimized the importance of structural inequalities, including both race and poverty. As one critic put it, in Banfield's view, 'those who suffer the most deserve their suffering . . . . It is the members of the incorrigible lower class who contribute most to the troubles of the city' (Rossi 1971: 818). Where should we place 'fun and profit' in our understanding of looting?

Looting and consumerism

Political commentators and even some academic observers sometimes take looting to reflect little beyond greed and the spontaneous exploitation of opportunities for free goods. The riots in England in 2011 became the focus for debates about the meaning of such activity and the alleged centrality of violent consumerism to the disorder. A range of journalists, politicians and academics pursued the idea that the scale and nature of the looting during the 2011 disorder was its signally distinctive characteristic. One journalist described them as 'shopping riots', and the justice secretary blamed the riots on what he termed a 'feral underclass, cut off from the mainstream in everything but its *materialism*' (Clarke 2011; emphasis added). It was an argument that was developed most extensively by academics, who talked of rioters' behaviour representing 'conformity to the underlying values of consumer culture, and show[ing] how far the diktats of that culture have been internalised by the participants'

(Moxon 2011). At greater length and depth, one group (Treadwell et al. 2013: 1) described the events in London after the shooting of Mark Duggan as 'destructive outbursts in which the protest was lost, or at least buried beneath the subjective motivations of those who, as the forces of law and order retreated, saw the opportunity to do some free shopping'. Consumer culture, they argued, supplied the young men involved 'with a compelling motivation to join the rioting', and they used the phrase 'aggravated shopping' to describe much of the disorder.

One early influential academic commentator was Zygmunt Bauman, who suggested that the 2011 riots should be seen not as bread or hunger riots (like their nineteenth-century predecessors) but rather as the demonstrable actions of what in earlier work he referred to as 'defective' or 'flawed consumers', these 'collateral casualties of consumerism' that are disqualified from consideration as 'fully fledged, right and proper' members of society through having failed the core social norm of 'consumer competence' or aptitude (Bauman 2007: 31). A combination of consumerism and rising social inequality lay at the heart of the aetiology of the 2011 riots, Bauman suggested, and, as a consequence, they should not be viewed as political – in the sense of seeking change – but, rather, were a misguided and doomed 'attempt to join, if only for a fleeting moment, the ranks of consumers from which they have been excluded' (Bauman 2012: 11). Both fun and profit are undeniable. As outlined earlier, the rioters' accounts of their experiences, reported in the *Guardian*/LSE research on the 2011 England disorder, were dominated by a sense of excitement and of the carnivalesque atmosphere that surrounded their initial involvement, including breaking into shops and helping themselves to free goods: 'I was just laughing because it was just hilarious like, seeing people running out of shops with their hands full of clothes and getting to the shops and there was actually nobody there, no police officers no nothing' (19-year-old, London). In addition to being opportunistic, much of the looting was highly ritualized and non-utilitarian. To the extent they were aware, could remember or could accurately articulate a motive, only a minority of those involved in looting had as their original motivation some general or specific desire to acquire material goods. In part, the 'collective' nature of such activity was a reflection of the brief sense of freedom many experienced in which '[l]ooting and destroying property is a relatively mild form of violence that arises within moral holidays when authority has broken down' (Collins 2008: 245). The experience provided a stark contrast with their everyday lives. Such activities were not, generally speaking, undertaken with much in the way of caution or any particular sense of needing to hide. As I have already noted, the looting was very public in character, often undertaken by participants who felt a generalized sense of invisibility and impunity (Katz 2016).

Rather than restricting analysis of looting to the field of consumption, it is important to place it in a wider context. First, we should consider it a form of 'political violence' (Mac Ginty 2004). Even if it does not involve violence directly, looting is facilitated 'by direct or indirect violence' (2004: 861). This is the context within which law and order breaks down and looting subsequently takes place. In order to occur, looting requires either violence or the threat of violence. The context of looting *is* violence. In the absence of violence, it is merely theft. Further, it is important to remember that rioters rarely specialize in their disorderly conduct, regularly being involved in violence, threats or theft alongside more general misconduct. For many involved, there were no clear-cut distinctions between looting and other activities. What may have started out as a protest, or as an opportunity to exact some form of perceived revenge on the police, may later turn to theft and associated criminal damage as opportunity arose. It is important, therefore, not to present looting as if it were effectively separate and therefore apolitical. This is not to argue that every act of looting has a political motive. Rather, it is to acknowledge that looting must be understood in the context of riots, elements of which have a clearly oppositional character. Relatedly, some of those involved in looting were also involved in other more obviously 'political' elements of the rioting or saw their actions, including looting, in part through a political lens, as this 24-year-old from Birmingham argues:

> We took stuff off shelves, and we took back what we think the Government owe us. That was the bottom line . . . . It was nothing to do with what happened in London [the shooting of Mark Duggan], it wasn't to do with anything, it was just people had enough of living the way they were living . . . . It just seemed like everyone was just having a bit of payback to the government.

Arson

Just as theft is a common crime but one that alters its character under conditions of civil disorder, coming to be referred to as 'looting', so one might make some similar observations about arson. The terminology doesn't alter; the burning of property during the course of a riot continues to be labelled 'arson'. Rather than being individual acts of fire setting, arson tends to be part of a wider repertoire of actions undertaken by many within the crowd, linked with aggressive claims-making, with resistance to law-enforcement bodies, with looting and with violence more widely. As such, arson can be thought of as part of the scene setting or early stagecraft of rioting, a moment in which certain motivations and oppositions are articulated and given substance. Arson, in such circumstances, is an oppositional signal indicating that civil disorder is underway and, via its targets, it may communicate elements of its purpose.

The traditional criminological literature on arson outside the context of civil violence tended to place considerable emphasis on clinical and psychiatric opinion, and while motivations may include financial gain and, occasionally, political objectives, the bulk of attention has tended to focus on pathological or mixed motives. One early study of over a hundred convicted arsonists found that roughly a quarter were regarded as having acted, in part at least, as a result of emotional or intellectual difficulties (Prins, Tennent and Trick 1985). Beyond a concern with psychological disorders, subsequent research on motivations focused on such factors as revenge, vandalism and excitement (Barker 1994; Horley and Bowlby 2011). When riot is the lens through which we view arson, the tendency is to see it simply as a further type of violence against property undertaken by participants involved in other forms of criminal damage (Gerell 2017) and, quite likely, also violence against the person. That is to say, in the context of rioting, there is rarely any suggestion that arson is a specialist offence or that it involves pathology or mental dysfunction or disorder. Arson during riot does not appear to be the product of a few isolated individuals. In this context, arson should be viewed as part of a collective endeavour and one that, under limited circumstances, may find some public support.

It is clear that arson is not simply a common element in riot and protest violence but is an endemic feature of the breakdown of order. It becomes hard to imagine rioting in the absence of such burning. In fact, from one perspective arson can been as a deliberately chosen 'escalation sign'. It is a symbol, almost a starting gun, signalling the inauguration of 'anarchy' (Katz 2016), operating as a means of assembling people as witnesses to the beginning of a moral holiday, and indicating to the police the wider violence that is threatened. Looking back a quarter of a century from the time of the Rodney King riots, the *Los Angeles Times* began its account of the Watts riot in 1965 in the following way: 'For six days, the black residents of Watts and surrounding areas burned, looted and battled with police, unleashing – in one fierce and frightening explosion – decades of pent-up frustration and anger. Raging men and women chanted a bitter chorus – "Burn, baby, burn!"' (*Los Angeles Times* 1992: 9).

The titles of numerous books on riots, such as Elizabeth Hinton's *America on Fire* (2021), Gerald Horne's *Fire This Time* (1997) and Mike Davis and Jon Weiner's *Set the Night on Fire* (2020), to take but three, indicate the centrality of arson to such events. In practice, relatively little attention is actually paid to arson itself in these and other analyses of protest violence. Accounts will quite possibly contain references to the extent of such damage and to its financial impact, but little is offered by way of insight into who starts the fires. We know the burning of particular targets, such as police vehicles and buildings, is a common and widespread early feature of riot, tending to be followed by more general attacks on property using fire. Given how easily fire spreads, documenting the targets of arson is not always a terribly precise matter. What local people know to their cost, however, is that arson will almost inevitably lead to very great, often lasting damage to their communities.

The consequences of arson can be dramatic. Small businesses were a major victim of arson in the sixties riots in the United States, with more than one hundred destroyed in Harlem in 1964, 600 in Watts in 1965, a thousand in Newark in 1967 and 2,500 in Detroit the same year. Small businesses are arguably particularly at risk, given they often have relatively low levels of physical protection (compared with big business), as well as regularly being sited in geographical areas which are not subject to high levels of routinized policing. In Detroit, a representative of the Small Business Association, hitherto very slow to become involved in riots response, said 'the devastation was almost unimaginable .... You could go through street after street where you could see the small retail shops were wiped out' (Bean 2000). In LA 1992, local residents lost over five thousand permanent jobs, and many lost all opportunity to shop locally for goods and services. The economic and social consequences for those who live in such disadvantaged circumstances are devastating. Hinds-Aldrich (2009), rightly in my view, sees arson in the context of riot as a form of 'performative violence'. Evidence from my study of the 2011 England rioters found respondents were often aware of the public nature of their acts and, more specifically, of the fact of the existence of an audience. This is an important marker distinguishing arson in the context of riot from its standard more private and hidden criminal equivalent. Again, just as they had done with violence more generally, respondents also drew parallels between their acts and the experience of playing or being in a game.

Performatively, there is also something ritualized about riot-related arson. Here one might point to the example of France, a nation where the torching of cars in particular is a now standardized symbol of protest and civil disobedience. Almost all riots in France since the 1980s have included widespread torching of vehicles, and the numbers have increased dramatically. Evidence from the French riots of 2005 suggests that over ten thousand cars were destroyed, more than 1,400 in one night, a great many by arson, together with 30,000 garbage containers. Such objects, both cars and garbage containers, are relatively unprotected items and easy to set alight. That this is understood by the police is underscored by their tactics. Indeed, vehicles are now an officially recognized, almost endorsed, ritual focus of violence in French rioting. To take some of the sting out of such attacks, the French government has even passed legislation to provide for compensation by the state specifically to the owners of vehicles lost in this way (Jobard 2014; see also Body-Gendrot and Duprez 2002). As Jobard (2014: 140) puts it, 'A few cars set on fire are so much less costly than a rampaged city centre, train station or shopping mall.'

Throwing stones and other missiles

Another common set of actions typical of collective disorder, yet generally little commented upon, is the throwing of stones, rocks and other missiles, or what Collins (2008) calls 'pelting the enemy'. The intensity of such activity varies considerably, but again it is all but ubiquitous within rioting. In some quarters, there is something of a debate as to whether such actions constitute violence at all (Pressman 2017). Certainly, there is often much such activity that is not violent in intent – inflicting injury on others, police officers for example, is not necessarily the ambition – but it is nevertheless dangerous and, from time to time, results in significant injuries (Heering et al. 1992). Stone throwing is part and parcel of the ritualized cat-and-mouse character of much rioting. Again, it is a broadly understood and well-rehearsed part of the performance. It's a form of public, explicit resistance, symbolizing one side's anger, its desire to move the police or others out of its streets and perhaps neighbourhoods, and to prevent, or at least make difficult, attempts at arrest and detention by the authorities. Pressman (2017) describes it as a form of unarmed violence. It is, as suggested, a very common element in almost all rioting. There have been few attempts at quantifying riot activity, but that by Abudu Stark and colleagues (1974) categorized over 1,850 separate riot activities in the Watts uprising in 1965. Of these, very slightly under one-tenth involved throwing rocks and other projectiles. In terms of geographical distribution, the researchers found relatively little overlap between rock throwing and other activities, such as arson and looting. This led them to conclude that much of such behaviour 'was an intermittent harassment of law-enforcement and fire-fighting units carried out as the latter were passing through peripheral areas on the way to areas of more intense fire and looting activity' (Abudu Stark et al. 1972: 421). Research on children's experiences of rioting in Northern Ireland found that five forms of violence dominated their accounts, one of which was stoning the police or the army (McWhirter 1982). A study of 'interface areas'[17] in Belfast found residents to be 'the subjects of persistent, of often low-level, violence' in which 'fifty-five per cent of residents [surveyed] had experienced stone-throwing as a problem' (Jarman and O'Halloran 2001). As one young person described it, 'It usually starts with someone slabbering at us – or us at them – or calling us names, and then this leads to stones being thrown.' Similarly, a study of interface violence in Derry found that it mainly involved 'various types of missiles, including bottles, stones, petrol bombs and blast bombs, being thrown over the interface barrier' (Hansson 2005: 18).

Rock and stone throwing is commonplace in the early stages of riot and, alongside fire setting, is part of the early scene setting in disorder, one of several in the initial riotous repertoire, including arson and often, subsequently, looting. Stone and missile throwing communicates violent potential without necessarily embodying violent intent. It has the advantage of involving a degree of physical distance between protester and police. This gives a degree of anonymity, separating the perpetrator from any injury caused.

Violence and protest

Some clear patterns emerge where riot and protest violence are concerned. As observed from the outset, riots vary markedly in intensity and extent. The toll in terms of physical injury was, for example, far higher in the LA riots and the sixties ghetto uprisings in the United

States than in the other main examples we've looked at in London, Paris and Hong Kong. Forty-three people were killed and over 1,200 injured in the Detroit riot; 26 died and over 700 were injured in the Newark riot. The fatalities that occurred during the riots in London and Paris – the most significant of the post-war era in England and France – were in single figures, with around 200 injured in England, and perhaps a similar number of police officers injured in France. As such, these differences in scale reflect the more general differences in patterns of violence between the United States and all other liberal democracies (Garland 2025b).

Within riots, it is violence against property that is most commonly found at the early stages and, leaving aside the throwing of stones and other missiles, tends to outstrip violence against the person at all stages of such disorder. Though the figures indicate that serious injury is far from uncommon during riot, where violence against the person is concerned a great deal of it is relatively minor. Serious or minor, what is clear is that it is citizens, not police officers or other law-enforcement personnel, who tend to be the victims. The vast majority of fatalities in the American riots were citizens. Not a single law-enforcement officer was among the 56 people who died in the LA riots in 1992, for example. In thinking about protest violence, we looked in detail at two particular and generally under-considered features of collective disorder: looting and arson. Both have equivalent criminal offences in non-riot circumstances (theft and fire setting), but their character or nature is altered in the context of the collective, more public nature of disorder. Both become more obviously performative and symbolic. Public protest has quite a clear choreography that gives structure to behaviour but remains under-analysed (Snow, Zurcher and Peters 1981). The major dramaturgical symbols of rioting include styles of dress (the 'black bloc' uniform, for example, together with masks, hoodies and keffiyehs), the importance of symbolic location and place (Tahrir Square, Zucotti Park, the Hong Kong LegCo (Legislative Council) Building or, further back in history, the Bastille Prison in Paris (see Sewell 1996)), activities that designate a particular culture of protest, such as the mass burning of cars in French rioting, or indicate attachment to a cause and solidarity in the face of police violence, such as the yellow umbrellas in Hong Kong (Lee and Sing 2019) or the *gilets jaunes* worn by blue-collar workers in Paris (Royall 2019). The violence of modern rioting is conducted in the full glare of the media, and much of the activity within it is consequently anything but private, and in many cases is not intended to be. The mediatization of rioting of course affects not just the rioters themselves but also law-enforcement officers, who, Katz observes, 'are increasingly sensitive to how their actions in response to anarchy are being picked up by media and responded to by people on the street' (2016: 17).

8
Blame the Police?

By its very nature, urban disorder involves conflict with the police. Crowds, with the potential for violence against people and/or property, almost inevitably come into very significant confrontation with those seeking to prevent or control such behaviour. Dealing with social conflict is central to policing and unavoidably so. Earlier in the book, specifically when discussing the idea of flashpoints, we noted the centrality of the police to the earliest stages of collective disorder. The institution most usually and most closely present when a spark apparently sets fire to existing tinder, is the police. The work of both sociologists (for example, Marx 1970; Waddington 1992) and psychologists (Reicher 1984; Stott and Drury 2000) has highlighted the often-critical role of the police in the emergence and spread of rioting, something acknowledged since at least the time of Peterloo in England in 1819 (Poole 2006). Direct or indirect police provocation of the crowd, or vice versa, is often found at the outset of disorder.[1] None of this is to suggest the police are necessarily to blame for urban disorder or even that changes in police practices would, in themselves, solve the problems that give rise to rioting. It remains the case, however, that the police are often blamed by protesters, and by political and scholarly critics, for fomenting violence (and rarely accept blame themselves). As a consequence, they often become the focus of such violence (Fogelson 1968; Joshua and Wallace 1983; Keith 1993; Roché and de Maillard 2009). One of the forms of collective violence that I pay little attention to in this book is what are sometimes referred to as 'police riots' (Abudu Stark 1972). These are cases such as occurred around the Democratic National Convention in Chicago in 1968, when 'the police rampaged through the streets, beating and gassing with abandon' (Abudu Stark 1972: 3). Although, as I will explain below, police violence is to be found within collective breakdowns in social order, my focus here is not primarily on collective police violence itself. No doubt such riots have elements in common with the types of rioting that are the focus here, but I have not the space to consider in detail those cases where what requires explanation is outbursts of relatively unrestrained police violence and aggression.

Protest policing

What is often referred to as 'public order policing' – though this is a misnomer, given that its focus tends to be public *dis*order – is contrasted with routine policing, the latter being concerned largely with response to public calls for service. Protest policing is concerned with managing crowds, particularly where there is the threat of disorder. It generally involves the deployment of large number of officers, who are prepared to use force in a coordinated way. Though unpredictability is a characteristic of all policing (Newburn 2022), it is perhaps especially so in protest policing. At the heart of all policing lies a fundamental challenge, and that concerns how robust it should be: when and how police should use force, and how much.[2] In connection with the protest over the proposed pipeline construction in British Columbia, Canada, mentioned earlier, the president of the Canadian Police Association captured the conundrum, saying 'If we enforce the law . . . we're criticized often for being too aggressive. On the other hand, if we don't enforce the law, then we're criticized for not enforcing the law. We're in effectively what's a no-win situation.'[3] In fact, it is more complicated than this because the police are faced with the question of whether or not to enforce the law, and also *how* to enforce the law, which laws, when and against whom. But the point is made.

The additional challenges facing public order policing may be briefly set out. What is the balance to be between protecting rights – freedom to protest, freedom of expression – on the one hand and the maintenance of order on the other? How do the police protect rights when the rights of different groups – protesters, counter-protesters and non-combatants – are in tension or perhaps even in conflict? Whose side are the police on? They are representatives of the state but also, in liberal democracies, somewhat independent of it. Yes, when challenged they will claim, inter alia, to be neutral, to be answerable to, and only to, the law. But what does such supposed neutrality mean in practice, and how is it managed and communicated? How the police go about their task of responding to potential or actual disorder may be profoundly consequential. This, again, may make the police the focus of protest, particularly where they are perceived to be favouring one side over another. The practice of public order policing may mitigate or exacerbate disorder and may have significant consequences for police legitimacy (Stott et al. 2020). Even more consequentially, as events in Hong Kong have illustrated, the success or otherwise of protest policing may have great significance for the legitimacy of the state (Ho 2020). Indeed, the consequences of police actions may even affect the likelihood of the survival of particular regimes, and here, for example, the uprising in Mubarak's Egypt in January 2011 offers ample evidence (Roberts 2024). In the end, despite its potentially huge consequences, there is an *inevitable fallibility* about public order policing, as there is about all policing (Newburn 2022). When it comes down to it, as Katz (2016: 8) correctly observes, 'riot control is inherently a business of interaction guessing'.

Understanding the history and nature of public order policing has been aided by the construction of contrasting ideal types – basic forms which it is asserted that such policing can take. Here, in recent times, the major contrast has typically been drawn between what is referred to as 'escalated force' on the one hand and 'negotiated management' on the other. There is a third ideal type – 'strategic' or 'selective incapacitation' – that we will come to in due course. McPhail, Schweingruber and McCarthy (1998) use these ideal types as a means of charting historical change, distinguishing between policing practices in the United States in the 1960s, which they see as being broadly characterized by 'escalated force', and the tactics employed in the 1980s and 1990s which came closer to 'negotiated management'. McPhail and colleagues' (1998) ideal types are constructed around five dimensions: police concerns with protesters' rights; police tolerance for community disruption; the nature of communication between police and demonstrators; the extent and manner of arrests as a means of crowd management; and the extent and manner of the use of force. Where escalated force is the influential mode of policing, concern with rights is low, as are tolerance for disruption and communication with protesters. There is considerable emphasis on the use of arrests, and the use of force is consequently high. The reverse, of course, is true where the ideal typification is negotiated management. Famous examples of demonstrations policed via escalated force include aspects of the Birmingham civil rights campaign in the sixties (King 2018), the famously violent policing of the Democratic

National Convention in Chicago in 1968 (Kusch 2008), and the protests at Kent State University in 1970 (VanDeMark 2024).

Successive governmental commissions in the 1960s were critical of American protest policing. Kerner, for example, proposed greater emphasis on police training and the importance of seeking to eliminate abrasive policing practices. The Eisenhower Commission on the Prevention of Violence identified 'excessive use of force' as an unwise tactic (though *excessive*, by definition, surely must be so), arguing that it often served to exacerbate problems, and proposed greater emphasis on a willingness to negotiate various aspects of protest. As such, it was particularly critical of the policing of the Democratic Convention in Chicago, holding it up as a model of how not to police public order situations (for an account of such policing in its wider political context, see Mailer 1968). McPhail and colleagues (1998) argue that, in the period between the 1960s and the mid-1990s, both the technology of public order policing and its general philosophy changed. Technological change included new defensive capabilities (riot helmets and face coverings, body armour and other protective clothing) and offensive technologies (baton rounds, tear gas and a range of 'less lethal weapons').

By the mid-1990s, the general philosophy in public order policing in liberal democracies had changed, its emphasis now being characterized by much less reliance on the enforcement of the law – even involving, della Porta and Fillieule (2004) argue, *under-enforcement* of the law. The desire, now, increasingly became to avoid coercive intervention wherever possible. Relatedly, therefore, authorities sought to identify and exploit opportunities for communication and bargaining and, as part of this, to place great emphasis on the collection of information and intelligence. This second ideal type – 'negotiated management' – became increasingly dominant by the end of the century and was generally the preferred option (della Porta and Reiter 1998; della Porta et al. 2006a). Nevertheless, considerable policing challenges remained, and in this context there emerged a third broad approach to protest policing. In its ideal-typical form, this approach, 'strategic incapacitation', utilizes surveillance as a means of monitoring risk, pre-emptive arrest and less lethal weapons to disrupt and incapacitate protesters, and the control of space as the basis for isolating and, again, disrupting protesters (Gillham 2011). The move towards risk management and more malleable policing strategies was partly a consequence of shifts in the manner of protest. As we will see in the next chapter, the emergence of what some referred to as 'new social movements', of leaderless, networked, fast-moving, unpredictable, social media-informed protest groups, brought new challenges for policing (della Porta 1995). Strategic incapacitation was more flexible than escalated force but involved greater use of intervention and force than negotiated management. There now exists quite an array of studies of protest policing in which these varying approaches are utilized: some intrusive and heavy-handed, others more flexible. A number of tactics, including preventive arrest, intelligence gathering, 'no-go' zones and 'kettling' (the containment by the police of large numbers of people within a cordon – protesters or simply those in the vicinity of a protest – often for many hours with no access to food, drink, toilets, etc.),[4] are being increasingly deployed as a means of managing crowds.

Militarization

On both sides of the Atlantic, in the United States and in Europe, the last decades of the twentieth century saw extended debates over perceived changes in the nature of protest policing and in particular as we've seen, controversies surrounding what some saw as the progressive 'militarization' of such policing. In terms of the *longue durée*, policing in the United Kingdom and elsewhere had seen a gradual demilitarization through the nineteenth and into the middle decades of the twentieth century (Newburn 2024). This reversed from the 1970s onwards, with protest policing once again becoming more violent and more controversial, in part as the circumstances being policed became more complicated and challenging. Two broad perspectives dominated debates around militarization. In one, the acquisition and use of new equipment and technologies was seen as a more or less direct and rational response to police failures to control increasingly difficult public order events, ones in which greater violence posed challenges both to public safety and to police legitimacy (Waddington 1987). Militarization, from this perspective, was seen as a form of disciplined and well-organized policing, its improved protective equipment, its specialized squads and its strategic deployment of force seen as better suited to modern public order conditions. Critics, on the other hand, saw in militarization a failure by police to exercise proper restraint, with the result that protest was met with unjustified repression, the almost inevitable consequence of which was that violence was exacerbated rather than mitigated (Jefferson 1987). Military discipline, it was argued, cannot be transferred to policing without changing its nature, and that is precisely what, it was argued, had occurred (Jefferson 1993).

It seemed to many observers that militarization of policing was at its most visible and, arguably, its most egregious during the riots in Ferguson, MO, and other US cities from 2014 onwards. Indeed, American policing is much more heavily militarized in general than, say, French policing which, in turn, is more obviously militarized than its British equivalent (Cyr, Ricciardelli and Spencer 2020; Linke 2010). American policing had been much affected by what was known as the '1033 program' (Delehanty et al. 2017), the formal name for processes by which obsolete or unneeded US military property was disposed of. Starting in 1990, after the wars in Iraq and Afghanistan, and ending under President Obama, the Department of Defense channelled billions of dollars of surplus military equipment[5] into state and local police departments. By 2014, the Pentagon had distributed 432 mine-resistant armoured vehicles, 400 other armoured vehicles, 500 aircraft and 93,000 machine guns to the police; between 1997 and 2014, the value of redistributed equipment was over US$5 billion. The sight of armoured vehicles and their like on the streets of Ferguson prompted Senator Elizabeth Warren to say, 'This is America, not a war zone.'[6] Not dissimilarly, Wacquant draws parallels between what has been happening in the United States over the past decade or more and the penalization of poverty in Brazil and elsewhere: 'Neighbourhoods of urban relegation – the decaying *favela* in Brazil, the imploding hyperghetto in the United States, [and] the declining *banlieue* in France – . . . turn out to be the prime physical and social *space within which the neoliberal penal state is concretely being assembled, tried, and tested*' (Wacquant 2008: 71; emphasis in original). Though Wacquant understandably skates over some vastly important national differences, at the heart of this process, he suggests, are innovations in and exhibitions of aggressive law enforcement. According to Graham (2010), such 'new military urbanism' involves the penetration of security into all aspects of public policy and social life. In such a context, the policing of public order, seen most visibly in developments surrounding the surveillance, management and control of transnational protest movements (della Porta et al. 2006), is of central importance and influence.

Anti-police sentiment and public disorder

On both sides of the Atlantic over the past half-century, official inquiries into and academic analyses of major outbreaks of public disorder have regularly found anti-police sentiment to have played an important role in the actions of those involved. It is important to unpack this a little, and to distinguish between the 'individual level' – how particular people experience policing – and the political or collective level where hostility towards the police among certain groups is the focus (Smith 1987). The Kerner Commission, for example, remarked that 'the police are not merely the spark' (Kerner Commission 1968: 206); rather, 'deep hostility between police and ghetto communities [was] a primary cause of the disorders surveyed by the Commission' (Kerner Commission 1968: 299). In the United Kingdom, a number of commentators took the view that the major urban disorders of the early 1980s – both in 1981 and 1985 – were fundamentally 'anti-police riots' (e.g., Clare 1987; Smith 1987). What emerged from these and a wide variety of accounts in the period – from the St Paul's riot in Bristol in 1980 (Joshua and Wallace 1983; Reicher 1984) to the riots in Birmingham in 1981 and 1985 (Field and Southgate 1982; King 2013), across London in 1985 (Keith 1993) and in Newcastle, Oxford and elsewhere in the early 1990s (Campbell 1993) – was that tensions between the police and particular communities, especially minority ethnic communities, were a significant element in the breakdown of social order.

A degree of caution is necessary here for at least two reasons. First, even when there is significant hostility directed towards the police during urban violence, this is rarely, if ever, the sole consideration in the minds of rioters (Gilje 1999; Kerner Commission 1968). In this regard, Lord Scarman in his famous report into the Brixton riot of 1981 noted that two views about the causes of the riots were put to him by many giving evidence. One was that the riots were 'anti-police'. A second was that they were a form of protest by the socially and politically marginalized who used their attacks on the police as a means of drawing public attention to wider grievances. In reaction to this, he said, 'I have no doubt that each view, even if correct, would be an over-simplification of a complex situation. If either view should be true, it would not be the whole truth' (Scarman 1981: 2, para. 1.4).

The second major reason for caution here is the one I have regularly flagged, the very clear danger of 'over-reading' social phenomena such as riots. One obvious way in which this may occur, as highlighted earlier, is in failing to pay attention to the ways in which rioters' accounts of their activities may be suffused with post hoc rationalizations and the application of 'techniques of neutralization' (Sykes and Matza 1957). It is vital to remain alive to such dangers, to be vigilant and to take care not to 'over-interpret' the accounts, statements and claims of those involved – whether protester, police officer or politician. Especial care was taken, for example, in the interviews that were conducted as part of the *Guardian*/LSE's (2011) *Reading the Riots* study that is reported throughout this book. From the organization of interviews, the style and nature of questioning, to the analytical processes involved, the dangers of misinterpretation, of taking too much at face value and of failing to adopt an appropriately critical approach to rioters' accounts, were never far from the forefront of the research approach. Bearing all this in mind, we can return to anti-police sentiment and, following Smith's (1987) observation, think more particularly about individual experiences of policing on the one hand and broader, culturally embedded relations between communities and the police as an institution on the other.

Historical legacies

In England in 2011 in each of the cities where riots took place, the rioters that were interviewed expressed considerable levels of antagonism towards the police. This varied in intensity – from poor relations and negative experiences on the one hand to an outright, visceral hatred on the other – but was audible everywhere. The roots of this hostility were complex. For many involved in the rioting, the police were a very deliberate and specific target. The origins of such feelings varied, but the antagonisms were long-standing. Some older interviewees remembered confrontation with police officers as an ordinary feature of childhood. One white man in his forties recounted regular violent encounters with police officers as a young person: 'I can only speak for Salford [where he lived], it was rife you know, you grew up just hating police.' Accounts of overt police violence were not uncommon, but more prevalent was the insidious disrespect and sense of illegitimacy that framed police–community relations in some areas. Mirroring much extant research (Jackson et al. 2013), some respondents depicted a situation in which the complete absence of trust in the police as a protective force meant that people would not call on them even in need, as emphasized by this 50-year-old white male from north London: 'people don't report crimes to the police . . . . They don't have the confidence that they're gonna help . . . with any of the problems that they've got. So, nobody wants to bring the police in their area.' Similar patterns of police overreach, misuse of powers, conflict with young people, low levels of trust and confidence, leading to eventual and substantial breakdowns in order can be seen in locations as widespread as Sweden, Turkey, Greece (Dikec 2017) and beyond.

In certain areas, poor police–community relations were informed by an ingrained historical narrative of enmity and were punctuated by violent confrontations and even riots. In England, neighbourhoods in cities from London, Bristol and Birmingham to Liverpool, Manchester and Leeds, all of which had seen rioting in the 1980s, and in some cases more recently, some respondents remembered events that had marked relations over the decades, like this 49-year-old Black woman from Tottenham: 'I don't like the police, I've never liked them, I don't want to have no communication with them. The reason is what we had to go through in Broadwater Farm' (where poor police–community relations and the death of local resident Cynthia Jarrett, during a police operation, led to very serious rioting in 1985).[7] Many others had inherited anti-police lore and accompanying distrust from older generations, as in the case of this 25-year-old Black British man, also from Tottenham:

> When we grew up in Tottenham we'd always hear you've gotta be cautious about the police. I was born in '86 so obviously the year after Cynthia Jarrett was killed in Tottenham so I heard from my family you gotta be wary of the police, people would get beaten up by the police and so forth .... From that time we heard stories about Roger Sylvester,[8] that kind of kicked off a lot of friction there, and then you had Mark Duggan,[9] it's like 'alright . . . wow', it's like a slap in the face.

While many of the more than one hundred police officers interviewed as part of the same study were very sceptical that a shooting in north London could possibly be linked to riots in geographically distant locations, occurring one, two, sometimes three days after the initial disturbances, the fact of it being the latest in a litany of deaths at the hands of the police is what appeared to give it its force. Respondents of all ages recited the names of previous victims as evidence of perceived police malpractice and their apparent impunity.[10] As one 19-year-old involved in the 2011 riots in north London said, '[M]y granddad told me about the Broadwater Farm riot [in 1985]. My dad told me about the Brixton riots [in 1981 and 1985], and now, like, I can tell my son, my daughters about oh yeah, the riots that happened. So yeah. It's a piece of culture, I think it's a bit of culture to pass on.' In this narrative, past riots were seen as both cultural heritage and as the basis of legitimate reactions to the contempt with which the police were believed to treat the community. The conduct of the police in 2011 was seen as the most recent indicator that little had changed. Antagonistic police–community relations, both past and present, clearly shaped attitudes in those areas affected by rioting and were a significant factor influencing not just their attitudes but also their conduct. A large public attitudes survey in London in 2011 offered further evidence, finding that respondents living in the London boroughs hit hardest by disorder had substantially lower confidence in the police locally and London-wide prior to the disorder (and still did after). They also had substantially lower trust in police procedural fairness (treatment) and police community engagement prior to the disorder, and again after (Hohl, Stanko and Newburn 2012).

Stop and search/frisk

Of all the issues that the 'rioters' had with the police, it was stop and search/frisk that tended to figure most prominently. In part, this is simply because being stopped and searched is undoubtedly the most common form of contact many such young people have with the police (Quinton 2011). Almost three-quarters (73%) of those interviewed in connection with the 2011 riots said they had been stopped and searched in the last year, and, of those, 71% had been stopped more than once. Among young men, the rate was much higher, and among young Black males a rate of twice a week or more was far from uncommon. The use, and arguably vast overuse, of the power stems from the police dual mandate – involving them in both force and service. Young Black men, for example, are clearly perceived by the police as a source of considerable risk or threat. They are also particularly at risk from violent victimization. Both feed disproportionate police contact, including stops.

The overuse of stop and search was at the heart of a broad narrative of police misconduct, and often police racism, that often tainted wider police–community relations in some neighbourhoods. There is now a vast literature, from numerous jurisdictions, illustrating the heavily disproportionate use of such powers against minorities (Bowling and Phillips 2007; Meares 2015). In practice, however, it is far from just the frequency with which stops occur that is the focus of complaint; it is often police conduct more generally during such interactions. Some respondents recounted instances of quite shocking violence, but more often they talked about lower-level rudeness and aggression frequently accompanying stops. Reflecting many of the findings from procedural justice research (Bradford, Murphy and

Jackson 2014; Tyler 2006), these interactions were often coloured by experiences of disrespect and humiliation, which clearly fuelled a sense of antagonism, as in this account from a 19-year-old Black man from Haringey in north London:

> [T]hey stop you and say, 'Ah, there's been a reported robbery', or the same lame old excuse just to stop you and search you . . . and being rude to you for like, no reason, and just finding little things to arrest you for. They'll push you on purpose . . . . Like they treat us horribly and then they don't understand . . . how we feel when we're getting treated like that.

A 22-year-old Black man from Stockwell in south London, who said he had been stopped between fifty and sixty times in the last year, described feeling threatened by the way the police use stop and search:

> [T]hese guys are always stopping us for no reason. Always. In their gangs . . . they're bullies. They'll jump out on me, batons out. That's threatening, that's intimidating me . . . . I understand if you're doing your job you want to stop and search me, fair enough . . . but don't jump out of your car, it's like, it's like someone jumping out with a knife.

One 29-year-old Black Londoner summarized what appeared to be the prevailing view, saying:

> I've been beaten up in the back of one of them territorial support group [riot police] war buses as we call them. These big black buses where they come and they kidnap us . . . . And they beat us in there . . . . They're monsters. Absolute monsters. And they don't have no law and justice in their heart. They look at us. They look at us as scum.

Stop and search is important both substantively and symbolically. There is clear empirical evidence both of disproportionate use and of aggressive and demeaning treatment. It is clear also that for many minority youth, such matters have come to represent all that is wrong with policing. This situation has held for decades and shows little sign of being subject to radical reform. In large part, this reflects the role it continues to play from a police perspective, generally being seen by officers, for whatever reason, as a crucial weapon in their armoury. Indeed, such is the attachment of the police to stop and search/frisk that it has become something of a sacred cow, symbolizing for them what is at stake in their daily professional lives.

One of the more shocking examples of the misuse of routine police powers was uncovered in Ferguson in 2014. A predominantly white police department had been issuing an increasingly large number of citations against local citizens, especially African Americans. The most common charges were those that gave police officers the greatest discretion, such as 'failure to comply' and 'resisting arrest' (Dikec 2017). Indeed, traffic citations became a leading indicator of police productivity. Municipal fines and fees were the second-largest source of income for the city, and the chief of police was regularly urged by city officials to generate increased income. A total of 90,000 citations were issued between 2010 and 2014, equivalent to 22,500 a year, in a city with a population of 21,000 (Dikec 2017). The police department was issued with a count of citations issued by each officer, and they were encouraged to reach individual targets, leading some to describe it as 'revenue policing' (Sobol 2015). Officer evaluations and promotions were inordinately affected by such measures of 'productivity', similarly affecting the culture of the department. The US Department of Justice (DOJ) concluded that this, in turn, influenced 'officer activities in all areas of policing, beyond just ticketing. Officers expect and demand compliance even when they lack legal authority. They are inclined to interpret the exercise of free-speech rights as unlawful disobedience, innocent movements as physical threats, indications of mental or physical illness as belligerence.' The outcome was a range of illegal practices which then combined with racial bias (Ferguson Police Department data from 2012 to 2014 showed that African Americans accounted for 85% of vehicle stops, 90% of citations and 93% of arrests made by FPD officers, despite comprising only 67% of Ferguson's population) to delegitimize the FPD in the eyes of the community. As the Department of Justice concluded:

> The confluence of policing to raise revenue and racial bias thus has resulted in practices that not only violate the Constitution and cause direct harm to the individuals whose rights are violated, but also undermine community trust, especially among many African Americans. As a consequence of these practices, law enforcement is seen as illegitimate, and the partnerships necessary for public safety are, in some areas, entirely absent.[11]

In practice, 'local policing was not an arm of justice but instead a form of state predation targeting the poor' (Garland 2025a: 8). While taking care not to assume that one can extrapolate from the Ferguson case to American policing more widely, let alone the policing of, say, European jurisdictions, it remains the case that one of the strongest themes emerging from research on riots is that those who become involved in the violence tend to be profoundly distrustful of the police, often viewing the institution monolithically as a single, hostile invading or occupying force. To some extent, this reflects long-standing, embedded problems in police–community relations, together with the more particular and immediate experiences that many citizens have of mistreatment and prejudice at the hands of the police. Their struggle is with an organization that many refer to as the 'biggest gang' (Newburn et al. 2018). As one 21-year-old white male in London put it, 'It's like the police, they're a gang. That's how people, like on the streets, that's how we see it . . . we say they're the biggest gang in the world.' That this phrase recurred with such frequency, and in so many of the different areas in which there were riots in England in 2011, suggested that it represented an established way of thinking about and understanding the police among certain social groups (see also Holdaway 1983). As a 24-year-old Black male put it, 'You don't really win fights against the police. You might win a few battles, but you don't win the war against them in the long run. And they're a bigger, biggest gang on the road, to be honest. That's what the police are. Because they are bullies.'

Empowerment and revenge

As I described earlier, a new, albeit fleeting, sense of freedom informed many rioters' emotional reactions to the disorderliness evident on the streets in London in 2011. Many protesters adopted the language of war when recalling the confrontation with the police. They described how they threw stones, bottles and other materials, rammed the police with wheelie bins and other things they could find to hand, and shouted 'Fuck the police', or something similar. Some spoke of how they targeted police property, setting fire to and vandalizing cars, vans and police stations, or attacked officers, some claiming they wanted to inflict serious injury. As highlighted earlier, this also made clear why those involved might have felt excitement at suddenly having the police on the run, with a carnivalesque sense of fun enveloping much of the whole initial experience. Many reported feeling empowered and, alongside this, because of a brief role reversal, of having a temporary sense of being in control, both of their territories and over the 'biggest gang'. Momentarily, they had the upper hand over the police.

As one 21-year-old woman put it, for those involved in the rioting,

> this was just their way of getting back at the police and having some kind of control. 'Cos when you're arrested, they can have the control, and they can talk to you how they want, do what they want. That day people could do what they wanted and say what they wanted to the police. And I think if they had the chance to do it again, they would.

It was an opportunity for payback, for some sort of revenge against an institution they viewed with great hostility. In our research, a substantial number of rioters talked about their action against the police, the majority talking of retaliation for various perceived grievances. As one 34-year-old Black male from Tottenham said, 'After all the brutalizing I have seen police doing to people it was . . . a sweet moment in my life to see police getting some of their own medicine.' Indeed, the strength of these feelings was one of the reasons that some condemned the looting and vandalism, feeling it devalued or distracted attention from what they saw as a legitimate fight against an old adversary. Similar sentiments were expressed in many of the protests that occurred in the aftermath of the killing of George Floyd, with some observers concerned that the 'real' purpose of the demonstrations was being lost among the widespread destruction of property and theft of goods.[12]

As noted, a short, sometimes very short, feeling of empowerment, of greater control, underpinned the excitement, often especially visible in the early stages of a riot. One 22-year-old white man who was involved in attacks on the police in Salford and Manchester in England described himself as 'buzzing, to be honest, was really happy, to be honest, 'cause we had total control of the precinct . . . we all hate them, we've all spent time in that police station, and you know it was ours for a day'. This was another example of the symbolic importance of territory and its centrality to feelings of empowerment, in this case focusing on a local police station, ordinarily a place to be feared. I reported earlier a 15-year-old girl saying she'd 'never seen the police so scared before'. For the police, of course, such a 'spatial incursion' was not only potentially dangerous itself, it was also a signal of potential future escalation. Just as the police feared loss of control, so the rioters derived excitement and satisfaction from the brief control they felt they had grasped. As a 16-year-old Asian boy from Birmingham put it,

> I felt like no one could stop us . . . it felt great, it felt, we could do what we wanted to do, we could break anything, we could do as much

> damage as we can, and we could not be stopped . . . . Normally the police control us, like, the police have more power, we obey the law, the law was obeying us, know what I mean?

And, while the police were often the initial, and sometimes the primary, targets of violence, rioters revealed wider frustration, not least with those in positions of political and financial power. Participation in the riots was often expressed as anger and frustration at their social invisibility, and it became an outlet for those who felt they did not have access to other, more obviously legitimate channels of communication or complaint. As one 26-year-old in the London riots summarized it, 'When no one cares about you, you're gonna eventually make them care.'

A quick caveat needs to be entered here. My focus has been on critical views of the police held, in particular, by young people – those most likely to occupy an oppositional position where the police are concerned. There is a perspective, and an important one, that is missing here, and that is the views of those residents in areas affected by the riots who were not involved in protest. Unsurprisingly, they held rather different views. As just one example, Siva Kandiah, 39, a shopkeeper in Hackney in East London who had been in business for eleven years at the time of the 2011 riots, said he had been watching the violence on television believing his shop would not be affected. However, eventually, as he said,

> my shop was broken into . . . . The next morning I come back . . . . My shop was completely open, . . . lights on, and the shop was mashed up completely top to bottom, from ceiling to electric wire . . . . You should ask what they left for me . . . . I cried that day, Tuesday morning, cried and I just went home . . . . I built this shop up as a convenience store so it's just like this is your baby and you just work for it, 11 years and you've worked and somebody mash [it] up in 11 hours . . . . I never had contents insurance either . . . . I lost almost £87,000 . . . . There is a reason for things, they say . . . . God will punish them, that's all I can say. I believe [in] karma.[13]

In understanding the conflict between protesters and the police, and in seeking to make sense of rioters' frustrations and grievances, it is important not to lose sight of the very real impact their violence and destruction has on the lives of other citizens living in the neighbourhoods most deeply affected. Non-combatants may spend hours, even days, fearing for their safety and security. Many will lose their homes and their livelihoods. Theirs is a perspective, though not a primary focus of this book, which it is important to acknowledge. Finally, and before we leave the subject of the police, we must think about their perspective also.

Behind the visor

The bulk of work in this field focuses on the police role in the aetiology of collective violence and as a focus for rioters' enmity. Accounts of the experience of officers themselves is much rarer, though exceptions include Peter Waddington's (1994, 1999) two in-depth quasi-ethnographic studies of public order policing and, in a more limited way, Didier Fassin's (2013) study of French policing. Even these, though they offer a behind-the-scenes view of elements of police decision making, remain limited where collective violence is concerned. After its first phase, which involved 270 interviews with rioters, the *Reading the Riots* study turned its attention to the police, spending several months interviewing 130 front-line police officers in the main cities where rioting occurred.

Much that the rioters had to say about their experiences found some echoes and parallels in police testimony. Rioters talked of their excitement and of the carnivalesque atmosphere surrounding at least the early period of rioting. Naturally, the experience of having to police a major breakdown of order is somewhat different, but for some there was nevertheless a sense of anticipation if not pleasure at the prospect. As one officer put it, 'Truthfully? Excitement! There was not one point [where I felt] scared or anything. My adrenaline was pumping.' There were others who expressed similar feelings about excitement, though this officer was pretty much alone in their claim of feeling no fear. The excitement centred on the promise of being able to utilize what had been learned in training, the thrill associated with the anticipation of violence, and the sense of the unknown. At the very start of the events in London in 2011, and other cities in England in the days that followed, as the fighting and destruction were beginning, officers wondered what they were heading towards. As one officer said, 'as we were making our way, I started to think to myself: oh my goodness, we are literally just going to drive straight into the eye of the storm'. On that first night of rioting in London, some vans had travelled a long way from the south-west of the city and then inadvertently into the very centre of the riot on Tottenham High Road: 'Suddenly bricks and bottles and scaffolding started being thrown at us. And we were like, jeez, OK, it's actually happening now. It's so loud in the van when those things hit the side, it echoes around a sort of big tin chamber.' In Manchester a couple of days later, as missiles started hitting the van, another officer said they were shouting at each other: 'Get your shields up – the window's gonna go in!' It is at this point that officers quickly become aware that they need all the protective equipment there is available. There was often a rush to check helmets, visors, shields and the rest. Inside one riot van, officers found themselves under attack, with a brick hurled through a window and officers desperately trying to keep the doors closed. One female officer reported, 'I don't think he'd got the bolt on properly, so he had his hand on the door. Obviously there was a big hole in the window now, and then suddenly this machete knife came through and started, like, hacking at his hand. Thank God he had his gloves on which protected him.'

Encouraged by this excitement, the line between bravery and foolhardiness was quite a fine one on occasions. One officer described how he got back to his feet, having been attacked, hit by missiles and knocked to the ground; in his words, the adrenaline, stupidity and a desire not to miss out on the action led him to decline treatment for his injured eye and instead plunge back into the chaos. Emotions were very much at the forefront of the accounts of all those on the 'front line' and, of these, as intimated, the most frequently and strongly expressed was fear. A sense that officers were one step from something disastrous pervaded their experience. One officer simply said, 'I just thought: how much longer will this go on? This is almost a living hell. If some of my officers start going down now, we'll get overrun. They will kill us.' Fear of serious injury or even death was widespread and was expressed both as fear for oneself and as fear for others. In the latter case, this was articulated in particular by more senior officers responsible for men and women on the front line. There were, of course, good reasons for such fear. In part, this was a straightforward reflection of what they were confronted with:

> I couldn't quite [escape] . . . . Next thing I knew, all I could feel were hands clawing down the back of my overalls, trying to grab me and pull me back. There was a moment where I thought: if I get dragged back, there's so many people here, it's so dark and it's so chaotic, that might just be it. I might just be gone. Just disappeared.

Similarly, another officer travelling in a riot van said to the driver:

> 'Whatever you do, don't stop.' Because I was literally thinking: in this road, if we came up to a barricade and we were forced to stop . . .

> I honestly believe they would have turned [the van] over. They would have managed to get the door out and, I honestly believe, got us out, one by one, and – I'm not exaggerating – I think they might have killed us.

One special constable, on his first day in uniform, got a phone call from his girlfriend, in tears, watching the disorder live on television. She said, 'Just don't die, please don't die.'

Though there were no fatalities among the police and, as I have shown, such outcomes are extremely rare, the scale of the violence on those four nights reflected the potential dangers involved. The fears that were articulated also reflected local history and knowledge of what had happened previously. In particular, the epicentre of the first night of rioting in Tottenham was only a short distance from one of the most high-profile riots of the 1980s, at the Broadwater Farm estate in 1985, where PC Keith Blakelock was brutally murdered, having become detached from his colleagues (Newburn 2024). His death, understandably, had become part of the history and folklore of local policing. Comparisons between the events of 2011 and the 1980s riots were regularly made, particularly by senior officers, the earlier events giving a sense of the dangers faced and the scale of the risks involved.

One constable said he was faced with a crowd of about 1,200–1,300 people standing in front of him shouting and screaming, some with balaclavas on, some with bandanas covering their faces, people dressed in shorts and T-shirts, some dressed in black; different ages, men, women, kids, launching things at the police. The sky went dark due to the sheer number of missiles in the air. One of the missiles – a breeze block – struck him on the head.

> I've dropped to the floor, my shield is on the floor. For that period of, like, five to ten seconds, I just took blows all over the body . . . . After I'd been hit in the head and [got] back up on my feet, somebody was shouting: 'Kill the fucking pigs!' That's when I almost felt a shiver through my spine.

As we have established, riots by their nature are unusual. They are relatively rare occurrences, and for most officers involved there will have been little in their experience with which to compare them. Under these circumstances, and rather in parallel with what we heard from some of the rioters, officers turned to cinematic or other visual representations when attempting to describe disorder or what Katz (2016) would label 'anarchy'. One constable talked of watching rioters make a hole in a fence, giving them access to a building site: 'And that was just this infinite source of brick and scaffolding and everything that you want to throw.' Some found it difficult to breathe or see with all the smoke around: 'The helmet steamed up immediately, so I could just about see where I was going.' The violence towards police often became intense very quickly: 'The instruction came to put your visors down, and everyone's shields come up then,' said a 35-year-old sergeant. 'It was like a scene from [the film] *Zulu* – you know, that scene when they all come over the hill? Three hundred people literally came round the corner into the side street and started attacking us .... Because I had my visor down, it was like watching a TV screen.' Just as rioters often did, many officers framed elements of their experience via comparison with movies and video games. The extent of the violence, against people but especially against property, the burnt-out cars, 'endless smashed windows' and the remoteness from everyday professional routines led one officer to observe, 'This is not real, this is like a movie set.' Similarly, the bronze commander[14] in Salford, a 45-year-old superintendent, who issued a 'van up and get out!' order to withdraw from the scene given the dangers faced, likened what happened that day to the movie *Black Hawk Down*, the 2001 war film about a disastrous operation by US armed forces in Somalia.

Excitement, fear and pride associated with the bravery shown in the face of extreme danger were experienced and articulated in different ways, but this appears to be a core part of policing serious civil disorder, and not surprisingly so. As Harris (2019: 201) observes, 'police officers have many more occasions to exhibit and act upon physical courage than the rest of the population does'. He notes that 'warrior culture' in American policing has long been an important frame through which officers see themselves: a buffer 'between society, on the one hand, and the rising forces of evil and violence on the other'. It is world-famously captured in Joseph Wambaugh's novel *The New Centurions*, published in 1971, in which he uses his experiences as a policeman in the Watts riot to convey the fear felt by officers as part of their mission. Famously, of course, our understanding of police culture is much influenced by early studies of police work (Westley 1970; Van Maanen 1978), not least that by Jerome Skolnick (1966). Importantly, Skolnick argued that there are 'certain outstanding elements in the police milieu ... [which] combine to generate distinctive cognitive and behavioral responses in police: a "working personality"' (1966: 42). Alongside authority and efficiency, one of these was *danger*. There is no quantum here; rather

Skolnick was rightly observing how the existence and perception of danger, alongside other matters, shape the way in which officers tend to see the world.[15] To deal with elements of this, Sierra-Arevalo (2021: 75) argues that there exists a cultural frame, in essence a cognitive lens that he terms the 'danger imperative', which 'emphasizes potential violence and the need to provide for officer safety at all times'. The 'danger imperative', the argument goes, shapes everyday policing, encouraging a series of accommodations which affect how policing is perceived and delivered. As we have seen, perceptions of pervasive danger in policing have led to a number of effects, and one of the most visible, particularly in the public order arena, is 'militarization creep' (Eisenberg 2023). As I have already indicated, militarization generally is fraught with controversy (Fassin 2013; Graham 2010; Newburn 2024), and in the United States, particularly since Ferguson, it has become a matter of almost continuous scrutiny in the public order arena. But the distinction drawn between 'everyday' and public order policing is important here, for the latter is undeniably fraught with danger. It is, to a degree therefore, unlike other policing.

Protest violence and policing

The police and social conflict go hand in hand. It is the job of the police to maintain order and, consequently, where breakdowns in order are threatened, the police will almost certainly be present. Consequently protest, particularly protest where opposition is likely, will necessitate police presence. Protest violence will bring police intervention and, on occasion, may even be a consequence of police intervention or of perceptions of police conduct. The study of protest violence and riots, certainly in the post-war period, suggests that a signal factor has been poor police–community relations, indeed often very considerable enmity between police and minority communities in particular. Those involved in such violence are often highly distrustful of the police, viewing the institution as a hostile force. Police actions are highly consequential in this context in two main ways. First, as already suggested, it is often police conduct, or perceptions of police conduct, that lie behind the anger fuelling some collective violence. Second, and subsequently, how the police go about the job of policing public disorder has important outcomes in terms of the exacerbation or mitigation of violence and in terms of the consequences for both individuals' lives and the communities involved.

The nature of protest policing has shifted markedly in the past half-century or so, sometimes characterized by a changing emphasis between two ideal types, 'escalated force' and 'negotiated management', this being taken to indicate, broadly, an increased concern with protesters' rights, increased emphasis on police–protester communication, and decreased reliance on arrest as a primary means of control. These being ideal-typical constructions, it is by no means the case that the historical trend is clear-cut or without counter-trends. Indeed, one such is the increased militarization characteristic of public order policing in the same period. Now, some commentators have argued that at least elements of this should be seen as necessary protective responses to increased dangers and as indicative of improvements in police organization and management in public order situations. Even so, there are plentiful examples, very obviously in but by no means confined to the United States, where public order policing has taken on not only the appearance but also the style of military activity.

9

Riots, Media and Social Movements

Towards the very end of 2010, widespread protests took place on the streets of Tunisia, leading to the eventual toppling of the authoritarian regime of Zine El Abidine Ben Ali in early 2011. Events in Tunisia were quickly followed by significant demonstrations and attempts to topple incumbent regimes in Libya, Egypt, Yemen, Syria and Bahrain, some of which were accompanied by violence. In addition to the end of Ben Ali's rule in Tunisia, leaders were also deposed in Libya (Muammar Gaddafi), Egypt (Hosni Mubarak) and Yemen (Ali Abdullah Saleh). There were also large-scale protests in Morocco, Iraq, Lebanon, Kuwait and Oman, among others, and smaller-scale demonstrations in a number of countries including Palestine, Saudi Arabia and Djibouti. Although regime change was not the focus of the protest, Western Europe also saw sustained rioting around the same time, with significant conflagrations occurring in France in 2009, England in 2011 and Stockholm in 2013, among others. These outbreaks, together with other significant protests, including those linked to the metamorphosing Occupy movement (SMSEC 2015), from Wall Street in Manhattan to Occupy Central in Hong Kong, and to the emergent Black Lives Matter movement in the United States, led to an extensive search for an explanation for such widespread upheaval. One left-wing UK-based journalist, Paul Mason, neatly encapsulated the extent of the turmoil in the title of his (2012) book, *Why It's Kicking Off Everywhere: The New Global Revolutions*. *Time* magazine even had 'The Protester' as its front-cover person of the year in 2011.

While by no means all of the examples cited thus far fall into this category, what the majority have in common is their link to another form of collective behaviour, that generally referred to as 'social movement' activity. More particularly, then, the focus of this chapter is on the intersection of social movements and collective violence. Social movements as political vehicles have a long history, but recent times have brought significant change, and one argument, widely rehearsed if not always accepted, has it that 'new social movements' or, sometimes, 'networked social movements', are a distinctive recent development which brings with it implications for the ways in which both protest and protest violence occur and, consequently, for the ways in which we should understand them. It is for this reason that my focus here is on developments largely occurring in the new millennium, including uprisings such as the so-called 'Arab Spring'[1] and social movements such as Occupy, Black Lives Matter and Defund the Police. Protests around each and all of these have seen occasions of significant violence, and we will revisit some previously discussed issues, not least the policing of such conflicts. One area, relatively little discussed thus far in this book but a matter seen by many as being at the heart of what distinguishes modern or new social movements from their earlier counterparts, is the role of the media and in particular the impact of the internet and new social media, thought by many to have affected the nature and shape of civil violence (Crossley and Krinsky 2015). The 2024 riots in the north of England are one recent illustration of where the spread of (dis)information over social media is thought to have been crucial both in fomenting violence and in shaping it (Ismail and Ardalan-Raikes 2025). Finally, this area brings into reasonably sharp relief the issue of how riots spread. In part, I will argue that it is a consequence of the strength of their 'narrative capacity' (Tufekci 2017), the ability of a movement to spread its worldview and frame its story in its own terms. It is regularly and widely observed, for example, that within the 'Arab Spring' the initial protests in Tunisia were a forerunner for what subsequently occurred in Algeria and Egypt and also that the 'Arab Spring' had a similarly direct influence on the emergence of Occupy Wall Street and on the spread of the Occupy movement across the United States and around the globe, and indirectly on the emergent Black Lives Matter movement. Thus do networked movements spread.

Social movements

Social movements, as generally discussed, lie somewhere between formal political institutions, such as political parties, and disorganized crowds or other collectivities. Calhoun (2013: 26) describes them as 'relatively long-term collective engagements in producing or guiding social change'. Herbert Blumer suggests they be viewed as 'collective enterprises to establish a new order in life. They have their inception in a condition of unrest and derive their motive power on the one hand from dissatisfaction with the current form of life, and on the other hand from wishes and hopes for a new scheme or system of living' (1951: 199). Social movements have a lengthy history. As Charles Tilly, their foremost historian, observed of their emergence,

> a distinctive way of pursuing public politics began to take shape in Western countries during the later eighteenth century, acquired widespread recognition in Western Europe and North America by the early nineteenth century, consolidated into a durable ensemble of elements by the middle of the same century, altered more slowly and incrementally after that point, spread widely through the Western world, and came to be called a social movement. (Tilly and Wood 2013: 7–8)

Painting with the broadest brush, it has been argued that, whereas protest in traditional society had been short-lived, highly localized and spasmodic, the development of the modern state offered a new target for popular demands and new means of seeking to achieve them. Campaigns increasingly became longer-term, with particular foci aimed at influencing or even challenging the authority of the state.

Most gatherings are peaceful, but where protest is concerned, and where challenges to state authority are involved, conflict is always possible. Occasionally, violence will be the outcome, and under certain conditions this violence will be intense and possibly extensive. Blumer distinguishes between two main forms of social movement: the reformist and the revolutionary. As it sounds, they differ in the scope of their objectives, the former focused on change in some aspect of contemporary order, the latter seeking to alter or reconstruct it. One would expect revolutionary movements to be more challenging than those that simply seek reform, and therefore to be more likely to be the site of conflict. Rejecting the term 'riot', Tilly and others focus on what he called 'contentious gatherings' and, more broadly, on the field of 'contentious politics' (Tilly 1995, 2003; Tilly and Wood 2013).

New social movements

It is suggested that from the late 1960s more traditional movements focusing on workers' rights and the like gave way to 'new social movements', 'oriented to autonomy, self-expression, and the critique of post industrial society' (Tilly and Wood 2013: 70). The category included such movements as feminism, gay rights, Indigenous peoples' rights and the environment or green issues. By the new millennium, something further had changed with the arrival of the internet, of new systems of information collection and sharing, and the emergence of new social media. For Manuel Castells (2015: 15), the primary theorist of such changes, the networked collectivities of the digital age represent a new species of social movement that has a number of features: an autonomous communicative capacity, enabling movement members to connect with each other and more widely 'via the new social media, mediated by smartphones and the whole galaxy of communication networks' (2015: 220). The core of networked social movement activity involves a connection between activity in the public cyberspace, bypassing mainstream media, and public urban space, which challenges institutional authority. Though he is careful to avoid technological determinism, Castells argues that, 'given enough social unrest and rebellious potential in a given society, the widespread use of social media allows individual rebellions to become social protests and ultimately social movements' (2015: 226). Taking the example of the Spanish *indignados*,[2] whose protests arose like so many others in 2011, Castells describes a movement that had no formal organization or programme, which had no leaders, locally or nationally (though see Gerbaudo 2012), or even spokespersons most of the time, and which had a horizontal, multimodal structure, creating 'coalitions of coalitions' (Kevin Danaher, quoted in Klein 2005: 18), leading Castells (2015) to label it a 'rhizomatic revolution'.[3]

Central to what Castells came to refer to as 'networked social movements' was 'mass self-communication' based on the 'horizontal networks of interactive, multidirectional communication on the Internet' (Castells 2015: 248). The backgrounds to these movements included the aftermath of the major economic crisis, a deepening crisis of legitimacy and increasing social inequality. The movements tended to be triggered by *outrage* or indignation and, in turn, *hope* of change. These networked movements, Castells argues, don't need formal leadership, are loosely connected by common goals and, though they usually start on the internet – what he refers to as the 'space of flows' – they concretize by occupying urban space – the 'space of places'. In principle, these are non-violent movements, generally beginning with peaceful, civil disobedience. Rarely are they programmatic, and demands, where articulated, tend to be multiple and varied. Castells argues that they are essentially cultural movements that connect the demands of today with the projects of tomorrow.

The 'Arab Spring', Occupy and Black Lives Matter movements

The term 'Arab Spring' came into popular usage after the fall of Hosni Mubarak and Egypt's regime in early 2011. It became linked to a range of events, starting with the Tunisian revolution the previous year. In Tunisia, it had been the self-immolation of Mohamed Bouazizi, a local vegetable-seller who felt he had been humiliated by the authorities, together with the heavy-handed response to the protests that ensued, which morphed into a popular campaign against the by then 23-year-long rule of Ben Ali. Demonstrations, initially in rural Tunisia, were the immediate response to Bouazizi's death, and these were largely 'spontaneous gatherings sharing emotion and passion of mutual deprivation and anger' at the former regime (Mabrouk 2011). They were followed by urban demonstrations organized by lawyers and unions. There was major miscalculation by the police, who responded with significant repression, including the killing of a protester in the first week of demonstrations. Rather than intimidating protesters, the violence inflamed them, providing a supposed 'second spark' (Bramsen 2018a).

Bouazizi's very public death also influenced matters in Egypt. There, the murder of 28-year-old Khaled Said was crucial in mobilizing opposition to the incumbent political regime. Arrested by the security police and seriously assaulted, Said died in police custody. His brother took pictures of his body, and the widespread sharing of the images of the brutalized corpse further heightened tensions. As Tufekci (2017: 140) observes, the use of the extreme photographic images of Said echoed earlier incidents, such as the murder of Emmett Till,[4] to which we might add, although different media were involved, the beating of Rodney King and the filming of the 2020 murder of George Floyd. A Facebook page, entitled 'We are all Khaled Said', was created by Google executive Wael Ghonim,[5] and acted as a focal point for the growing protests. 'From internet networks, the call to action spread through the social networks of friends, family and associations of all kinds' (Castells 2015: 56). Protests began in Cairo's Tahrir Square, with two million people gathering in what became known as the 'day of rage'. If the original spaces of resistance were on the internet, the fundamental core of the protest movement involved the occupation of symbolic public space.[6] The battles between protesters and Mubarak's regime continued both on the internet, which the government initially sought to shut down but was eventually forced to concede, and very publicly in Tahrir Square, which was the subject of repeated attacks and attempts to evict those occupying it. Furthermore, though the use of the symbolic locations has a long history in social movements, '[t]his communal solidarity created in Tahrir Square became a role model for the Occupy movements that would spring up . . . in the following months' (Castells 2015: 60).

Occupy Wall Street (OWS) began in September 2011, in Zuccotti Park, located in New York City's financial district. With the financial crash of 2008 in the background, the Canadian anti-consumerist and pro-environment magazine, *Adbusters*, was behind the initial protest call.[7] Calhoun (2013: 26–7) suggests that, even at its height, Occupy Wall Street 'was a loose-knit coalition among activists with a variety of different primary concerns: labour conditions in Walmart, fracking and energy policies, financial regulation and indeed inequality itself'. It was 'unwilling to make specific demands or to agree on a simple charter' (Gitlin 2013). Milkman, Luce and Lewis (2012), like others, describe OWS as a 'floating signifier' in which, like a Rorschach blot, different people saw different things. It was, they suggest, a 'post-identity movement'. From the outset, it was in effect a leaderless movement. As David Graeber, an academic anthropologist, and originator of the 'We are the 99%' slogan, said of OWS, 'The first decision ensured that there would be no formal leadership structure that could be co-opted or coerced; the second, that no majority could bend a minority to its will, but that all crucial decisions had to be made by general consent' (Graeber 2011). In the absence of formal demands, it was clear from the outset that there was much about the Occupy movement that was fundamentally dramaturgical in character – offering symbolic oppositions rather than making concrete demands.[8]

Gitlin argues that the social movement that 'erupted' in Zuccotti Park in downtown Manhattan in 2011 'was organized, but not in any obvious way.' Its master stroke, in organizational terms, 'was to devise a form of action, occupation, that parlayed electronic networks into the forming of face-to-face community in public places', as had happened inter alia in Tahrir Square (Gitlin 2013: 9). The Occupy movement only really took off 'after it hit the epicentre of American capitalism', spreading across North and Latin America all the way to Europe and South Africa. 'For a moment, it seemed the youth of America had spearheaded a global revolution in their wholesale rejection of the liberal economic and political system their elders had spent the last 30 years imposing on the rest of the world' (Graeber and Hui 2014). By mid-October, there were demonstrations underway or planned in 951 cities in 82 countries (Tedmanson 2011).

In New York, it is possible, as some observers such as Gitlin have it, that the city administration was caught off guard and dithered. Initial tolerance was not to last, eventually being replaced by brutality and forced dispersal. The actions of the authorities in policing the protest, and particularly in clearing the park, served to publicize OWS, not least through the example of indiscriminate pepper-spraying of non-violent protesters in New York and subsequently, and notoriously, at the University of California, Davis, once again all captured on camera and widely publicized. As Todd Gitlin put it, 'when the police went for overkill – pepper spray, mass arrests – pictures of official abuse flew around the world through the movement's own media and then via the mainstream.[9] Support for the movement mushroomed', at least for a while (Gitlin 2013: 13). It remained in the public eye for a couple of months before the NYPD forcibly evicted the protesters from the park. Alex Vitale, a prominent academic police critic and author of *The End of Policing* (2017), said that while many of the OWS demonstrations had been disruptive, they were generally non-violent. 'The police response, however, [has involved] heavy-handed enforcement actions, which in some cases exceed their legal authority and violate protestors' basic rights to free speech and assembly' (Vitale 2011: 78).

Many critics focused on the particular style of policing adopted by the NYPD, linking it to elements of Wilson and Kelling's famous 'Broken Windows' article of 1982 and to the reliance on 'stop and frisk' as a core tactic. Increasingly, as attention shifted away from the Occupy movement, criticism in the United States focused more on police violence towards Black citizens. Though African Americans had been dying in large and disproportionate numbers at the hands of the police for many years, this issue was becoming gradually politicized and subject to the *outrage* that Manuel Castells suggests provokes action by modern, networked social movements. The criminologist Franklin Zimring (2017) details how newspaper coverage of 'police shootings' and 'police killings' rose sharply from late

2014 onward. The Black Lives Matter (BLM) movement, started in 2013 by three women – Patrisse Cullors, Alicia Garza and Opal Tometi – was, at least in part, a response to the acquittal of George Zimmerman of the killing of Trayvon Martin.[10] It was the following year, however, that the movement really seems to have taken off, largely as a consequence of the death of Michael Brown, and the riots that developed in Ferguson, MO, thereafter (Hagan, McCarthy and Herda 2022). Keeanga-Yamahtta Taylor (2016) argues that Brown's death was a breaking point, not only in Ferguson but across the United States: 'Perhaps it was the inhumanity of the police leaving Brown's body to fester in the hot summer sun for four and a half hours after killing him, keeping his parents away at gunpoint and with dogs' (2016: 153). Disorder broke out in the hours and days that followed, with 172 people arrested and 132 charged with 'failure to disperse' during the demonstrations (Taylor 2016: 155).

Only a matter of weeks before Brown's death, a video had circulated of a New York City Police officer choking 43-year-old Eric Garner into unconsciousness – Garner was clearly heard to say 'I can't breathe'. He was pronounced dead at the hospital. Although the medical examiner ruled Garner's death a homicide, the officer, Daniel Pantaleo, was not indicted. Tens of thousands of people took to the streets. Some months later, in Ferguson, the eventual failure to indict Officer Darren Wilson, the police officer charged with causing the death of teenager Michael Brown, led once again to large-scale rioting. Two days prior to the decision over Darren Wilson, a 12-year-old boy, Tamir Rice, was shot and killed by the police in Cleveland, Ohio. He had been playing with a toy gun. The slogans 'Black Lives Matter' and 'I Can't Breathe' became all but ubiquitous. Somewhat like Occupy, however, even at this point a certain amount of controversy arose over tactics, structures and leadership, and the need to give everyone a voice (Taylor 2016). By early 2016, the movement had somewhat faded from public consciousness. Occasionally, cases broke through, not least the killing of 17-year-old Laquan McDonald in Chicago and the initial decision not to bring charges against the officer concerned. This changed when video footage was eventually released to the public, ending with the conviction of that officer, Jason Van Dyke, for second-degree murder. Even the regularity of such deaths did not guarantee continued focus on the matter as a social problem, however. As the journalist Wesley Lowery observed, 'in each instance Americans' focus on race and justice landed like another strong wave, only to recede right back into the wide ocean' (Lowery 2016: 221).

It was at this point that very significant and sustained rioting broke out and, under the banner of 'Black Lives Matter', would come to a great many American cities, as well as to Europe and beyond. In 2020, on Memorial Day (an American public holiday), 46-year-old African-American George Floyd died at the hands of the police. He had been accused of passing a counterfeit US$20 bill and was arrested by two rookie officers. During an ensuing tussle, a more experienced officer, Derek Chauvin, intervened, pulling Floyd to the ground. There he pinned him, and kept him face down, despite Floyd voicing the same words uttered by Eric Garner, 'I can't breathe', many times, and 'Don't kill me!' In all, Chauvin had his knee on Garner's neck for nine minutes, once again all caught on camera. Even after officers had tried and failed to find a pulse, Floyd was kept pinned to the ground. By the evening, differing accounts of what had occurred were circulating, but the name George Floyd was coming to symbolize the claims of the social movement. The historian Michelle Phelps (2024: 108) suggests that the demonstrations that the video of Floyd's assault and death inspired 'were the largest in recorded US history' – no small claim, given the scale of the urban riots in the sixties (though see Buchanan, Bui and Patel 2020) – spreading, it seemed, even to 'small-town white America'.[11] Half a million demonstrators took to the streets on 6 June 2020, and she estimates that by mid-June roughly twenty million people, or 6–10% of the whole US population, had been to at least one George Floyd-focused demonstration. The movement's 'narrative capacity' (Tufekci 2017) seemed exceptional.

Violence quickly followed, and in Minneapolis the mayor initiated an 8 pm curfew. The police response was extraordinarily aggressive, involving the use of tear gas, flash-bang grenades and a range of other 'less lethal' munitions, often without warning. At least 89 people were injured (Phelps 2024: 110), with even journalists sometimes targeted. As we have noted in earlier chapters, in such circumstances, the civil violence that ensues often begins with rock and stone throwing, and is followed by violence from and against the police (and other agencies such as ICE). It also often includes looting, and what occurred in Minneapolis was no exception. The looting drew widespread criticism, with President Trump weighing in, tweeting: 'Those THUGS are dishonoring the memory of George Floyd, and I won't let that happen .... Any difficulty and we will assume control but, when the looting starts, the shooting starts' (quoted in Phelps 2024: 112). Large numbers of arrests were made but, fortuitously perhaps, there were few fatalities. The spread outside Minneapolis was not only extensive, but international, and it was suggested that within weeks protesters were demonstrating and marching against racism and cognate issues in at least 93 other countries and territories. Among these, the most prominent in terms of the number of protests were the United Kingdom (179), Germany (67), Canada (66), Australia (46) and the Netherlands (39) (Pressman and Devin 2024). In terms of examining diffusion, Pressman and Devin show there to be clear temporal links between Floyd's death and the US protests and what happened abroad subsequently, as well as evidence to support the hypothesis that it was media coverage of US events that played a primary role in the process of transmission. Some adaptation was visible too, with the focus in some countries being on local victims of police violence rather than on George Floyd, and there were changes to hashtags to reflect this. Furthermore, it is not just the protests but the newsworthiness of the violence associated with the protests – i.e., the fact that there were riots – that undoubtedly contributed to the spread. As Phelps (2024) noted, they certainly raised concern about the persistence of racism in the United States but also, she suggests, helped the Democrats' visibility in the 2018 electoral contests. As earlier research had indicated, while many raise doubts about the effectiveness of disruptive protest tactics (McAdam 1983; Tarrow 1994), there is some empirical evidence for the effectiveness of violence and disruption, particularly in increasing the extent to which protesters are viewed as legitimate claimants (Gamson 1975).

Within the United States, the goal of at least some of the protesters quickly coalesced around the demand to 'defund the police'. As anyone even passingly familiar with the politics of policing would have been aware, this was a challenging aim, and it was not one that was either widely accepted or that travelled easily. In what Phelps describes as a 'landmark' *New York Times* op-ed in June 2020, the campaigner Mariame Kaba[12] entitled her piece, 'Yes, We Mean Literally Abolish the Police'; the subtitle – 'Because reform won't happen' – captured the reasoning.[13] This and a great many other interventions took the idea of 'defunding' seriously. Minneapolis became something of a testbed for the possibility of radical change. Meanwhile, Derek Chauvin's case was coming up, as were those of his fellow officers. By the time the court ruling was expected, the city had already agreed a civil settlement of US$27 million with the Floyd family. In April 2021, after a trial at which fellow officers testified against him, Chauvin was convicted of second-degree murder and sentenced to 22 years in prison. All four officers were eventually convicted of violating Floyd's civil rights.

The killings continued, however, including in the week of the verdicts themselves, when a mixed-race man involved in a struggle with officers who were attempting to get him out of his car was shot, seemingly mistakenly, when one policewoman shouting 'Taser!' drew her service revolver instead. The killing sparked further rioting in the Twin Cities. In the end, Mariame Kaba's caution was correct, with Phelps summarizing the Minneapolis experience in the following way:

> In the three years following George Floyd's murder, everything and nothing seemed to change with the MPD [Minneapolis Police Department] . . . [I] asked how the MPD was (not) held accountable for its violence. The answer, in short, was that even as the mobilization of summer 2020 produced a groundswell of support for radical changes in public safety, it was not ultimately enough to dismantle the police department. (Phelps 2024: 171)

A number of factors were in play. The absence of a single or obvious core voice articulating the protesters' objectives was one: '*Abolitionism* [wa]s the name of a diffuse, decentralized social movement rather than a well-defined theory' (Garland 2025a: 120). The lack of clarity about the objective itself – the meaning of 'defund' – and what an alternative might look like, were others. There were then, of course, powerful voices and interest groups in opposition, and Phelps's impressive account slowly unpicks the gradual dismantling of radical possibility and its replacement with watered-down reformism. According to the not-for-profit organization Mapping Policing Violence, the numbers have been worsening in the years since George Floyd's murder. Although there was a slight drop in 2021, numbers have risen from the 1,155 killed in 2020 to 1,314 in 2025, the worst year on record. They found that Black people were disproportionately more likely to be killed by the police (Black people represent 12% of the US population and 24% of those killed by the police) and were also more likely to be unarmed and less likely to be threatening someone when they were killed.[14] That something more radical hasn't come to pass in Minneapolis, or elsewhere in US policing, doesn't mean that it can't or won't. But, for the time being, the picture is far from positive (see Sherman 2020). The United States is also far from alone where what are perceived to be disappointing outcomes are concerned. In the Middle East, notwithstanding the impact of the Tunisian revolution, the outcome in Egypt, Libya and, most recently, in Iran in 2026, has been the reassertion of authoritarian or military rule, the crushing of protest movements and the widespread stifling of human rights. The Occupy movement, which flourished and spread so impressively, has almost entirely disappeared from view. We have seen what has occurred with the Black Lives Matter and Defund the Police movements. Is this negative picture a reflection of something intrinsic to the nature of modern social movements, or must we look elsewhere?

Social movements in the internet age

In a classic statement, Frances Fox Piven and Richard Cloward (1977) argue that disruptive protest, including violent protest, was more likely to succeed than less violent forms, certainly as far as poor people's social movements were concerned, but this impact diminished as organizations formalized, bureaucratized and their leaderships increasingly eschewed disruptive tactics. Certainly in the short term there is evidence for the success of disruption and violence, as we have seen with both Occupy and BLM, for example, but over the long term the consequences are less clear. This discussion raises two sets of questions. The first and most obvious concerns the efficacy of violence and disruption, but there is also the question of variation in organizational structure and its implication for movement achievements. We noted earlier that commentators such as Gamson (1975) viewed organizational stability as important to movement success, both in terms of recognition of the movement and the wider benefits of their activities for the population. He was, in turn, critical of the use of violence as part of what Tilly would call the movement's 'repertoire of action', seeing it as undermining the chances of success. In this chapter, I have focused, in the main, on modern social movements – 'networked social movements', as Castells calls them – which have tended to be broadly horizontal in structure, to eschew traditional leadership, especially charismatic leadership, and to avoid statements that are manifesto-like, or anything approaching clear, unshifting goals and objectives. They are 'networks of outrage and hope' – driven by outrage and encouraged by hope – and are much influenced by and organized around internet-based and social media activity. As Klein (2005: 17) says, 'What emerged on the streets of Seattle and Washington was an activist model that mirrors the organic, decentralized, interlinked pathways of the Internet – the Internet come to life.' It is vital not to overestimate the degree of organization involved. As Klein observed of protests in Quebec, it was true that there were well-organized groups:

> the unions had buses, matching placards and a parade route; the black bloc of anarchists had gas masks and radio links. But, for days, the streets were also filled with people who simply said to a friend, 'Let's go to Quebec', and with Quebec City residents who said, 'Let's go outside'. They didn't join one big protest, they participated in a moment. (Klein 2005: 146).

Each and all of these movement characteristics have divided opinion, some seeing them as the source of flexibility and advantage, others as undermining the ability of modern social movements to sustain their activities and drive home their messages.

Hugh Roberts (2024), in his book on Egypt and the 'Arab Spring', argues, for example, that the fall of Mubarak was a consequence of a military coup rather than coming on the back of the protest movement. That movement, he argues, had 'for the most part no sense of direction, no precise idea of where to go from Tahrir Square, demanded the departure of Mubarak as an end in itself – that is, as a fetish' (2024: 153). While what happened in Egypt was much influenced by the ploys, tactics and general example of those involved in the Tunisian uprising, elements of the protest were imitation, he suggests, rather than emulation. Many in Egypt were ill-prepared to achieve anything lasting. In this context, hugely difficult though it would have been, they failed to challenge the real source of power in Egypt, the army. What then occurred, while revolutionary in spirit, fell far short of revolution. As Roberts among others notes, part of the failure was the result of the absence of leaders. This 'yielded power to the government, allowing it to usurp the choice of negotiators' (Tufekci 2017: 72) – an underestimation of the concessions Mubarak was willing to make, and a failure to negotiate. Western commentators tended to view and present the lack of leaders as a virtue though, ironically, they subsequently tended to valorize the work of particular individuals, such as Wael Ghonim, the Google executive who started the Facebook page, 'We are all Khaled Said'.

Critiques of social movements that are apparently leaderless and have less than clear structures are far from new. Writing in 1970, the feminist critic Jo Freeman said of second-wave feminism that

> the idea of 'structurelessness', however, has moved from a healthy counter [to an overly structured society] to becoming a goddess in its own right . . . . [I]t has become an intrinsic and unquestioned part of women's liberation ideology . . . . If the movement is to grow . . . , it will have to disabuse itself of some of its prejudices about organization and structure. There is nothing inherently bad about either of these. They

> can be and often are misused, but to reject them out of hand because they are misused is to deny ourselves the necessary tools to further development. (Quoted in Chenoweth 2021: 124; and see Rock 2023)

The journalist and public intellectual Malcolm Gladwell, for one, is doubtful of the power of networked movements, suggesting that hierarchical bodies tend to be more effective, and in doing so he sets himself up directly against the likes of Clay Shirky whose book, *Here Comes Everybody*, he describes as the bible of the social media movement. As already noted, networked movements tend to have, at best, loose aims and objectives, and this is where Gladwell sees the major problem: 'The drawbacks of networks scarcely matter if the network isn't interested in systemic change – if it just wants to frighten or humiliate or make a splash – or if it doesn't need to think strategically' (Gladwell 2010: 48). In fact, it is not simply that aims and objectives may be loose, but in reality, far from being the child of a sizeable social movement, many protests are made up of a great many smaller ones. That they may each have their own ambitions helps explain why overall objectives often look plural and malleable. The subtitle of Shirky's book is 'The Power of Organizing without Organizations', and in it he outlines some of the changes that have occurred in this field in the new century. Some care is due here, too, because the continuing importance of 'leadership', even in times of apparently weakened central authority, should not be underestimated and, in consequence, ideas such as the 'iron law of oligarchy' continue to have resonance in modern times (as has the cognate work of Pareto[15] and Mosca).[16] These include improvements in the nature and velocity of information sharing, the speed with which groups can form and change, the removal of a number of barriers to collective action – the avoidance of certain social and geographical boundaries, for example – as well as the hugely reduced costs of communication. Shirky says:

> One way to think about the change in the ability of groups to form and act is to use an analogy with the spread of disease. The classic model for the spread of disease looks at three variables – likelihood of infection, likelihood of contact between any two people, and overall size of population. If any of those variables increases, the overall spread of the disease increases as well. This model also applies well to the spread of gossip and other word-of-mouth opinion. (Shirky 2008: 159)

At the heart of all this lie modern forms of communication. The protesters who took to the streets of Moldova in 2009 to signal their disapproval of the country's communist government had their actions described as a 'Twitter revolution'. The same year, the State Department in Tehran in Iran sought to avoid a scheduled maintenance shutdown of Twitter in the midst of ongoing student demonstrations, fearing the consequences. As Gladwell (2010: 42), with a degree of hyperbole, suggested, 'Where activists were once defined by their causes, they are now defined by their tools. Facebook warriors go online to push for change.' Noting that the bulk of protest movements now tend to use social media, Shirky (2011) suggests these are not a 'replacement for real-world action but . . . a way to coordinate it . . . . In fact, the adoption of these tools (especially cell phones) as a way to coordinate and document real-world action is so ubiquitous that it will probably be a part of all future political movements.'

Certainly, the internet and social media have enabled forms of organizing that are quite different from those typical of earlier decades. What we have come to know as a 'flash mob' – a sizeable group coming together suddenly in a public place, taking part in some specific activity and then quickly disappearing – came into being, as in the nomenclature being established, around 2003 (Walker 2013).[17] Initially, it was utilized by comedy and theatrical groups, many commentators considering it to be a new art form (Vanderbilt 2004). As with much crowd activity, there was much about flash mobs that was carnivalesque. Quite quickly, it became clear that the tactic could be used for political purposes. By 2011, a journalist from the *San Francisco Examiner* was calling it the 'year of the flash mob' (Downs 2011). It was also the point at which the authorities started to take stronger measures to crack down on flash mobs (see Kaminski 2013).

In recent times, political leaders facing riots and protest have often been quick to focus their attention on the internet and on social media, believing them to be the heart of the problem. As Recep Tayyip Erdoğan, the president of Turkey, put it, 'Twitter is the enemy of the people' (quoted in Castells 2015: 223). In Egypt, at the beginning of the protests in Tahrir Square, one of the major governmental responses was an attempted shutdown of the internet. It blocked text messaging and BlackBerry messaging also. As a consequence, 93% of Egyptian internet traffic ceased, some small internet service providers (ISPs) continuing to communicate. The impact, however, was significantly lessened by the activities of people and systems from outside Egypt sympathetic to protesters. Television networks, dial-up phone lines, ham radios and fax machines all provided alternative options for mass communication.

Landlines outside Egypt were utilized to forward messages to foreign-based internet networks. As Castells (2015: 65) summarizes, 'old-fashioned technology became instrumental in overcoming government censorship. Altogether, these different means added to the formation of a dense, multimodal network of communication that kept the movement connected within Egypt and with the world at large.' Within days, internet access in Egypt was restored. The movement, anyway, had reached a stage of development in terms of its size and its activities that meant the shutdown would have been of limited impact: 'once the movement has extended its reach from the space of flows to the space of places, it is too late to stop it, as many other networks of communication are set up in multimodal forms' (Castells 2015: 67).

Governmental attacks, verbal and physical, on the internet and social media have arguably contributed to exaggerating the importance of these technologies to the nature of contemporary protest. In the midst of the England riots of 2011, just a few months after the uprising in Egypt, the prime minister, David Cameron, said in parliament that businesses such as Facebook, Twitter and BlackBerry should show greater responsibility, and he implied that the government was consulting with the security services and would intervene if their actions didn't change, though he didn't specify what this meant. Opposition politicians supported Cameron's position. In fact, research at the time showed that while BlackBerry messaging was used to aid coordination and played a significant role in communication within the disorder, Twitter (now X) had little effect on how the riots themselves played out, its greatest influence being on the clear-up afterwards. Similarly, a survey of Tahrir Square protesters showed that platforms such as Twitter and Facebook were important in pushing the early turnout of people to the streets, not least as the source of information about the nascent protests (Tufekci 2017). Ignorance was widespread. While it is true that social media helped form a significant element of communication and community building, claims that social media *caused* either the 'Egyptian revolution' or the England riots involve significant overreach (Fuchs 2013). Both the cyber-utopianism that accompanied some of the early accounts of the uprisings in the Middle East in particular (Mason 2012) and the techno-determinism that characterized some of the responses to the activities of new social movements should be firmly rejected.

Social movements and the challenge of violence

As observed earlier, where public order policing itself is concerned, the long-term historical trend has been away from militarized and repressive forms of policing towards those that pay greater regard to the right to protest, are more tolerant of the disruption that protest may bring, and emphasize the importance of negotiation and communication. This shift, sometimes summarized as a move from *escalated force* towards *negotiated management* (McPhail, Schweingruber and McCarthy 1998), has to varying degrees occurred across liberal democracies in this period (della Porta and Reiter 2006a; Halloran, Elliott and Murdock 1970; Newburn 2024; Waddington 1994). The activities of 'new social movements' have provided significant challenges to policing and have provoked reactions that fit uneasily with this broad secular trend in public order policing. I have discussed in some detail, for example, recent trends in the militarization of policing. Some of the challenges are held to derive from the organization of new social movements and the nature of their contentious repertoire. Such movements, as we've seen, tend to be characterized by flatter structures, an absence of traditional leadership, aims and objectives that are malleable, sometimes in conflict with each other or perhaps simply unstated, and repertoires of contention that, similarly, are plural and flexible. Their activities are much influenced by the availability and impact of the internet and by new social media, and, according to Castells, combine activities in this 'space of flows' with more traditional occupation in the space of places. As della Porta and Reiter (2006b: 186) suggest, in consequence it appears we are witnessing 'a general and not yet concluded (re)negotiation of demonstration rights and accepted or tolerated protest repertoires'.

In Bonn in 1985, the first of the major global political meetings (it was the G6 at the time) was the focus of mass demonstrations. Subsequent meetings of the World Trade Organization (WTO), the International Monetary Fund (IMF), the World Bank and the G8, among others, have become significant sites of contestation. These meetings illustrate the classic problems of public order policing. The societies hosting such meetings have to appear to be open and democratic, including enabling protest while simultaneously engaging in a sufficient level of suppression to allow the meetings to take place under conditions of guaranteed security – all in the glare of the world's media. Most observers argue, however, that securitization has tended to trump other concerns, with policing generally becoming more repressive. Increasingly, meetings have been held in remote locations but, whether rural or urban, the defensive strategies adopted have included substantial levels of spatial management and exclusion, including reinforced perimeters restricting access and, within these, a highly controlled 'red zone', marked by more fencing and highly militarized policing, providing and indicating a no-go area for the uncredentialled. What this has produced has been highly fortified sites and 'exclusionary fortress-oriented policing' (King and Waddington 2006; see also Graham 2010). Those being policed are themselves quite highly differentiated, and their repertoires are varied, ranging from the highly provocative actions of 'black bloc' groups that tend to be most obviously intent on violence through to other much less confrontational elements that tend to locate themselves a long way from the 'red zone'. Reflecting on both the WTO protests in Seattle in 1999 and the G8 protests in Genoa in 2001, della Porta and Reiter suggest that

> conflict around breaches of the Red Zone became ritualized, with an escalation of police strategies to defend summit sites, but also with a multiplication of tactics tried by demonstrators aiming at penetrating them: some threw paint balls (or garlic in the Genoa case); the non-violent contingent lay down in front of the entries; the civil disobedient people attempted physical pressure on the gates. (della Porta and Reiter 2006b: 24–5)

Consideration of how best their aims might be achieved necessarily invites social movements to reflect on the efficacy of the different elements of their contentious repertoires. Centrally, this is likely to include an examination of what role, if any, there might be for violence. Some modern social movements are particularly mindful of the potentially negative consequences of the use of violence and have deliberately eschewed such tactics. The conduct of the authorities around the turn of the millennium, particularly in the context of the policing of anti-globalization protests, reinforced such views.[18] Della Porta, Andretta, Mosca and Reiter suggest that since the protests at the G8 in Genoa in 2001, 'debate within the [anti-globalization] movement on the dangers of using radical forms of action has intensified. Criticism within the movement . . . often focused on the negative effect that clashing with the police, setting fire to cars, and smashing windows has on the public image of protesting' (2006: 147–8). They cited the hugely disproportionate media coverage given to the violence of a small minority of protesters in Seattle (at the anti-globalization protests in 1999), which virtually drowned out coverage of the main issues. Non-violent civil disobedience became the preferred strategy. A spokesperson for the Genoa Social Forum (GSF) (a coalition of anti-globalization movements, political parties and societies) said, 'we emphatically repeat that the demonstrations and actions which we shall promote during the G8 summit shall be peaceful . . . we solemnly declare that we have chosen to act in a wholehearted respect for the city and we have chosen not to carry out attacks on any person whether or not he or she is wearing a uniform' (quoted in della Porta, Andretta, Mosca and Reiter 2006: 139).

Della Porta and colleagues argue that 'The harsh behavior of the police in Seattle and Genoa was attributed to the growing tendency on the part of the police to lump civil disobedience and violence together' (2006: 149). Police action in Seattle was fairly indiscriminate, with the eventual response being generally directed against the entire movement – precisely the danger anticipated by the social identity model of collective behaviour. In consequence, for many involved, police actions felt highly disproportionate as well as indiscriminate. As Naomi Klein (2005: 150) observed, 'At that time, it was already clear that the police were running out of control, getting their excuses ready for a major civil liberties crackdown and setting the stage for extreme violence. Before a single activist had taken to the streets, a pre-emptive state of emergency had been essentially declared.' In Genoa, there was also little trust in negotiation. Lines of communication between protesters and police were often interrupted; there were occasions when police were uncontactable, not least when there were concerns that a 'black bloc' group was approaching a sensitive part of the city. The police, in turn, complained that protesters failed to communicate clearly. Furthermore, the movement's loose structure and rejection of leadership fed police distrust of crowds that were unable to 'police themselves' (della Porta and Reiter 2006a). As with Seattle, a combination of somewhat inchoate protest strategies utilized by the protesters, together with indiscriminate police surveillance and information collection, led to a police approach based on an undifferentiated image of the 'no-globals' as "bad demonstrators"' (della Porta and Reiter 2006a: 25).

In the event, as one newspaper summarized it, many of the 200,000 who came to demonstrate 'were beaten to a pulp by seemingly out-of-control riot police'.[19] The 'most severe attack, however, was launched against the TB [Tute Bianche or 'White Overalls'] demonstration of "civil disobedience"' (Azzellini 2009: 1308). Alongside baton charges and the use of hundreds of gas grenades, live ammunition was fired, with 18 bullet casings later collected. On the Saturday night, a police operation, which had all the hallmarks of a 'forward panic' (Collins 2008), involved the storming of a school in which protesters and journalists were camped and led to injuries to 82 of the 93 present, including fractured skulls, compound fractures to limbs and broken teeth (Azzellini 2009). This led della Porta, Andretti and colleagues (2006: 161) to argue that Genoa seemed to mark 'the culmination of the escalation of coercive strategies employed against the [anti-globalization] movement'.

In short, the long-term trend from *escalated force* strategies towards approaches broadly approximating *negotiated management* came under pressure in the context of transnational protest around the turn of the millennium. New social movements, with their malleable forms and repertoires, offered a new challenge and one that contributed to a number of changes. To unpick this slightly, della Porta and Reiter (2006a) draw a set of further distinctions where policing strategies are concerned. In this case, they identify three main strategies, which they term *coercive* (the use of force), *persuasive* (control attempts via communication and negotiation) and *informational* (all information strategies with a control or preventive aim). These they then apply to contemporary transnational protest policing. In addition to the clear reappearance of coercive strategies outlined above, they highlight the fact that much such force is oriented towards temporary incapacitation. Where persuasive strategies are concerned, they say that what is striking is the strong deterrent, if not intimidating, nature of the approaches employed, combined with low levels of trust in negotiation. Finally, in relation to information strategies, the trend towards large-scale data gathering and proactive, and increasingly panoptic, forms of information surveillance similarly indicates intentions that are repressive, even if the analytical capacities of police forces and other bodies are often insufficient to make such information strategies a reality. The dangers are very real but can be overstated and, once again, the work of Halloran, Elliott and Murdock (1970) and Waddington (1994) should alert us to the need for due care when assessing such arguments. Della Porta and Reiter (2006b: 182) acknowledge 'that it might be rash to conclude that the negotiated management model has been replaced by a new protest policing style', though clearly there are aspects of recent practices that depart quite significantly from that model.

Social movements in intense times

Explaining such shifts requires quite a broad perspective and includes, at the very least, changes in the organization of policing and developments in police 'knowledge'. This would require shifts in the nature of governance – the declining influence of national systems of accountability alongside a broader democratic deficit at the international level. Growing emphasis on proactive information gathering and surveillance has been a dominant characteristic in contemporary policing (Ericson and Haggerty 1997; Ratcliffe 2026), with notions such as 'intelligence-led', 'evidence-led' and 'proactive', policing becoming increasingly prominent. To these shifts, and in tandem, we must also add the developments in social movement characteristics explored in greater detail in this chapter, not least their horizontal, often leaderless, somewhat inchoate nature, as well as their hybrid or multiform character, with broadly peaceful movements potentially harbouring small violent groups within them. Finally, it is important to acknowledge that modern social movements now operate in times of extraordinary political and social upheaval, what della Porta (2025) calls 'intense times'. This is not the moment for a lengthy discussion of what is meant by this but, rather, it is important here simply to acknowledge that the period since 2010 has been one involving an especially extensive 'protest cycle' – 'a phase of heightened conflict and contention across the social system' (Tarrow 1994: 153) – and one that has seen considerable change in the understanding, presentation and use of violence both by protest groups and by control institutions.

10
Reaching Judgement

I began this book with a brief riff on the subject of Rorschach tests. The fundamental point was that much of what we see in riots appears to lie in the eye of the beholder. Political perspectives come to the fore. Prejudices about particular groups are played out as if they straightforwardly reflect some truth about the causes or nature of riots and protest. But fundamental questions remain about how riots and protest violence are seen and talked about, how narratives are constructed, how certain events come to be seen in particular ways and why one way of presenting events comes to be the dominant one. This is of central importance for, as Kenneth Burke reminds us, a way of seeing is always, simultaneously, a way of not seeing. This raises the question of who has the power to influence or perhaps even determine how things are perceived. One obvious source is the state and, indeed, I will argue later that where a government makes a decision to launch some form of 'official' inquiry, its outcome will often come to form the dominant narrative. Nevertheless, this is rarely straightforward, and there is always some form of competition over meaning, a tussle to create claims to 'truth', or what Bourdieu would have called a 'doxa' (Bourdieu and Wacquant 1992), a pattern, common sense or conventional wisdom that comes to be established and provides the basis for understanding a particular set of events.

It is this basis for understanding, this competition over meanings and ideas, and what it tends to comprise, that is my focus here. What, for example, do the political, public and media responses to protest and violence generally involve? What are their parameters, do they differ or overlap, and what is revealed in the choices that are made to frame matters in particular ways and to utilize certain sorts of language? Indeed, we may start at the very beginning again with the word 'riot'. Is it used and, if so, by whom and to what effect? What alternatives are offered and by whom? How is collective violence talked about, defined, attacked and defended by politicians, pundits, other professionals and the public? Such issues deeply affect popular conceptions of disorder and are matters that vary considerably over time and place or, if one prefers, historically and comparatively. In this regard, however, and as the subjects of the two chapters that follow also make clear, it is important to recognize that the influence of these reactions to rioting often continues far beyond the period of the disorder itself, serving to settle particular narratives and providing the foundation on which formalized responses to the violence, or its absence, can be explained, built and justified. In this context, media framing may have a very significant impact on public images of protest, establishing understandings that are both pervasive and durable (Halloran, Elliott and Murdock 1970; Snow, Vliegenthart and Corrigall-Brown 2007). It will often be the case that there are differing, indeed competing, accounts from different sources. There were some significant differences between the ways in which the alleged motivations behind the Southport riots in 2024 in England were presented in initial social media accounts and the picture that later emerged from the police and other authorities (Home Affairs Committee 2025).[1] Political framing can affect almost everything, including the penal and public policy responses that I explore in the remaining chapters.

The proximity of violence

When discussing my research project in 2011 in which we planned to conduct interviews with rioters out on the streets of London and other English cities, we wondered how to reach people and how best to open the conversation once we had. We aimed for extended interviews with people who had been involved in the riots. Establishing trust with them was going to be important and, in all likelihood, not easy. We wanted to know all about people's involvement, what they'd done, how and, to the extent such things can be known, why. In the event, we decided on the simple formulation of asking people, 'When did you first hear about the riots?' This quickly led to a discussion of where they were at the time, how they heard, and what they then decided to do. It was a successful interview strategy. Most commonly, people would say that they'd been out and about and they witnessed incidents at first hand or, more likely, that they had heard of things via television or radio or through friends. And this, it turns out, is typical of the natural history of riots. Beginning with pamphleteering, the circulation of handbills and the like in previous centuries, and then, as societies grew in complexity, the arrival of newspapers, journals and, later, radio and television became the key channels through which news of the breakdown in social order circulated. Beyond the immediate context of witnessing things at first hand, media in various forms are how knowledge of disorder, and therefore messages about disorder, are disseminated (see Quarantelli and Dynes 1968).

In setting out their views of disorder, politicians, policymakers, journalists and others offer both diagnosis and prognosis. To do so, there is no need for particular elaboration, though that may be offered, for even the language that is adopted will give some indication of the views therein. Often there will be some embellishment, however, and this will offer a view backwards – what happened and why – and forwards – what should be done, what is necessary, now and possibly in the future. The tussle that subsequently ensues is over the power to define both the past and the future and, where the latter is concerned, to shape and mould it. I'll begin by looking in a little more detail at political responses to riots. Given that it is clear by now that *all* responses to riots are political in *nature* and, for the most part, also in *intent*, my focus in this next section is on the responses to breakdowns in order by politicians, elected representatives and the like. What type of witness are they? How, typically, do they respond? We begin with politicians' commonest responses, the tropes they reach for, before moving on to examine the work and impact of official inquiries.

Political tropes

There are three primary tropes invoked by politicians when there is an outbreak of serious disorder. They are by no means entirely distinct, and they overlap in several ways. Overall, they form the basis for what tends to be, though is by no means always, political condemnation of rioting or violent protest.[2] The first is to portray rioters, or at least those who are thought to foment the violence, as *outsiders*. Here we immediately encounter overlap, for in all three cases the trope is of an outsider, of someone who, by dint of a particular characteristic or characteristics, is not of the mainstream. In this first case, however, the fundamental element of outsider status is something literal; they are portrayed as being *from elsewhere*. These are people who have come from other geographical locations in order to undertake their activities, persuade others to become involved, encourage particular courses of action, and so forth. They are not *of* the place. Linked with this, the idea of 'agents provocateurs' is well established in accounts of riots and rioting (Waddington 2000).

As one example, in the 1967 Detroit riot it was regularly argued that it was people new to the community, who had only recently arrived in Detroit, who were primarily responsible for the violence, though research later showed this to be false (Fine 2007). In a wide range of examples, from the 1980s urban riots in England (Scarman 1981) to Ferguson, Missouri, in 2014,[3] it has typically been suggested that people from outside those communities had deliberately travelled in order to instigate or take advantage of the violence. Caplan and Paige (1968: 18) found that, in Detroit and Newark in 1967, those most likely to riot were not migrants but long-term residents, with 59% of rioters in Detroit being born in the city compared with 35% of the non-rioters – the discrepancy being even greater in Newark. Similar claims had been made in the case of the 2011 England riots.[4] In such accounts, the riots became the work of 'professional criminals', 'opportunists' and 'copycats', the implication being that there was little link with local neighbourhoods and, more especially, with local 'respectable' citizens, and consequently, any claim to legitimate grievance was removed.[5] Again, no solid empirical evidence was produced.

The second trope, linked to the first and widely used politically during breakdowns in order, is that wherever they're from, those involved are distinguished simply by their criminal and antisocial nature. As President George H. W. Bush said of the Rodney King riots in 1992:

> What we saw last night and the night before in Los Angeles is not about civil rights. It's not about the great cause of equality that all Americans must uphold. It's not a message of protest. It's been the brutality of the mob, pure and simple. And let me assure you: I will use whatever force is necessary to restore order. (Quoted in Camp 2016: 98)

Bush's phrasing, all the way down to the 'pure and simple' construction, was repeated by the British prime minister, David Cameron, a couple of decades later when, responding to the 2011 England riots, he talked of 'sickening scenes – scenes of people looting, vandalising, thieving, robbing, scenes of people attacking police officers and even attacking fire crews as they're trying to put out fires. This is criminality, pure and simple, and it has to be confronted and defeated.'[6] A few years earlier, in 2005, the French interior minister, Nicolas Sarkozy, described rioters as 'thugs and scum', later saying he regretted using the term 'scum' as it was too 'weak' to describe the young people involved (Dikec 2017: 127). In Turkey, the then prime minister, later president, Recep Tayyip Erdoğan referred to protesters as 'marauders', 'vandals', 'marginals' and 'terrorists' (Dikec 2017: 175–6). The underpinning view here is that the riots involve people who are insufficiently socialized or perhaps who, as classical psychology would have it, have lost their inhibitions and have returned to a more primitive form. Anything more fundamental is excised from explanation. From the outset, empirical research has undermined such arguments, beginning with the historical scholarship of Rudé, Hobsbawm, Thompson and others which illustrated that far from being the conduct of some disorganized rabble, the mob or the dangerous classes, protests in the eighteenth century were dominated by working people, shopkeepers and labourers drawn from local communities and integrated into common customs, norms and expectations.

The third and final trope, and one easily linked with the others, sees rioters as socio-economically separate. They are viewed as part of the lumpenproletariat or, more colloquially, the 'riff-raff'. In the mid-1960s, a combination of the second and third tropes came to dominate the view of the McCone Commission, which had been charged with inquiring into the Watts riot in LA. Its report, *Violence in the City*, claimed the rioters were marginal people and the riots meaningless outbursts. The LA rioters were portrayed as a small and unrepresentative fraction of the Black population, as criminal and delinquent, as well as unemployed and under-educated (Fogelson 1967). In Detroit in 1967, the rioters were seen 'as being peripheral to organized society, with no broad social or political concerns', and the view was that the frustration that led to rioting was little more than part of 'a long history of personal failure' (Caplan and Paige 1968: 15). A range of data sources, on income, unemployment and occupation, however, suggested that rather than being cut off from employment and having given up hope where job opportunities were concerned, many rioters were continually on the margins of the job market. Furthermore, there was little evidence of differential values at play. There were few differences in levels of group membership reported and, if anything, they were slightly higher among the rioters, a group who did not obviously seem to be 'bowling alone' (Putnam

2000). This held for both levels of interaction with neighbours and levels of church attendance. Their conclusion was 'that Negroes who riot do so because their conception of their lives and their potential has changed without commensurate improvement in their chances of a better life' (Caplan and Paige 1968: 21).

All three primary and interlinked political tropes find limited empirical support yet continue to enjoy widespread political popularity. In large part, this no doubt stems from their respective strengths as easy means of rejecting more complex and convincing forms of argumentation. In addition, no doubt, it also partly lies in the power that derives from well-established, embedded and continuing fears of outsiders (Elias and Scotson 1965) or 'strangers' (Schutz 1944; Simmel 1971). Looming large behind all of these common political tropes lies the influence of classical views of the crowd or the mob. Such portrayals generally involve an explicit contrast with the political claims that might otherwise be assumed were the source of grievance and anger. A recent example can be found in England where, responding to the looting and violence seen during the 2024 riots, the secretary for health, Wes Streeting, said, 'Don't tell me that people are just expressing legitimate grievances while they have got their hands full of stuff from Lush' (a high street cosmetics store) before going on to describe the violence as 'the mindless thuggery of the far right'.[7] A local senior police officer used exactly the same phrase while also deploying the 'outsiders' political trope: 'In Blackpool, we have witnessed some mindless thuggery from individuals, who we believe to be from outside of the county, intent on causing issues in our communities.'[8] Despite the absence of empirical support, classical views of the crowd continue to have considerable resonance, then, and not just in relation to riots and rioting. The neoconservative cultural commentator Douglas Murray, for example, reaches for precisely such ideas when seeking a means of explaining what he sees as the mass delusion associated with modern rights and identity movements. To understand the contemporary attraction to what he refers to as 'woke culture', Murray suggests that we are experiencing 'a great crowd derangement. In public and in private, both online and off, people are behaving in ways that are increasingly irrational, feverish, herd-like and simply unpleasant' (2020: 1). This is the power, indeed the 'madness of crowds'.

Official inquiries

Where matters of judgement and agenda-setting are concerned, among the more consequential actions governments can take in the context of riots is the establishment of some form of official inquiry. Such commissions are generally sizeable, costly and often somewhat slow-moving, so they are by no means a common response to disorder. But under certain conditions – often where an authoritative response is believed to be required – they are deemed expedient.[9] In what follows, I'll briefly examine the nature and impact of four such inquiries, that in LA in 1965, the Presidential Commission in the United States that reported in 1968, Lord Scarman's inquiry in south London in 1981 and the report into the policing of Hong Kong's protests, published in 2020. A certain cynicism is occasionally evinced where such inquiries are concerned, with critics considering them to be repetitive, unoriginal and overly time-consuming, there often being more talk than action. In evidence to the Kerner Commission in 1967, the psychologist Kenneth Clark said that he had read many of the reports of previous riot investigations and found them to be 'a kind of Alice in Wonderland – with the same moving picture reshown over and over again, the same analysis, the same recommendations, and the same inaction' (Kerner Commission 1968: 483).

The McCone Report was published in late 1965, a mere one hundred days after the inquiry had been established by California's Governor Brown.[10] It quickly looked out of kilter with the times. In contrast with almost all the riot analyses that followed, it referred to the outbreak of violence in south-central Los Angeles as a 'spasm', with the rioters 'caught up in an insensate rage of destruction' (McCone Commission 1965: 1) and as an 'explosion – a formless, quite senseless, all but hopeless violent protest – engaged in by a few but bringing distress to all' (1965: 4–5). According to Scoble, McCone saw the riot as being 'perpetrated largely by the criminal element of the Negro community, with others egged on by an extremist leadership which subverted the normal attachment of non-criminals to law and order in the ghetto' (Scoble 1968: 171). It thus played on the most basic political tropes, using language closer to that of classical psychology than to the more obviously sociologically informed scholarship that was coming to dominate in the sixties. McCone was widely criticized for its failure to understand the local community – indeed, its apparent lack of attempt – its shoddy social science, its inconsistent use of data offering weak speculation in place of rigorous analysis and producing an outcome that was as predictable as it was without much foundation. This was the last gasp of the conservative view, or 'riff-raff theory' (Graham 1980), so far as official inquiries were concerned. McCone's failure, Fogelson (1967: 342) suggests, was a reflection of the mainly upper-class, white background of the Commission's members and their associated 'preconceptions about violence, law enforcement, ghettos, and slums' (additional criticism can be found in Akins 1968; Blauner 1970; Scoble 1968).

Whereas McCone, indirectly, brought the curtain down on 'riff-raff' theories and other means of marginalizing the significance of the experience of disorder for those involved in it, Kerner, established only two years later, presented a view of the disorder that became *the* established view of riotous behaviour for the next three-quarters of a century or more.[11] Again, as previously discussed, Kerner's understanding of the riots helped cement the 'tinder and spark' approach in public, political and academic discourse. Underpinning the disorder was a 'reservoir of grievances', varying from city to city but in general relating to 'prejudice, discrimination, severely disadvantaged living conditions and a general sense of frustration [among African Americans] about their inability to change those conditions' (Kerner Commission 1968: 117).

The Kerner Report had a huge impact, its various editions selling more than two million copies before the end of the decade, with one commentator describing it as having become 'a basic document in the platform of American liberals for social reform, a catalogue of problems and a program of solutions' (Kopkind 1971: 378). By the end of the 1960s, the established view from Kerner and subsequent reports, such as Skolnick's to the Violence Commission set up the following year (Skolnick 1969), saw such conduct fundamentally as acts of political protest (see Fogelson 1967; Graham 1980).

In short, Kerner helped establish an approach to the aetiology of protest violence that has dominated public and scholarly understanding ever since, even if political interpretations continue to draw on now unfashionable classical psychological approaches. A further example of the influence of official inquiries can be found in England in the early 1980s. In this case, the violence broke out in one of England's largest African-Caribbean communities in the south London neighbourhood of Brixton in April 1981, in the early years of a new Conservative government under Margaret Thatcher. Lasting little more than 48 hours, there was widespread violence against people and property, and this was followed later that year, and then later in the decade, by further rioting in London and other English cities (Newburn 2024). An inquiry was established under a leading judicial figure, Lord Justice Scarman, who used his independence of government to focus on controversial subjects including racism and racist policing in Britain, as well as the wider social policy context – education, housing, opportunity, employment – facing Britain's minority youth. It was a balancing act. As Scarman put it,

> I identify the social problem as that of the difficulties, social and economic, which beset the ethnically diverse communities who live and work in our inner cities. These are difficulties for which the police bear no responsibility . . . . But, unless the police adjust their policies and operations . . . they will fail, and disorder will become . . . endemic. (Scarman 1981: 2 para 1.7)

Scarman's report, published within a year of its commission, had a huge impact, particularly within policing. Indeed, it effected 'a reorientation of police thinking on a wide front', and by the end of the decade its analysis had come to represent 'the predominant conception of policing philosophy' among chief police officers (Reiner 2000: 205–6). It heralded the arrival of organizational, tactical and philosophical changes that placed greater emphasis on community involvement, service orientation and the overriding importance of order maintenance – in short, what many subsequently came to call 'community policing'. It was a settlement that was to see British policing well into the new millennium. Scarman's report was distinctive for several reasons, not least that 'it broke the prevailing law-and-order consensus by firmly locating the sources of unrest in "insecure social and economic conditions and in an impoverished physical environment" – a "set of social conditions which create a disposition towards violent protest"' (Hall 1999: 190).

Having considered three official inquiries – one that missed the changing mood and spirit of the times and was rapidly superseded (McCone), one that encapsulated, mirrored and cemented the contemporary zeitgeist (Kerner), and one that influenced a single but nevertheless important element of social functioning, policing (Scarman), with lasting impact – my fourth example is a state-sponsored inquiry established with particular political intentions in mind. In this case, the inquiry was produced by Hong Kong's Independent Police Complaints Council (IPCC) in 2020, whose aim was to frame analysis in a particular way, to drive it in a specific direction and in the process justify extant and future repression while undermining the legitimacy of alternative viewpoints. The immediate background lay in the increasing frequency of protest in Hong Kong, and widespread claims of police harassment, repression, heavy-handedness and brutality, leading to both domestic and international condemnation. The IPCC report's position was steadfast, however. The escalating disorder was viewed as 'lawlessness', 'incipient terrorism', 'urban guerrilla tactics' and 'vigilantism' (IPCC 2020: paras 16.5–16.7). Police action was simply reactive, responding to 'the need for law enforcement action' (2020: para. 16.4) in connection with 'illegal action by protesters and for the protection of themselves and others when attacked by violent protesters' (2020: para. 16.22). The IPCC's world was a Manichean one in which the police represented safety and security in the face of continuous and unjustifiable violence from those intent on destruction.

Hong Kong's chief executive, Carrie Lam, described the report as 'comprehensive and objective' and rejected all criticism. The criticism was widespread, however, with the director of Amnesty International Hong Kong, for example, talking of a 'misleading report [that] makes no attempt to establish accountability for the gross police misconduct seen on the streets since last summer. It also demonstrates the Hong Kong government's effective refusal to address the widespread and systemic human rights violations that have taken place during protests since last June.'[12] A group of British psychologists brought in to help with the IPCC's research eventually resigned, the principal investigator saying, 'We were in the end manipulated and put in an awkward position. There is no way I could have stood by the [IPCC's] report.' When asked if he thought he would be allowed to visit Hong Kong in the future, he said, 'I don't think I'd feel safe.'[13] This final case is an example of an official inquiry being established and organized to head off criticism of the state. Although it claimed to be independent and objective, few believed it to be so, seeing it, as the *Daily Express* put it, as 'a puppet for Beijing'.[14]

Media responses to riot

We have considered the political reactions to riots and rioting and, via politics, official inquiries and their contributions to what John Kingdon (1984) would call 'agenda-setting'. The major remaining consideration is the role of the media. What forms do media reactions take? How do they interpret events, and what influences their decision making and with what consequence? In examining this, it is useful to consider where information tends to be drawn from, who are the 'primary definers' (Hall et al. 1978) or 'key informants', who is believed to have credibility, and which values, not least 'news values', affect the choices that are made, and to what end.

At various points along our journey, we have stopped to consider the language of riot and protest violence. Which terms of art are used and are considered appropriate? It is in mainstream media coverage that some of the clearest and bluntest contrasts can often be found. The mainstream media often play an important role in 'diagnostic framing', establishing, explicitly or otherwise, some sense of causation and blame where civil violence is concerned. Traditional mass media coverage, the reports from major newspapers and radio and television stations, for example, tend quite quickly to use the terminology of riot, to shift from talking of 'crowds' to presenting the idea of 'mobs', and of deploying other terminology more associated with the classical psychology – 'irrationality', 'mindlessness', 'thuggery', 'criminality', hooliganism' and 'anarchy'. There is, however, relatively little empirical analysis of such media activity. Some assessment was undertaken by the Kerner Commission, which expressed mixed opinions. It was generally impressed with the seriousness with which the media approached the 1960s riots, but concluded that the picture eventually produced contained unreasonable exaggeration, a view that has been shared by many other observers over the years (Abudu Stark et al. 1974; McCone Commission 1965; Myers 1997; National Advisory Commission on Civil Disorders 1968). This led them to say that they were 'deeply concerned that millions of other Americans, who must rely on the mass media, likewise formed incorrect impressions and judgments about what went on in many American cities last summer' (Kerner Commission 1968: 363). What were the processes that led to this situation? In part, Kerner thought, it was the pasting of sensationalist and misleading headlines onto otherwise more nuanced stories that contributed to confusion – what Cavell (1982) calls the 'theatricality of scripted news recitation'. It was also concerned that there tended to be an overreliance on information drawn from officials who lacked skills in the management and interpretation of relevant data.

One of the constant concerns or refrains of critics of the media is that they may, directly or indirectly, be responsible for the ways in which violence spreads. Here, notions of 'copycat' riots, of direct emulation or some other forms of osmosis-like contagion are often invoked, typically without much thought as to what mechanisms might be involved. Lord Justice Scarman, with little evidence for his claim, said of the 1981 riots in England that, 'The media, particularly the broadcasting media, do in my view bear a responsibility for the escalation of the disorders (including the looting) in Brixton on Saturday, 11 April and for their continuation the following day, and for the imitative element in the later disorders elsewhere' (Scarman 1981: 111, para. 6.39). In all such discussions, there is something of a tendency, whether it is officials talking or the public, to treat 'the media' as more homogenous than is the case. In reality, of course, the media, even mainstream media, do not speak with one voice or work in one way.

Kerner's analysis had asked how news coverage was perceived and received by people locally, and here they found more widespread criticism – something articulated regularly where protest violence is concerned. Black readers and viewers distrusted much of what they were offered, with one saying, 'The average black person couldn't give less of a damn about what the media say. The intelligent black person is resentful at what he considers to be a totally false portrayal of what goes on in the ghetto' (Kerner Commission 1968: 374). At heart, the mass media were viewed as another manifestation of the white power structure. This should cause little surprise, given the almost complete invisibility, for example, of Black life from LA's mainstream media. Johnson, Sears and McConahay (1971) suggest that coverage in the LA press, for example, was almost entirely absent between 1892 and the Supreme Court's school desegregation case of 1954. Less than 1% of the total news space was devoted to Black economic and social life, except for a brief period in the early 1900s when there was conflict over Jim Crow. Though the emergent civil rights movement began to elicit coverage, including some that was sympathetic, Johnson and colleagues suggest the difference was far from profound and had even declined prior to Watts in 1965.

In a very small but important study of the media coverage of the England riots of 1981, Howard Tumber (1982) examined the role of television, offering a breakdown of news coverage, its broad parameters and what this indicated about how news was constructed and to what effect (building on the basic but vital sociological observation that mainstream media are never homogenous in approach). The focus was primarily on television news, finding that twice as much time was spent on studio footage as on actual film of the rioting itself. As time passed, the concern shifted from reporting on events towards *reaction* to those events, and it was here that decisions about which opinion to include came especially to the fore. Initially, much focus was on equipment, with clear agenda-setting attempts made by both police and government to bring this to the forefront. Greater attention was paid to injuries to police than to the public, and to the destruction of property by rioters than to police violence. Police representatives were the most frequently interviewed, followed by government ministers, who spoke for longer, and local residents. Politicians and police, of course, are institutionally advantaged when it comes to responding to events such as riots, both being 'well known' to journalists, relatively easy to contact and, indeed, often proactive in their relationships with the media. In this manner (Schlesinger and Tumber 1994), 'official' sources come to be the primary definers, and under such circumstances it is of little surprise that studies find rioters' voices to be much less frequently heard. Cottle's study of the Midlands riots of the same era found the police appeared on nearly 30% of all occasions, with government representatives making up another 20%. Three-quarters of all police comment came from senior officers; only 2% from the rank and file. There tend to be three predominant foci for the designatory work undertaken by the media in the context of the riot: the nature of the events; how people involved are to be portrayed; and how the neighbourhoods and communities in which violence occurs are themselves to be seen – usually negatively. Cottle (1990: 367–8), in line with many others, rightly observes that where the police are concerned, they often 'appear as an "external" agency confronted by the riot, an agency reacting to the event, rather than as an agency routinely involved in inner city policing and therefore possibly an "internal" protagonist in a complex process in which they have had a pronounced role'.

In Cottle's (1990) Midlands study in the mid-eighties, as in similar studies in the United Kingdom at the time, and in the United States in the sixties and more recently, accounts of riot and protest violence are deeply racialized. Matters of race infuse the sense of place – the 'ghetto', the 'inner city' – the histories of the neighbourhoods concerned, and their backgrounds of immigration and diaspora, as well as the contrasting identities of those caught up in the conflict as protesters, witnesses and 'defenders' of order. These racial histories are, naturally, often significantly more complex than notions of 'race riot' might imply: to take one important example, in the LA riots in 1992, there were multidimensional racial dynamics, with conflict not just between Black and white Americans but also, notably, between Black and Korean Americans. In significant part, therefore, it was an 'interethnic conflict' (CovertAction Information Bulletin 1993). Indeed, Darnell Hunt (1997) shows how 'reading' the media varied, often markedly, among different ethnic groups. His study of KTTV/Fox news coverage of elements of the Rodney King riots found 'relatively low salience of raced subjectivity among Latino-raced and white-raced informants', reflecting a wider divide in which Latino-raced informants 'were *more* likely than black-raced informants to condemn the looting and fires and to support the arrests' (1997: 141). Tensions between the communities had long been strong but had significantly increased in the period prior to the riots as a consequence of the death of a young, unarmed African-American girl, Latasha Harlins, shot and killed by a Korean store owner, who accused her of shoplifting and shot her in the back of the head as she tried to flee the store (Stevenson 2015). The subsequent failure of the courts to return nothing stronger than a conviction for 'voluntary manslaughter' did little to calm tempers. Mediatized choices shaped interpretation and understanding from the beginning but by the time of the acquittal verdicts for the four officers charged with assaulting Rodney King, it is estimated that the video footage of the shooting of Latasha Harlins was being shown at ten times the rate of the Rodney King beating and, indeed, was the footage that was first shown when the verdicts were delivered (Oh and Hudson 2017).

Media accounts are not simply imposed from outside but emerge from in and around the community itself, with NGOs, community newsletters and journals – increasingly internet-based – offering first-hand accounts of events and directly presenting points of departure from official channels and their attempts at the establishment of hegemony. And, while news sources may generally favour majority groups and will often approach community leaders, as Budarick (2011) shows with regard to the Redfern riot in Australia, alternative viewpoints are sometimes available and, albeit with limited reach, they may provide some resistance to the dominant narratives otherwise in play.

Much of the discussion thus far, and very deliberately so, has focused on traditional media such as newspapers, radio and television. Though they have been dominant forms for a very considerable period, the pace and extent of change in the media landscape is in danger of pushing them to the sidelines of analytical attention. The impact of the internet, of new social media, of 24-hour rolling news media and of a plethora of information-sharing systems and platforms has multiplied the numbers of producers of news content. Indeed, with the rise of 'citizen journalism' (Wall 2015), everybody is potentially such a source. This has led 'to the creation of an unprecedented amount of potentially newsworthy information and a remarkable number of "news spaces" in which to broadcast/publish it. In the process, increasingly sophisticated, interactive news audiences are reconstituted as consumers' (Greer and McLaughlin 2010: 1044; see also Colbran 2023).

In their analysis of changes in the media landscape, Greer and McLaughlin (2010) focus on the 2009 G20 protests and associated violence in the city of London. The story they tell begins as a fairly standard one of the development of an inferential structure (Lang and Lang 1955) dominated by a police perspective underpinned by fears of 'protester violence'. There were regular police briefings outlining likely threats and risks, with these being repeated and rehearsed regularly in mainstream press and television. Initial reaction to the major police operation that was eventually put in place was that it had been a success, even though there had been one death. A combination of police credibility and the firmly established inferential structure already in place meant that the death was placed and understood firmly in the context of 'protester violence'.

But this was by now a very different media landscape, characterized by an incredible 'density and variety of recording devices being used by professional and citizen journalists, private businesses, demonstrators, the police, and passers-by' (Greer and McLaughlin 2010: 1050). The circumstances of the protest meant the interactions between police and protesters took place in very close proximity to non-involved members of the public. This produced further witnesses and in due course the beginnings of an alternative narrative relating to the man who had died. Ian Tomlinson had been attempting to make his way home from work, appeared have come into contact with the police and had been thrown to the ground. Once this became clear, it began to change the public attitude towards the policing of the event as a whole and prompted calls for independent scrutiny. Under earlier conditions, there things might have remained. Think back 40 years or more to the death of Blair Peach, believed to have been killed by a London Metropolitan police officer long before that was eventually, and formally, established. By 2009, however, there was considerable mobile phone footage available, including, it turned out, some taken by a tourist that included Tomlinson's fall to the ground. The footage was placed on the website of the *Guardian* newspaper and quickly amassed around 400,000 views. The footage showed that Tomlinson had been injured as a consequence of an unprovoked attack by a police officer. Still more footage of the violent policing tactics that had been used generally to manage the G20 protest came to light, and criticism of the Metropolitan Police Service (MPS) intensified, creating an increasingly dominant and new inferential structure of 'police violence'. The new and proliferating information and news sources had begun to trump the institutional authority of the MPS in the 'hierarchy of credibility' (Becker 1967). This particular event concluded with the dismissal of the police officer concerned, though he was found not guilty of Tomlinson's manslaughter.

As the Tomlinson case suggests, and as we have seen in previous chapters, notably through the example of the so-called 'Arab Spring', the new media landscape is argued to have had a significant impact on modern social movements, on modern protest, and therefore on protest violence. Khamis and Vaughn (2011) suggest, for example that new media were crucial in three important, interleaved ways in the Egyptian revolution: enabling cyberactivism (not least through public mobilization via Wael Ghonim's 'We are all Khaled Said' Facebook page), encouraging civil engagement, and promoting new forms of citizen journalism. One consequence was the undermining of state media services, as alternative sources, including transnational satellite television channels such as Al Jazeera, increased in visibility, importance and impact. One ought not to overstate this impact, however, and reductionist claims of a 'Twitter revolution' in Iran in 2009, a so-called 'Facebook revolution' in Egypt in 2011, and the 'Twitter revolution take two' in Libya the same year all require some mitigation, and perhaps majorly so. Social media have been important, sometimes vital, as in the Tomlinson case, but they always operate in a wider context, being one set of tools among many (Ali and Fahmy 2013). Nevertheless, as Castells (2009: 413) puts it, 'The greater the autonomy of the communicating subjects vis-à-vis the controllers of societal communication nodes, the higher the chances for the introduction of messages challenging dominant values and interests in communication networks.'

Reaching judgement

At the start of the chapter, I quoted Kenneth Burke's dictum that 'a way of seeing is always a way of not seeing', and I return to it here as concern with the claims and counterclaims that surround protest and protest violence, though present throughout the book as a whole, has been a specific focus here. Much of this chapter has been primarily concerned with the political claims made about such contestation, and the role of the media in this regard also. In putting forward a particular view of a protest or a riot, one of the aims that constituencies have is to develop narratives, frames or tropes that will influence, challenge and perhaps even come to dominate the way such events are seen and understood.

Any form of narrative that is told about protest and protest violence is, of necessity, a simplification, an edited version of a more complex set of events (Fernandes 2017). In such processes, the messiness of everyday life is reduced to certain selected, key characteristics. In this context, as we have seen, and drawing on Goffman, thinking in terms of 'framing' is useful, referring to 'interpretive, signifying work that renders events and occurrences subjectively meaningful' (Snow, Vliegenthart and Corrigall-Brown 2007: 387). A frame is an 'interpretive [schema] that simplifies and condenses the "world out there" by selectively punctuating and encoding objects, situations, events, experiences, and sequences of actions within one's present or past environment' (Snow and Benford 1992: 137). As the metaphor implies, frames work to help identify what lies within or outside the viewer's gaze. The two primary framing techniques we have used are the 'diagnostic' and the 'prognostic' (Snow and Benford 1988): the former identifies a problem and potentially attributes blame; the latter articulates a potential solution.[15]

Where protest and protest violence are concerned, I have identified three primary (diagnostic) political tropes that are utilized when order breaks down. These concern the issue of *who* riots and, by implication, *why* they riot, focusing on claims about what the nature of those involved and what their demographic and social characteristics might say about them and therefore about the events themselves. As we have seen, it is regularly claimed by the authorities that participants are *outsiders* in one of three main ways. The first is as outsiders to the community, either geographically or, more generally, as in having little sense of commitment or belonging. The second sees those involved in the disorder as dominated by the criminal and the antisocial, and thus as being guided by a different moral code than the majority. Third, participants are presented as being drawn from the socio-economically marginal, who in another context might be referred to as an 'underclass' (Wacquant 2022). In each case, the consequence of the deployment of the trope is the marginalization of the political claims made by those involved in protest, relegating those involved, and their concerns, to the margins. The language of 'riot' rather than 'rebellion' or 'uprising' tends to underpin such dismissal.

In the context of claims-making, we have seen that official inquiries can be of great significance, though such inquiries are rare and by no means always effective, even when established. That said, a governmental imprimatur and all that goes with it may occasionally have a very substantial influence on the impact of narrative claims, though the context is important. The McCone Commission in 1965 entirely misread the zeitgeist and was quickly and almost entirely forgotten. The Kerner Report, by contrast, a mere three years later, took a very different stance, one that was in line with the emergent mood of the times, and served to concretize a view of that decade's riots in particular, and collective urban violence more generally, for years to come.

We now live in radically changed, mediatized times. The new media landscape means that social media and the internet have become the focus of much analytical attention. We now have a plethora of information-sharing systems and platforms and a vast increase in the numbers of producers of news content, as well as the rise of so-called citizen journalists. At the very least, all this complicates the contest for narrative dominance and arguably reduces the state's ability to dictate how events will be seen. One consistent theme of commentary about networked social movements has been that the new communicative and technological environment has increased their ability to organize and to influence. A consequence is an expansion in what Tufekci (2017) calls their 'narrative capacity' – the ability of a movement to frame its story in its own terms and to spread this (world)view.

As with assertions about new social movements, however, it is important not to overclaim where the extent of change is concerned. Protest and protest violence, and the ways in which they are represented and understood, continue in the main to conform to long-established patterns. Frame variation is common, and perhaps the central analytical question for us remains why it is that one or more diagnostic frames will become the ones around which common understandings crystallize. Is it because they are empirically credible, ideologically in tune with the times or proffered by sources with particular resonance and power? The preceding discussion implies some support for all of these, reinforcing the importance of understanding the role of narrative, not simply in relation to generalized understandings of events but also to more particular matters, ranging all the way from policing practices to collective identities (Polletta 1998) – each and all of which reinforces the importance of thinking carefully about the medium- and long-term consequences and legacies of such events.

11
Protest, Violence and the Penal State

Having considered some of the primary means of post-violence claims-making, my concern here and in the following chapter is with social and political responses to the violence, in particular in this chapter with the wider response or impact of the 'penal state'.[1] How are the courts and systems of punishment mobilized, and to what effect? What will the scale of punishment be, what messages might this send and what are the consequences? One can begin with questions about the numbers arrested, punished, imprisoned and so forth. Beyond the immediate reaction, there is the issue of ongoing consequences. Punishment, especially custodial punishment, is likely to have significance for those punished, and those close to them, for many years after any formal sentence has been completed (Western and Pettit 2010). These are concerns which we should take seriously and see as part of the wider 'life cycle' of protest and riot. Protest and protest violence leave a legacy, some of which derives from the costs that result from criminal justice and penal involvement.

The nature of this state response may also have implications, sometimes significant implications, for how protest and violence play out. Such actions may serve to ameliorate or to exacerbate what is taking place and may reveal, to a much greater degree than hitherto, the problems confronting contemporary authorities (see, for example, Butler, Adonis and Travers 1994). It is generally the hope of the state, of course, that the actions of its penal arm will bring violent action to an end (on how de-escalation can potentially be managed, see Halloran, Elliott and Murdock 1970), but it may also have the reverse effect. Here, and we will consider this in greater detail below, the recent history in Hong Kong is instructive. As we rehearsed earlier, the past decade and more in Hong Kong has seen several significant public protests involving, among others, the Occupy movement (Graeber and Hui 2014), student demonstrations (Wong 2020), the Umbrella Movement (Lee and Sing 2019), resistance to the Legislative Council's attempts to reform the extradition law (Pang 2020) and, latterly, to the new Beijing-imposed security law. In each case, there have been large-scale policing operations, often involving highly repressive tactics. In this context, there is a strong case to be made that the successive waves of protest from at least 2012 were influenced by the handling of earlier events, and, in the anti-extradition case, strong evidence that the penal response was a driving force in the growing scale of the protest as well as its changing tactics and focus (Stott et al. 2020; Wong 2019). This seems of undeniable social scientific importance and is something that should become a more standard part of our analysis and understanding of how protest and violence play out over time.

We may unpick this slightly. As outlined, I have noted perhaps two primary ways in which we might think about the consequences of the reaction of the penal state. First, there is the impact of punishment on the individuals caught in the penal net, as well as the reaction of those watching from near and far, together with their wider networks of kin, kith and community. Second, there are the implications for the protest itself of the state's reaction to protest violence – what will be the effect on the political or other causes espoused by the protesters and others? In the former, the concern is with the protesters and their community, and how repression affects their lives and well-being. In the latter, there is the question of what we might think of as the cultural consequences of the reaction to protest. What are the implications of the formal reaction of the state for the subjects of that protest, for its perception, its legitimacy and its future, and for those more distant who may be its audience? In this connection, I will focus in particular on what has become known as the 'Stonewall riot' of June 1969 – which occurred in New York City, and which, accurately or otherwise, has come to be seen as a turning point in the history of LGBTQ+ rights in the West. This provides, I think, a useful case study in the collateral cultural consequences of protest policing and violence. I begin, however, by examining a little of what is known about the reach of the penal state during and in the aftermath of protest violence.

Riots, social marginality and the penal state

In 2011, England's largest riots in the post-war period caught many by surprise, both the numerous politicians who were abroad and enjoying their August holidays when the violence began and the police who were also, it appeared, caught somewhat flat-footed by the suddenness and scale of the disorder (Home Affairs Committee 2011). In the immediate political reaction to the riots, there were many senior political figures who were critical of the police, and particularly of what many saw as too slow and insufficiently robust a policing response. Quite quickly, the agreed political view was that a tough penal reaction was what was required. And this was exactly what ensued.

In response to what felt like unprecedented pressure, the courts introduced all-night and weekend sittings both practically and politically to deal with the large numbers of people held on custodial remand. Although defended by those running the prosecution system, they were dismissed by some critics as 'kangaroo courts, dispensing "conveyor-belt justice"' (Bawdon and Bowcott 2012). In their sentencing of rioters, the judiciary increased penalties markedly and also abandoned the conventional sentencing guidelines 'that should have acted as a restraint on its punitive impulses' (Lightowlers and Quirk 2015).[2] That riot cases were treated differently to all other types of offending could be seen in a range of ways, not least initially through remand in custody in the vast majority of cases rather than a presumptive entitlement to release on bail. Then there was a frequent uplift in charging – often opting for the most serious alternative where two or more possibilities existed. This, and the decision to depart from sentencing guidelines, led both to increased use of custodial sentences and, where they were imposed, to significantly longer custodial sentences (Ministry of Justice 2012; Pina-Sanchez, Lightowlers and Roberts 2017). The immediate custody rate tripled from 12% to 36% in magistrates' courts and rose from 33% to 81% in the Crown Court (the higher court) (Bell, Jaitman and Machin 2014). Similarly, the average custodial length went from 2.5 months to 6.6 months in magistrates' courts and from 11.3 months to 19.6 months in the Crown Court. The outcome was a significant spike in the prison population in late 2011.

The impact of penal involvement is socially concentrated, of course. Riots tend to occur in poorer communities, though as we've seen they may also coalesce around other symbolic locations

(Tahrir Square, Trafalgar Square, The Champs-Élysées). The data on those arrested and charged in England found that approximately 70% came from one of the 30% most deprived areas. In a study of the capital, Kawalerowicz and Biggs (2015: 19) found that material deprivation was significant in any explanation of variation in involvement in rioting across London. Government data show that in relation to the riots, 42% of those prosecuted were in receipt of free school meals – eligibility for free school meals being regularly used as a proxy for poverty – compared with 16% of the overall population (Ministry of Justice 2012: 27). Department of Education data showed that two-thirds of the juveniles appearing before the courts during the riots were, broadly speaking, teenagers whose verbal, numerical and reading skills were low and whose future employment opportunities were likely to be severely compromised before any prison penalty was imposed on top.

Similar trends and similar criticisms to those identified in England in 2011 can be found in a range of other riots. Sidney Fine (1987), looking back on the 1967 Detroit riot, quotes the deputy director of the Lawyers' Committee for Civil Rights Under Law: 'for all practical purposes, the United States Constitution was absolutely suspended from sometime during the evening of Sunday, July 23rd, to Tuesday, August 1, 1967'. The police had arrested a total of 7,231 individuals during the course of the 1967 Detroit riot, compared with just under four thousand arrests during the 1965 Watts riot, and 1,510 arrests during the Newark riot that immediately preceded the Detroit riot. By any measure, it was a huge intervention. The arrestees were overwhelmingly Black, male and young. Much of the police operation was effectively street-sweeping. There was little success in arresting snipers or arsonists. On the streets, however, the police often made arrests on a wholesale basis, non-combatants being swept up along with rioters. The police, in effect, sometimes 'spread a huge net over the riot area, and seized everyone caught within it' (Fine 1987). None of the Detroit Police Department, the prosecutor or the Recorder's Court was prepared for the sheer number of people apprehended. The number of felony defendants added during the first five days of the riot was the equivalent of a normal six-month caseload. The result, according to Fine, was a virtual breakdown in general administrative and legal processes. Booking became an 'assembly-line' operation, with clerical employees working 12-hour shifts. Of 700-plus juveniles processed, the vast majority had had no previous contact with the Juvenile Court. They were subject to prohibitive bonds, and the Juvenile Court judge boasted that he had not released 'a single juvenile . . . back into the community to feed the riot' (Fine 1987).

Prisoners suffered considerable physical abuse and discomfort, and often could not even be located by the authorities. According to the deputy United States Attorney General Warren Christopher, relatives were left in ignorance as to where family members were being held. Some prisoners simply 'sort of vanished' for a few days. 'As a result of their fear of the potential of the violence, the judges saw the court's role as assisting the police in law enforcement rather than being a check on police activities . . . . In fixing bail, Recorder's Court judges left no doubt that their purpose was "to stop the rioting"' (Fine 1987). Fine goes further and suggests that Recorder's Court judges virtually suspended the writ of habeas corpus during the disorder, further indicating their unwillingness to let people go. Only about 3% of the guilty received jail sentences extending beyond time served, and fewer still received true felony sentences of one year or more. Fine suggests that this pattern of punishment reflected the 'indiscriminate character of the arrests, [and] the sketchiness of the evidence against many defendants' (Fine 1987). Crucially, the number of people coming before the courts meant huge pressure to dispose of cases and not to continue or increase the strain on a system that had already suspended a great many of its standard operating procedures.

The 43 homicides in the riot led to three convictions. The prosecutor issued two homicide warrants to two police officers involved in the riot's most infamous affair, the killing of three young Black men in the Algiers Motel. Both confessed to firing the fatal shots. In the other, an 'all or nothing' ('first-degree murder' or 'acquit') option was put before the court, and the officer was eventually acquitted. In the other cases, the charges were dropped. The executive secretary of the Detroit chapter of the NAACP alleged that the judge had used the law to 'protect the image' of the police department. The criminologist Jerome Skolnick says that the criminal courts in these cities had become an 'instrument of political needs relatively unrestrained by conditions of legality'. In other riot cities, as in Detroit, there were 'recurring breakdowns in the mechanism of processing, prosecuting, and protecting arrested persons' (Skolnick 1969: 228–9). A post-riot survey of African Americans around the central area of rioting found nearly nine in ten of them did not think that the laws were '"fair to all people," and 92% did not believe that the police enforced the laws "equally"' (Skolnick 1969).

Prosecutorial creativity

Creative use of prosecution is a regular hallmark of contemporary state reactions to riot. A couple of brief examples: one significant protest in South Dakota in April 2016 involved several thousand people, led by tribal members serving as 'water protectors' and gathering at camps near the Missouri River in a bid to stop the construction of the Dakota Access Pipeline (DAPL). The protest movement (#NoDAPL) claimed that the pipeline posed a risk both to local water quality and to the cultural heritage of the Dakota and Lakota peoples of the Standing Rock Sioux Tribe (Whyte 2017). A wide palette of approaches was used against #NoDAPL activists, including by now well-established militarized forms of policing. Macy (2024) reports that in a single day in late November 2016, 300 people were injured and 26 hospitalized as a result of a police operation. By early 2017, when the National Guard and other law-enforcement officers had evicted the last remaining protesters, there were over 800 criminal cases in the state courts against water protectors. Creative approaches to prosecution saw terrorism charges (under the Patriot Act) brought against a protester who had sought to dismantle part of the pipeline, and charges of attempted assisted suicide were brought against two 'water protectors' who entered the pipeline in a bid to halt construction. Finally, in this regard, activists were also prosecuted for their passive resistance in locking arms with other protesters when police attempted to arrest them. In other protests, similar conspiracy charges have been brought against protesters for displaying 'Black Lives Matter' banners and insignia. The pressing of charges, and all that goes with it, with little eventual follow-through, is fairly typical of riot-related cases. In addition to creative prosecutorial practice, non-application of the law is a long-standing tactic when seeking to favour one side in a conflict. Robinson (2022) points to the example of the Tulsa Race Riot of 1921, where not a single white Tulsan was convicted of rioting or spent any time in jail for any offence, even though inter alia a group of white Tulsans attacked and devastated the city's Black community (see also Ellsworth 1982; Messer 2021).

Just as police officers must make sense of and deal with the often extreme violence they are confronted with, it is important to remember that prosecutors and others responsible for the running of the penal system are also faced with the challenge of bringing the violence to an end – or, at least, this is how many come to see their role in times of riot. As is the case more straightforwardly with the police, the work of the courts and wider systems of punishment become focused on bringing culprits to justice and contributing to the reassertion of order.

The collateral consequences of punishment

Earlier, in the case of the 2011 England riots, we saw increased levels of imprisonment and lengthier sentences given to those coming before the courts. Those riots, along with the other examples above, illustrate the often high levels of punishment and the relative absence of standard legal protections in such times. Judicial order comes under strain at the same time as social order is challenged. My focus here is on the legacy of riots and, more particularly therefore, on the impact and consequence of punishment. Punishment leaves a footprint. It makes a mark in people's lives and on the wider community, one that is substantial and often long-lasting. This is my concern here.

This impact of punishment, and incarceration in particular, is now well-trodden territory and it doesn't require lengthy rehearsal here. In their review of this field, Kirk and Wakefield (2018) make reference to a wide range of effects, including among them the following consequences of penal engagement: worse physical and mental health outcomes for those who have been imprisoned; declining employment prospects and future earnings; the break-up of fragile families; reductions in civic and institutional engagement; increases in material insecurity and reliance on public assistance; rising legal debts; housing and residential instability; and poor educational and health outcomes for children of incarcerated parents. To this, they add the fact that high rates of incarceration and the social churn that such levels of imprisonment place on communities have a number of negative consequences for neighbourhood informal social control and collective efficacy, with a tendency, consequently, to increase levels of cynicism towards the law and legal authorities among local residents. The consequence, predictably enough, is higher rates of crime and recidivism in those already badly hit communities. This, in turn, reminds us once again that the burdens of contact with criminal justice and penal systems are 'heaped disproportionately on men, racial and ethnic minorities, and those already severely disadvantaged' (Kirk and Wakefield 2018: 176).

To this startling list of personal, family and community consequences we may add the forms of social and political restriction and exclusion that are increasingly a part of the package of punishment as meted out by modern nation-states. As Uggen and Stewart (2015: 1874) note of the United States, for example, 'People convicted of crime are subject to a growing list of federal, state, and local restrictions affecting their economic, political, and social activities. These are often called "collateral consequences" because they are typically located outside the penal code, implemented by non-criminal justice institutions, and interpreted by the courts as civil regulations rather than criminal penalties.' These exclusions, disqualifications, ineligibilities, banishments, restrictions, deportations and record-based surveillance, for example, have a wide range of impacts including further limiting the educational, training and employment prospects of those who have been subjected to severe punishment, especially imprisonment (see Goffman 2014). A requirement of disclosure of previous criminal histories is becoming more common and more consequential in many jurisdictions – often leading to further disqualification. Such histories are also linked to reductions in eligibility for state support and public assistance, not least in the housing market. There is now a wider literature on the subject of banishment (Beckett and Herbert 2010) with, for example, probation and parole conditions leading to a range of restrictions on which geographical areas are in or out of bounds, and where entry can lead to violation of the terms of supervision or release. There are double dangers here for immigrants, with violation potentially leading to detention and deportation. Finally, Uggen and Stewart (2015) remind us that healthcare access is strongly interwoven with employment and associated benefits in the United States, as it is in many jurisdictions, so a lack of stable employment or other prospects may dramatically constrain healthcare choices and lead to long-term negative effects. The collateral consequences of punishment are particularly notable and visible in the United States because of its experiment with mass incarceration. Indeed, such is its extent that there are scholars now examining its wider impact on citizenship more generally and, indeed, on democracy. Terms such as 'custodial citizenship' (Lerman and Weaver 2014) and 'carceral citizenship' (Miller and Stuart 2017) are used to capture the forms of second-class status that now exist for poor Black Americans in particular. In relation to all these developments, the United States may be something of an outlier, and an often egregious one at that (Garland 2025a), but the point remains a generally applicable one: punishment leaves a lasting mark, the scale of penal intervention during and after riots is often very sizeable and, as a result, the impact of riot-related punishment for individuals and communities is often vast and ongoing.

Riots and the rise of mass incarceration

For much of the twentieth century, the incarceration rate in the United States, though on the high side internationally, was relatively stable at around 100 to 120 per 100,000 population. It started to rise steadily in the 1970s, and by 1995 had reached 600 per 100,000: a sixfold increase. It would eventually reach over 700 per 100,000. To put this in perspective, the rate in the mid-1990s in England and Wales, one of the higher incarcerators in Western Europe, was around 100 per 100,000. It was 85 in Germany and Italy, and only 37 per 100,000 in Japan. Whereas in 1972 there were under 200,000 Americans in federal and state prisons, this figure had risen to over one and a half million by the mid-1990s. With a further 700,000 prisoners incarcerated in local jails, it meant that well over two million Americans were imprisoned annually by the millennium's end. It was not just the scale of imprisonment in the United States that led commentators routinely to refer to this as a policy of 'mass' imprisonment or incarceration, but the 'systematic imprisonment' of African-American men (Garland 2001). By the mid-1990s, one in three Black men in their twenties was either in custody or in some other form of penal supervision and long-term trends meant that 30% of all Black males born in America around the turn of the millennium were likely to spend some of their lives in prison (Mauer and Huling 1995).

The growth in numbers incarcerated in the United States together with those under other forms of penal supervision – probation, parole and so forth – has spawned an enormous social scientific literature. Much of this has focused on the question of aetiology. How is it that the world's second largest democracy came to imprison so many of its citizens and, more particularly, its citizens of colour? In part, the 'war on crime', announced by President Johnson and continued under President Nixon, together with the latter's announcement of the 'war on drugs' in 1971, are seen as important supply-side factors (Simon 2001). Second, there are features of what David Downes (2001) labelled the 'macho penal economy' itself, not least the expanding private corrections sector, which tend towards expansionism (Christie 2000). Third, and one of the most important factors, is the general transformation of political culture that has occurred in America and elsewhere. Crime is now a staple of political discourse and of electoral politics. Crucially, as numerous commentators have noted (Beckett 1997; Downes and Newburn 2023), those closing decades of the twentieth century saw a progressively intensifying battle by the major political parties to be viewed as the party with the toughest message on law and order. Initially in the United States, and subsequently in many other jurisdictions, a 'tough on crime' stance came to be associated with electoral success, and its opposite, being 'soft on crime', with electoral failure (Newburn 2008). Finally, a growing body of work, particularly comparative criminological scholarship, has focused on matters of political economy, arguing that American exceptionalism finds its roots in the country's history of inequality, its labour market practices and its limited welfare provision (Lacey, Soskice and Hope 2018). Building on such work, David Garland (2025a: 2) argues that 'the USA is a comparative outlier in policing and punishment – and in criminal violence and social problems more generally – because, as compared to other developed nations, its economy is more unequal, its working people more insecure, its welfare state more inadequate, and its poor neighborhoods more disorganized'.

Intriguingly, this now vast literature on American penal exceptionalism, the history of an experiment that began in the sixties, which has a great deal to say about 'crime', crime levels and crime rates, generally has little and often nothing to say about the country's urban riots (see, for example, Zimring 2020). At this point, we should remind ourselves of some of the basic 'facts' of America's riots/urban uprisings in this period. Riots, as I have regularly repeated, are generally rare phenomena. There are many hurdles to be overcome before people will take to the streets, set buildings and vehicles on fire, attack police officers and steal goods from shops, often in broad daylight. Mass violence, as Bramsen (2024: 80) observes, needs mobilization or, as Collins (1988: 249) puts it, 'everyone coming in on the beat'. Whatever one might say of riots in sixties America, however, it would not be that they were rare. Indeed, they were comparatively common. Quite what constitutes a riot is, as rehearsed, open to debate, but whatever criteria we use, it is the case that there were hundreds of riots in America between 1964 and 1972 and, by one estimate, thousands (Hinton 2021). Hundreds of lives were lost, thousands of injuries sustained and hundreds of millions of dollars in damages caused. The 1960s riots can only be one small part of the overall aetiological picture where explaining the shifts in America's penal politics and practices is concerned, but it seems odd to ignore them.

The primary exception to this picture lies in the scholarship of the contemporary historian Elizabeth Hinton (but also, importantly, Flamm 2007). Initially, in *From the War on Poverty to the War on Crime* (Hinton 2016) and subsequently in *America on Fire* (Hinton 2021), she moves away from the work of researchers that has focused on the rise of free-market economics and neoconservative politics and argues that the changes in the American system of punishment have their origins earlier in the nature of President Johnson's 'war on poverty'. The riots, from Watts onwards, together with the worsening crime problem and the continuing issue of Black poverty and segregation, formed the building blocks for a renewed sense of urban crisis in the United States. The 'long mobilization' of the war on crime was not a reconfiguration of the extant racial caste system. It was not a 'new Jim Crow' (Alexander 2010; Wacquant 2001), she argues. 'Rather, the effort to control and contain troublesome groups with patrol, surveillance, and penal strategies produced a new and historically distinct phenomenon in the post-civil rights era: the criminalization of urban social programs' (Hinton 2016: 25–6). In short, Hinton argues that Johnson's Great Society programmes provided a clear pathway to the later law-and-order expansion that emerged under Nixon and his successors. The penal state expanded as the War on Poverty programmes shrank. In a similar vein, Peter Levy (2018: 312) concludes, 'Unfortunately, the nation adopted the wrong lessons from these tragedies [the riots]. Rather than redoubling federal efforts to address the social and economic ills which underlay the revolts, the nation as a whole decided to construct . . . a carceral state.'

The riots were by no means central mobilizing events, but they were nevertheless important bits of context when, for example, Congress came to consider Johnson's Safe Streets Act in 1967. Both the riot in Detroit and that in Newark, in terms of duration and proximity, coupled with the growing anti-Vietnam War protests, 'reinforced the Johnson administration's sense that the United States was under attack from within' (Hinton 2016: 106). Hinton quotes one White House official who wrote to the president saying, 'It suddenly seemed as if the whole country had come unglued'; and, indeed, Johnson deployed 5,000 soldiers to assist the local police department in Detroit. In an address to the nation, the standard political tropes came to the fore. Speaking on the second night of rioting, the president said, 'The apostles of violence, with their ugly drumbeat of hatred, must know that they are heading for disaster . . . . There is no American right to loot stores, or to burn buildings, or to fire rifles from the rooftops. That is crime' (quoted in Hinton 2016: 107). As we saw earlier, however, the vast majority of fatalities and injuries were suffered by local Black citizens, and in both Newark and Detroit, the latter particularly, the evidence of police violence is plentiful. Johnson's administration turned a blind eye to the bulk of such misconduct and this, Hinton argues, enabled the encouragement of 'the widespread implementation of the policing tactics that had been used to suppress rioting on an everyday basis. Indeed, the experience of fighting urban uprisings deeply shaped the strategies White House officials embraced as they developed the national law enforcement program' (2016: 110). As she puts it more forcefully still in her book on the sixties 'uprisings', 'Mass incarceration is one consequence of the draconian police ethos born in the 1960s and 1970s in response to mass violence' (Hinton 2021: 3). Here we have the clearest statement linking the urban riots with the emergence of mass incarceration, the midwife in this case being the increasingly repressive strategies adopted by American police departments, particularly where African-American communities were concerned.

Hinton's argument revolves around what she refers to as 'the cycle': a 'recurring pattern of over-policing and rebellion, of police violence and community violence, that helped define urban life in segregated, low-income, Black, Mexican American, and Puerto Rican communities in the late 1960s and early 1970s' (Hinton 2021: 21). In her words, the 'cycle began with the police, who moved through the ghettos of America "like an occupying soldier in a bitterly hostile country," as James Baldwin had observed in 1960, so that their presence – their perceived callousness to the inequality around them – felt violent in itself' (2021: 44–5). Unnecessary or inappropriate police action – actions perceived thus – could quickly tip into more widespread violence and even crowd violence, leading to the arrival of militarized police riot-control techniques. The late 1960s and early 1970s she describes as 'the crucible years', the years when the War on Crime ploughed huge resources into urban police departments, leading to a dramatic escalation of 'surveillance, harassment, and violence in American cities' (2021: 45). It set the tone for what was to become so-called 'zero tolerance' and 'broken windows' policing (Newburn and Jones 2007; Westley 1970), characterized by the aggressive policing of low-level misconduct, and the rise of what Kohler-Hausmann (2013: 353) refers to as the rise of 'misdemeanor justice'. This trend may be linked also to what I discussed earlier as the 'return of banishment'. In their analysis, Beckett and Herbert focus on the range of new techniques that have emerged as the basis for the creation and enforcement of zones of exclusion. These new codes, they argue, 'enable a significant increase in the power of the police . . . to monitor, arrest, charge, and jail those considered disorderly' (2010: 37). The consequences of 'banishment' are severe and include, as we have seen, 'impaired geographic mobility, diminished safety and security, loss of income and access to work, diminished access to social services, police harassment, and frequent entanglement in criminal justice institutions'. Banishment, as is the case with all policing activities, is differentially imposed, affecting what Soss and Weaver (2017) call 'race-class subjugated communities' most particularly. In such circumstances, a 'social disciplinary model' of policing comes to the fore, one that has 'abnormality' rather than 'crime' at its core, and is one in which police coercion is a reminder to individuals or communities that they are under constant surveillance.

Hinton's thesis is that the urban riots of the sixties and beyond, alongside other factors, helped feed the reorientation of law-and-order politics via the various metaphorical 'wars' – on poverty, drugs and crime – leading inexorably in the direction of what we have come to see as America's experiment with 'mass incarceration'. Intriguingly, not only does Hinton locate the beginnings of US mass incarceration in the 'socioeconomic conditions that lay at the root of the rebellions' (2021: 204) and in the new policing strategies that the rebellions gave impetus to, she also argues that it was the beginning of mass incarceration in America that helped bring the riots to an end: by the mid-1970s, she argues, three-quarters of Black people in American prisons were aged under 30, and the numbers of incarcerated people of colour increased by half in the decade to 1980. This 'systematic imprisonment of young Black men', which began in the late sixties/early seventies, 'effectively removed from cities a significant portion of the young people who had committed and sustained the violence' (2021: 204). Their absence reduced the likelihood of further uprisings.

Much of this chapter, and not least this relatively brief overview of America's experiment in mass incarceration, has focused on the negative consequences of protest and protest violence. More positive forms of impact are also possible, however, and it is to these we turn next. As writers such as the Chicago sociologist Robert Park noted in the early decades of the twentieth century, the crowd could be a source of positive social change. Such an observation was arguably particularly important at a time when the dominant view of the crowd was that it was a source of danger and something requiring suppression. Even where suppression is the general reaction, it remains the case that protest and, indeed, even protest violence, may have medium- and long-term outcomes which lead, directly or indirectly, to new, positive social relations.

The impact on protest and protest community

On 27 June 1969, New York police raided the Stonewall Inn, a Greenwich Village bar whose customers were primarily gay men. There were very few, if any, women at the Stonewall. The bar was widely known to be mob-run,[3] and the police raided regularly to receive their pay-offs. Despite such bribery, the club made considerable profits – rents were low and the business was all cash (Duberman and Kopkind 1993). On this particular night, a riot took place, not a particularly large riot, but one that has established itself in history. Most straightforwardly, this riot is seen as an especially consequential outbreak of disorder because it is viewed as the spark that lit the gay liberation movement. Notwithstanding its undoubted importance, some profound overclaiming goes on where this particular slice of history is concerned. One activist has absurdly suggested that 'No event in history, with perhaps the exception of the French Revolution, deserves more [than the Stonewall riots] to be considered a watershed' (quoted in Armstrong and Crage 2006: 724).[4] Although there has been considerable revisionism since, Stonewall continues to stand strong in the collective memory, with its commemorative success being celebrated annually in marches and other events, leading Armstrong and Crage (2006: 725) to suggest that the story is 'better viewed as an *achievement* of gay liberation rather than as a literal account of its origins'. Nevertheless, for our purposes here, it plays a useful role in illustrating the potential power of protest violence for understanding the consequences for community in the aftermath.

Plain-clothes officers had entered the club around 1.20 am on the night of 28–29 June 1969, with a warrant enabling them to close the Inn as a consequence of accusations of selling liquor without a licence. The Inn was regularly raided by the NYPD. From the outset, this raid was different from the norm: officers in uniform were absent; those present weren't from the division that usually undertook such actions; the raid occurred at the height of the night and with little warning. Employees were arrested and customers told to leave, many gathering outside on the street. In due course, some officers became trapped within the bar. The Tactical Police Force (riot police)[5] arrived in buses, with around 150 on the streets near the Stonewall Inn (Leitsch 2019). Officers were widely accused of being rude, aggressive and violent, though eventual numbers of injuries were low. Around thirteen arrests were made, including the high-profile one of the folk singer Dave Van Ronk, and seven employees of the Inn. Raids, as suggested, were far from uncommon, as were arrests. On this occasion, however, the failure to adhere to standard expectations led to more of a fightback, to greater resistance. As is typical, the reasons for the escalation given by those present were very variable, with the examples proffered including times in the evening when, it was claimed, 'the police had difficulty keeping a dyke in a patrol car' (Smith 2019), an officer hit a Stonewall waiter with a nightstick (Duberman 2019), a police van arrived (Truscott 2019), or the actions of some of the 'scare drags' against the cops provoked a reaction (Boyce 2019). Duberman takes up the story outside the Inn in the early hours:

> By now, the crowd had swelled to a mob, and people were picking up and throwing whatever loose objects came to hand – coins, bottles, cans, bricks from a nearby construction site. Someone even picked up dog shit from the street and threw it in the cops' direction . . . . Stunned and frightened by the crowd's unexpected fury, the police . . . retreated inside the bar [and when one was injured] the fear turned abruptly to fury. (Duberman 2019: 244–6)

The Inn was dreadfully damaged overnight and the police, it is claimed, had cleaned out almost all the money inside. For some, this was the moment that both organizing and mythologizing began. Holly Woodlawn, best known perhaps for acting in a couple of Andy Warhol's films, described it as 'a milestone for the gay community . . . because it was the biggest gay riot in history' (Woodlawn 2019: 165). Gradually, the movement radicalized, the moment was exploited. Media contacts were utilized, flyers printed and distributed and an annual commemoration planned. Estimates suggested there were between 5,000 and 20,000 marchers at the first New York event in 1970, with Chicago and LA also hosting slightly smaller events. Armstrong and Crage (2006: 742) suggest that a 'parade proved to be ideal for the affirmation of gay collective identity and for the production of feelings of pride central to the emotional culture of the movement. The emotional impact granted the parade lasting cultural power.' Intriguingly, and paralleling much of what we have had to say earlier about riots and diffusion, the spread of the 'myth' of Stonewall also rests on the idea of a 'spark', followed by a sense that something spontaneous, almost magical, occurred. A counter-narrative, however, is equally possible and, indeed, plausible. As already noted, New York was by no means alone in the process of memorialization. Furthermore, if one looks a little further back, then there are events preceding Stonewall that deserve their place, at least an equal place, in LGBTQ+ history.

Armstrong and Crage (2006), for example, mention inter alia Compton's cafeteria disturbance in LA in August 1966, the raid on the Black Cat bar in early 1967, also in LA, and the New Year's Ball raid in San Francisco in early 1965. Two of Los Angeles' better-known historians, Mike Davis and Jon Wiener, describe a march on 11 February 1967, more than two years before Stonewall, as 'the first gay rally against police violence in America, the earliest gay street demonstration, and the historic beginning of the gay liberation movement' (2020: 167). The raid at the Black Cat gave rise to the publication *The Advocate*, 'the oldest and biggest gay magazine in the nation' (2020: 168). To this list, Davis and Wiener add the opening of the first gay church, the first protest march, the first invocation of 'pride' and the first official gay parade – all in LA. Gay men, they say, were treated worse by the LAPD than those in New York by the NYPD; indeed, the Department had been notoriously corrupt for decades. The mob was not buying off the cops in LA in the way they were in Greenwich Village. There are, in short, many reasons to see the history of gay liberation in the United States as being very much more complex than the simple narrative that has Stonewall at its centre. Nevertheless, such a narrative has taken hold and, though it is challenged, it has proven hard to disrupt. In the end it matters not, and this is a moment once again to be reminded of the Thomas dictum that 'things defined as real are real in their consequences'. Wherever one stands on the extent to which the Stonewall riot was central to emergent gay consciousness and to the expanding movement now referred to as LGBTQ+, most seem agreed that protest violence occupies an important constructive role in the history of gay liberation in the United States and beyond.

Protest, violence and punishment

Arrest, prosecution and punishment are predictable responses to many of the behaviours found in riot and protest violence. A considerable body of criminological research has by now established the medium- and long-term impacts of punishment generally and imprisonment more particularly. Riots often result in very large numbers of people being imprisoned, with impact on their subsequent life chances. But the consequences of punishment may also be felt community-wide, the incarceration of large numbers of young males – not untypically the most likely to be involved, arrested and imprisoned – leaving many families fatherless and living on reduced incomes. Frequently, these are communities that suffer very considerable property damage during rioting, some of which may reduce the available amenities (shops, leisure facilities, etc.), further reinforcing the social marginality of the neighbourhoods affected. In several of the examples examined above – the United States, England and France – one of the reactions to the rioting was a reinforcement or even intensification of law-and-order politics and practices. At their most extreme, as in the United States, Hinton (2021)argues that the urban riots of the sixties played a significant role in stimulating the initial emergence of what was to become the country's experiment with mass incarceration. In both France and England, the riots in the early twenty-first century bolstered law-and-order rhetoric by those in power and in the case of England led to at least a temporary spike in the prison population. Alongside these very obviously negative consequences for both individuals and local neighbourhoods, more positive community outcomes are also possible. As we've seen, for some, the experience of riot and protest violence involves a sense of community, of being in it together and of having a broadly common goal or set or goals, however vague (as, for example, in St Paul's in Bristol, England). For some, there may be some reinforcement of a sense of community. There may also be positive impacts on protest movements themselves, as the example of Stonewall and the LGBTQ+ community illustrates. It matters not that the history of the LGBTQ+ movement is more complex than the Stonewall 'story' would have us believe; the reality is that movement solidarity was much influenced by protest and, more particularly, by the heavy-handed policing response to that protest. The legacy of protest violence is clear.

12
Policy Response and Impact

In this, the third and final chapter on the legacy of riots, my focus is the public policy response to protest violence. I established earlier the importance of understanding the contested claims-making that occurs during and, especially, in the aftermath of riots and which seeks to establish how such events are to be understood. Among their many functions, these narratives affect the legitimacy of particular reactions to disorder. They help us make sense of such significant events, and in doing so shape any substantive change or, at least, the potential for substantive change that might occur. As E. P. Thompson (1971: 120) reminds us, it is all too easy 'to forget that riot was a social calamity, often resulting in a profound dislocation of social relations in the community, whose results could linger for years'. Indeed, as he goes on to point out, 'The "order" which might follow after riot could be an even greater calamity' (1971: 122). But, naturally, positive social change is also possible. My focus here will primarily be on state-level government and on the economic, industrial, cultural and social reactions to disorder and on what influences such responses.[1] In particular, narrative construction around riots affects the perceived legitimacy of different claims. Are the neighbourhoods and communities in which riots occur, for example, considered to have needs that require addressing and, if so, which among the no doubt many potential claims are the ones given priority? Does rioting lead to the recognition of certain claims or, alternatively, their relegation or absence of acknowledgement? Where, if anywhere, is reform required? There is almost no end to the potential implications of urban violence. The Rorschach blot nature of the riot means there tends to exist almost endless scope for interpretation, and this applies to policy making as it does to all else.

Throughout this volume, I have been concerned with how violence is understood, or 'framed', both diagnostically and prognostically. The straightforward argument underpinning this chapter is that such frames play a vital role in influencing governmental responses to major protest violence. Governments themselves do not stand outside this process, of course, and are themselves one of the major claims-makers operating during and after riot. There are potentially many claims-makers, however, seeking to influence not only how the violence will be understood but also what shape any response to the violence should take. Much of this is therefore a contest over 'policy narratives': 'those stories – scenarios and arguments – that are taken by one or more parties to a controversy as underwriting (that is, establishing or certifying) and stabilizing (that is, fixing or making steady) the assumptions for policymaking in the face of the issue's uncertainty, complexity or polarization' (Roe 1994: 3).

In exploring the policy legacies of protest violence, I will once again focus on the four main examples that have formed the backbone of analysis throughout this volume. As we will see, in Los Angeles in 1992 much of the immediate post-riot focus was on city leadership, in terms of both the role of the mayor and, more particularly, the command of the LAPD, before it eventually shifted to rebuilding the city. In Hong Kong in 2019, the focus was on political arrangements and the limits of democratic participation. In France, the basic political reaction was to push back against any suggestion of deep, underlying causes of the riots, though a range of modest policy impacts can be identified. Similarly, the England riots of 2011 provoked little direct policy reaction, with government intent in deviating as little as possible from the trajectory of its already established policies in policing, criminal justice or broader welfare reform. I finish with a few further reflections on the Black Lives Matter and Defund the Police movements as further examples of the legacy of riot.

Leadership in Los Angeles after the Rodney King riots

To remind ourselves, the 1992 'Rodney King riots' left more than 50 people dead and nearly 2,500 injured, 249 of whom were critically injured. There were over 16,000 riot-related crimes recorded, of which nearly 10,000 were 'serious', leading to more than 6,500 arrests. Property damage amounted to more than US$446 million across 1,120 buildings, of which 377 were completely destroyed. The political reaction to the riots was complex. Los Angeles County is huge, covering an area close to the size of the state of Connecticut. It is the most populous county in the United States and has become one of the nation's most diverse. By the beginning of the new millennium, its population was nearly half (47%) Latino, 30% white, 11% African American and 10% Asian. As Cannon (1999: 527) observed, 'the political demography of Los Angeles in the early 1990s sharply conflicted with the census'. Anglos held far and away the most offices. Blacks were somewhat over-represented, Latinos under-represented, and deliberately excluded, with Asians barely visible at all.[2] As a consequence, one of the most frequent, and sometimes fractious, post-riots conversations concerned what progress, if any, had been made where race and race relations were concerned. A local university study carried out a decade after the riots found approximately twice as many Angelenos believed the city had made progress on that front than those who saw little change. Nearly three-quarters believed minority ethnic groups were getting on well, compared with only one-third five years previously (Marks 2002). That said, surveyed at the same time, one half of all Angelenos nevertheless said they believed that riots similar to those of 1992 would occur within five years (Marks, Barreto and Woods 2004).

Much of the most consequential 'reading' of post-riots LA was made by journalists. National media, and influentially the *New York Times*, quickly framed the riots through the lens of race rather than class (though there are times when one stands in as a proxy for the other – see Wilson 1978), and focused on presidential, federal politics rather than local, city politics or social relations when considering the reaction to the violence. Unfortunately, notwithstanding the extent to which the scale and consequences of the riots were registered by the federal government, it seemed clear that there was little appetite in Washington, DC, to plough time and resources into urban policy. This was something of a shock to powerful Angelenos. As Mike Davis (1993a) observed, the absence of federal government concern may have been old news to Detroit or Buffalo, but in LA, 'which until recently had been preoccupied with fantasies of becoming the Byzantium of the Pacific Rim, it was a brutal shock'.[3] Beyond the general sidelining of LA, little if any consideration was paid to the lived realities of those in south/south-central LA. Much national coverage, such as President Bush's eventual statements on the verdicts, and President Clinton's subsequent unwillingness to offer any alternative, served to normalize the violence (Bernard-Donals 1994).

Closer to home, the *Los Angeles Times* in its overview of the riots concluded. 'There is no one answer, and there is no one story' (quoted in Twomey 2004). The newspaper focused, initially at least, on the epicentre of the rioting in south-central LA and what it took to be its 'tragedy' – what often appeared to be a lack of hope or promise that continued to dominate that part of the city. At the time of the Rodney King riots, the mayor, Tom Bradley, and governor, Pete Wilson, having been largely cut adrift by Washington, DC, launched an ambitious programme entitled 'Rebuild LA: An extra-governmental task force'. The scale of the destruction in the riots was going to require something equally sizeable in response, it argued. With weighty business, political and private-sector figures involved, under the leadership of the man who had overseen the 1984 LA Olympic Games, Rebuild LA had a number of failings. Eventually, it had a bloated board of 94 people, a consequent lack of focus, and a programme that was 'less an agenda than a series of pronouncements'.[4] As an initiative, it tended towards over-promising and underachieving. Circumstance didn't help, for within two years the Northridge earthquake caused a further US$20 billion in damage to the city's infrastructure and left huge numbers homeless. As one local historian put it, '[t]he story of South Los Angeles since 1992 is a cautionary tale, one that reminds us of the profound limits of planning and policy making in regions of extraordinary demographic dynamism'.[5]

Much of the post-1992 literature on the LA riots is suffused with negativity in relation to the fate of the city and the more particular issue of the LAPD and the attitudes of Angelenos in the years that followed the riots. Mike Davis (1993a), always one of the keenest though also one of the more dystopian observers of the metropolis, suggested that 'the national and local responses to the 1992 Los Angeles uprising have revealed a doom-ridden inertia and shortage of reform resources at every level of the American political system'. Min Hyoung Song (2005: 2), with a degree of hyperbole perhaps, says that the 1992 rioting, 'perhaps more than any other event marking out the passage through the dark years of the 1990s and beyond, has been exemplary in its ability to spark imaginative and critical works of profound pessimism'. In film (from the Hughes brothers' *Menace II Society* to Robert Altman's *The Player*), literature (from Paul Beatty's *White Boy Shuffle* to Ryan Gattis's *All Involved*) and music (of which there is much, including 2Pac's 'Hellrazor', Dr Dre's 'The Day tha Niggaz Took Over', all the way to Branford Marsalis's 'I Heard You Twice the First Time'), a highly and consistently negative picture emerges of LA and, indeed, of America, in the early nineties. The 1992 riots, Song argues, have become 'a cultural-literary event, an important source of tropes for imagining the seemingly endemic social problems plaguing the United States and the country's possible futures' (2005: 3). As such, the riots came to form an important building block in the New Right vision of national decline.

Far from being progressive, the initial policing reaction to the riots was essentially one of clampdown. As Mike Davis summarized it:

> In practice, the . . . doctrine of 'rapid containment' has involved the retraining of both the LAPD and the National Guard in modern riot-control technologies including armoured vehicles, plastic bullets and pepper gas. Crowd suppression, in turn, has been coordinated with toughened curfew laws, LAPD regulation of local airspace, and Highway Patrol control of freeway access to ensure that Black and immigrant Latino neighbourhoods can be quickly and comprehensively sealed off from the rest of the world. Elite Marine units at nearby Camp Pendleton, meanwhile, have trained in recent manoeuvres to storm 'urban terrorist strongholds' that bear a striking resemblance to ghetto housing projects. (Davis 1993b)

If the broad policy response focused on the promise of 'rebuilding' LA, narrower reform concerns concentrated on policing, and police leadership in particular. Most Black politicians had clamoured for Police Commissioner Daryl Gates's removal after the King beating and the Christopher Commission report. In the aftermath of the riots, 'with Willie Williams at the LAPD helm, blacks who felt frozen out of City Hall found a welcome mat at Parker Center' (Cannon 1999: 537). Williams was initially a huge success, with a 73% approval rating at one point compared with Gates's disapproval rating of 81%. It was a false dawn, however, for Williams failed to provide the leadership that the LAPD so desperately needed. He eventually became another chief who ended up mired in scandal of his own making, though the city council also contributed to the ongoing problems.

Morale in the LAPD had been in decline for a long time, even before the King beating – and attrition from the force spiked as low pay compared with other sectors took a toll. Arrests dropped, as did their quality, and patrol officers increasingly abandoned both the side-handled baton and the taser. Just as the earthquake had contributed to derailing the impact of Rebuild LA, so the O. J. Simpson case helped undermine any degree of improvement in policing that was detectable after the riots. Lou Cannon's (1999: 549) acerbic view was that the defence team 'managed to turn this case into a trial of the LAPD as much as of the icon-athlete Simpson. And unlike the defendant, the LAPD was convicted.' Willie Williams, who arrived with formidable institutional and political capital behind him, had had an opportunity to oversee historic change in the fortunes of the LAPD, and blew it. Taking over in 1997, new chief Bernard Parks overhauled the citizen complaint process, a long-standing reformist goal, with much greater Internal Affairs involvement, something studiously avoided by his predecessors, and leading to a much higher level of sustained complaints. Potentially more significant change was to come with the appointment in 2002 of ex-NYPD chief Bill Bratton as chief in LA, and the establishment of a wide reform package undertaken as part of a consent decree,[6] emerging, in part, out of the egregious misconduct of the anti-gang unit and the Rampart Division scandal in 1999.[7] By way of shorthand, the consent decree essentially mandated a very wide range of reforms, almost equivalent to those recommended after the Rodney King case. Bratton sought to embrace it. In 2009, the Harvard researchers who were evaluating the changes reported significant increases in public satisfaction with police services. Increases in the use of stops together with better outcomes from those stops were identified (Stone, Foglesong and Cole 2009), though concerns about under-policing continued. Researchers also concluded that what they referred to as the rift between the LAPD and its communities had narrowed, and stated 'the communities across the City of Los Angeles are increasingly confident in the professionalism of the LAPD' (2009: 52). It presented a fine picture, underpinned by a very considerable quantity of research. It just wasn't a picture that matched many people's experience and sense of LA's policing, with concerns lingering about the rising use of stops, and claims of racial profiling felt by some to be a ticking time bomb.[8]

In short, the problems that had plagued LA for decades were not significantly affected by the post-Rodney King riots policy reforms. Federal government largely washed its hands where the city was concerned, and the fine rhetoric that accompanied Rebuild LA turned out largely to be hubris. More narrowly, even minimal progress was slow to come to the LAPD, requiring several changes of chief and a consent decree. Meanwhile there were other disturbing developments, most obviously public order policing. Mike Davis (1993b) described the shifts in the LAPD's approach as the '"Ulsterization" of riot control', and its urban safety orientation as 'the creeping "Israelization" of residential security', with the LAPD 'inching closer toward outright legitimation of white vigilantism'.

Law and order, immigration and urban policy in France after 2005

Impacts in France in the months and years after the 2005 riots were varied and by no means always substantial. The first concerned urban policy or, more strictly, 'city policy' (Epstein, Guenot and Jobard 2023), which focused on increased resources in the *banlieues*. The aim was an 'unofficial goal of pursuing a form of affirmative action toward ethnic minorities' (Bonnet and Le Derff 2024), though of course in a context where it was necessary to respect, or at least work within, the republic's colour-blind ideals. Faith in such a programme seemingly was not long-lasting for, although there was further significant rioting in 2007 which might have been expected to act as a reinforcement, from 2010 the framing shifted towards law and order. Although less emphasis was now focused on the *banlieues*, France remained one of the EU countries with the most generous redistribution policies, providing a strong buffer effect on poverty.

The riots appeared to stimulate some political changes. Vornetti, Fauvelle-Aymar and Abel's (2009) study of the political impact on France's 'deprived urban areas' during the presidential election in 2007 found that in the places where the protest violence was especially severe, voter turnout increased and, significantly, support for the extreme right declined. In addition, the aftermath of the violence saw the rise or emergence of activist groups in some of the most riot-affected areas. Thus in Clichy, ACLEFEU (No More Fire) was established, which focused attention primarily on police misconduct. Alongside 'city policies', some areas developed youth policies aimed at empowerment, and some of the founders of ACLEFEU received their political education through that vehicle. The political legitimacy of some of the associations promoting empowerment increased, not least in Clichy and Seine-Saint-Denis. Despite this, the groups tended to remain on the political fringes, with the consequence that responsiveness to their demands tended to be limited.

Beyond impact on urban policy and on aspects of political functioning, it appears the most significant shift in France in the early twenty-first century in the aftermath of the riots concerned the rise of 'law-and-order' politics. The state of emergency that had been called at the time of the disorder continued well into 2006. The burgeoning law-and-order agenda saw a range of developments: the creation of local prevention and security contracts (empowering new, localized agencies in surveillance and crime prevention and control, as well as engaging in social prevention; see Roché 2005), increased video surveillance, tougher minimum sentences for repeat offenders (though the latter were abolished in 2014) and procedural changes which, in many cases, permitted 16– to 18-year-olds to be tried and sentenced as adults, all in the context of increased emphasis on harsh political rhetoric (Bonelli 2010). Notwithstanding the substantive 'law-and-order' developments and the focusing of policy attention on matters such as parental responsibility and immigration, President Chirac made some fairly positive public statements about young people and Prime Minister de Villepin reinstated some funding for *banlieue* NGOs. In the context of greater law-and-order rhetoric, some on the far right blamed large Muslim families, arguing that they should have their child benefits withdrawn, as should families of children found guilty of participating in the riots. Rap music was a predictable folk devil, with more than 150 members of the French parliament urging the justice minister to take legal action against seven rap groups whose lyrics were alleged to be 'anti-white' and which incited anti-French sentiment. A final proposal was that a law be introduced by which recently naturalized citizens found guilty of committing a criminal offence would be stripped of their French nationality. Sarkozy, as interior minister, pledged support for such a change, a move according to one poll that was supported by 55% of French citizens. Though there was some recognition of issues of racism and discrimination, the findings from the polls, together with the language that increasingly surrounded such debates, suggested that willingness to confront such matters was not strong (Murray 2006). One must be careful, of course, not to draw too heavy a line between the disorder and such political and cultural change, for a number of other countries displayed comparable trends where both welfare chauvinism and increased incarceration were concerned, and these did not experience rioting.

Broadly speaking, France made little attempt to respond positively to the riots and, having dismissed many of the claims being made about the causes of the disorder, in 2007 the newly elected president, Nicolas Sarkozy, was the source of much negative political rhetoric. On the policy front, he introduced 'obligatory integration contracts' for migrants that focused 'on assimilation, including language and culture requirements for long-term (ten-year) resident permits' (Koff and Duprez 2009: 717). It is worth noting that France was not alone here, and similar developments can be found elsewhere in Europe. Moreover, of course, such changes cannot be entirely reduced to the impact of the riots. On a more progressive front, Bonnet and Le Derff

(2024) suggest that a further consequence of the 2005 riots was legal initiatives aimed at improving minority representation in the media. Such under-representation had been an issue prior to the riots, and President Chirac had observed, 'We are well aware that discrimination undermines the very foundations of our Republic' (2024: 414). He emphasized that fighting discrimination and recognizing 'the diversity of French society' were crucial for the success of the country's integration policy. Chirac urged both public and private media to 'better reflect today's realities', leading to a 10 million euro fund to the National Centre for Cinema and the Moving Image to promote work in support of 'national cohesion'. Overall, however, there is little to suggest that the 2005 disorder in France provoked much in the political or policy worlds that was positive.

The 2011 London riots and the absence of reform

The riots were by any measure a huge political moment in British civic life. They were a major 'focusing event' (Kingdon 1984) and, naturally, raised both opportunities for change and questions about directions of travel. In some respects, the story that then unfolded was quite a straightforward one in which a small number of themes were developed and rehearsed by government, tied closely to existing ideological or policy preferences, and then were pursued relentlessly in a manner that largely precluded consideration of alternatives. Four major narratives developed during and after the riots. First, and following classic political tropes, the behaviour of those involved was reduced to its criminal content, excising any reference to the social conditions out of which the rioting emerged, for example. Second, such behaviour was taken to be indicative of a moral breakdown, and in this case one that was argued to have its roots in dysfunctional families and inadequate parenting. Third, the criminal conduct of the rioters was linked to long-established problems of urban gangs and knife crime, and tackling these was consequently identified as a governmental priority. Finally, it was argued that inadequate policing – in terms of both the nature and the scale of the response to the riots themselves, including poor preparation – had contributed significantly to the rapid spread of the rioting and to its consequences.

Despite no little initial contestation, including a largely overlooked government-commissioned inquiry, some unusual, large-scale and prize-winning research[9] and an array of commentators from differing points of view,[10] governmental narratives remained largely undisturbed in the weeks, months, even years, after the riots. As we saw earlier, the 'criminality pure and simple' diagnosis underpinned an intensive punitive reaction. The prime minister's primary diagnostic frame was also hooked to a wider observation that the behavioural and moral problems identified were indicative of what in advance of the riots he had come to refer to as 'broken Britain' (Hayton 2012). The governmental prognostic frame was that further decline was inevitable if action were not taken in at least two areas. Though there was never the slightest serious intent to disguise the absence of anything new, the government dusted down its Troubled Families policy agenda and attached it to its reading of the riots. The Troubled Families programme, in train at the time but held back by bureaucracy, was now to have the 'rocket boosters' put under it, 'with a clear ambition that within the lifetime of this Parliament we will turn around the lives of the 120,000 most troubled families in the country' (quoted in Newburn, Jones and Blaustein, 2018: 347). A link to the riots was briefly utilized to give the programme a symbolic boost, only to be completely dropped when there no longer appeared to be a need for such an organizing rationale.

Finally, there were two other brief developments. In the first, a pre-existing interest in urban gangs led to the UK government's latest flirtation with US 'supercop' (ex-Commissioner of the NYPD and LAPD) and moral entrepreneur Bill Bratton (Bratton 1998), who was briefly appointed 'gangs tsar', much to the dismay of many in British policing. The circumstances of the riots, and the scramble to catch up by many senior political figures, led to a more general political assault on the reputation of British policing, and public order policing in particular, a far cry from the typical response to riots which has tended to be highly supportive of the police. In the main, this was a deflection, and as it turned out a successful one, closing down dissent wherever possible and freeing the space for other 'initiatives'. There was one positive, research-related impact following the England riots. As I have outlined, our research showed consistent evidence of anti-police sentiment in all the towns and cities in which rioting occurred, and that police (mis)use of their stop-and-search powers was a significant contributor. In late 2011, and unexpectedly, the Home Secretary Theresa May announced a review of stop and search and, subsequently, sought and achieved substantial reductions in the use of stops. Though the drop in use was only temporary, it was significant (House of Commons Library 2022).

Before leaving the example of England 2011, and the policy reaction, there is one further brief set of observations to make. This concerns another aspect of the fate of communities affected by such protest violence, not least as a consequence of property damage. A number of neighbourhoods were faced with potentially huge rebuilding programmes in the aftermath of the riots, with opportunities, of course, to initiate something progressive. Again, however, as with policy change, this did not appear to be the governmental priority. It is not possible here to do more than give two fleeting examples, but both serve as illustrations of a wider point. The two are, first, the 'regeneration' of Tottenham in north London, near the epicentre of the start of the riots; and, second, the fate of Croydon in south London and, more particularly, the Reeves carpet store, its burning hulk captured in so many photographs at the time.

In 2012, the Mayor's Office released a report, *It Took Another Riot*, which laid out its thinking in relation to the regeneration of Tottenham. It noted the importance of curtailing inward migration and urged a focus on providing for a much greater mix of dwellings, particularly through housing regeneration. In this, as Dillon and Fanning (2015) put it, there 'was a running inference that regeneration would squeeze out some of Tottenham's most marginal residents, or at least prevent others like them from moving to the area'. As they go on to put it, the subsequently released Plan for Tottenham 'unambiguously supported the place-shaping approach' adopted by the Mayor of London's Office. In this, the local Premiership football team Tottenham Hotspur's new stadium was to play a leading role, and the local area would be transformed by 2025 from being one of the most deprived wards in England into 'north London's premier leisure destination with new high-quality housing and improved transport options' (Dillon and Fanning 2015). There was local resistance to some of the change and, though assessed over a decade ago now, Dillon and Fanning (2015) concluded that there was 'little concrete evidence of property-led regeneration leading to significant change in the socio-economic profile of Tottenham's deprived localities'. The writers were prescient. There had been a proposed joint venture between the local council and a private company to redevelop a local estate and to build more than six thousand new homes. Within a few years, however, having become entangled in local political squabbles, it collapsed amid claims that millions of pounds of investment had been wasted.[11] Rather like south-central LA, what happened – or didn't happen – in north London after the riots was in part a reflection of the lack of interest at national governmental level, and a general unwillingness to invest politically and financially in the poor minority communities most affected by the disorder.

The second example concerns the borough of Croydon, this time in south London. It was an area that was perhaps thought of as one with less obvious connections with the types of problems associated with large-scale breakdowns in order. That said, Croydon had a significant problem with youth violence and knife crime, something that worsened for a period after the riots (see Fraser et al. 2026). Indeed, a report written ten years after the riots by a panel chaired by the local Member of Parliament found few causes for optimism. Across a wide range of measures – children's vulnerability, educational attainment, crime and risk, family functioning, and skills and employment – the panel found that service delivery had altered, but there was little to nothing to report in terms of positive outcomes.[12] It was stasis at best.

One of the most emblematic bits of destruction in the 2011 riots in London was the arson attack on the Reeves furniture store in Croydon. On the night of the Croydon riot, Maurice Reeves had been out at a restaurant with his wife, celebrating their twenty-first wedding anniversary. Returning home, he switched on the news and watched what appeared to be his store going up in flames. Opened by his great-grandfather in 1867, the store had survived the Great Depression and two world wars. It had given its name to the road junction it sat on, as well as the nearby Reeves Corner tram stop. Images of Croydon's oldest independent furniture shop being burnt to the ground were beamed around the world in August 2011 and came to symbolize aspects of the scale and apparent senselessness of the damage and the generally negative legacy of the riots. Plans to rebuild the Reeves store proved unviable, and the site still stands empty. In response more recently, London's Somerset House[13] – a high-profile centre for culture and the arts – sought to commemorate the Reeves Corner story. An artist, Imran Perretta, was commissioned to capture the legacy of this particular part of the Croydon riot through sound, sculpture and performance. He describes the spot where the store stood as now being 'a patch of gravel with some concrete planters and some battered old trees and a white picket fence sort of encircling it. It sort of looked like this since 2011.'[14]

The artist hoped that his commission, *A Riot in Three Acts*, would encourage audiences to reflect on the legacy of 2011's events. In essence, this ambition was born of the absence of any substantive legacy. Perretta described his installation as a symbol of the riots and of 'the collateral damage of this righteous anger of the public who had been disenfranchised by the state'. The site of the fire had today become a 'wasteland' and a 'graveyard for the dream of change'.[15] In such circumstances, how does one respond? One way, as Somerset

House indicated, was via art in its various forms. Indeed, using such media may have the advantage of inviting direct emotional engagement with what has occurred, a form of response that is easier to capture via visual and other art forms. In Perretta's case, the combination of an installation and a musical requiem offered a passionate emotional and visual reminder of state inaction, and of events that might otherwise lack much in the way of legacy or memorial.

Collective identity in Hong Kong

As Lee and Chan (2018: 196) observe, 'No matter whether a large-scale protest movement can achieve its proclaimed goal, it can have an impact on the dynamics of contentious politics in the future.' And this, at least in part, is one important way we should see developments in Hong Kong. The wider battles over democratic representation can hardly be said to have been successful. Formal state responses have become increasingly repressive, and protest is now a significantly more dangerous proposition. The Chinese state has utilized a variety of tools, many encouraging the Hong Kong institutions to crack down where protest occurs, others, not least the framing strategies adopted by Chinese media, discouraging domestic audiences from sympathizing with the protest movements (Ma and Weiss 2023). At the peak of the 2019 protests, they note that hashtags such as Protect Hong Kong and Officers, We Support You became extremely popular on Weibo, the Chinese equivalent of Twitter/X. Rather than simply relying on a traditional tactic such as censorship, two alternative productive mechanisms were utilized; the first sought to demobilize protesters by illustrating the state's repressive capacity and by framing the protests as a 'foreign-backed threat to national sovereignty and social stability'; the second aimed to rally the masses. At heart, the objective was to signal the high cost of anti-regime activities. Naturally, there have been claims and counterclaims. The battle over narrative construction has been particularly hard-fought, with pro-democracy activists continuing to pursue electoral and other gains, and the Hong Kong and Chinese governments claiming the movement has entirely failed. The fact that observers in Taiwan are increasingly nervous is one indicator that the direction of travel in Hong Kong is seen as generally portentous.

And so, perhaps for now, as far as we are concerned, the story in Hong Kong is how the pro-democracy movement has transformed itself, slowly radicalizing and shifting the nature of its contentious repertoire. Bennett and Segerberg examine the processes by which movements without high-level centralized leadership and coordination can nevertheless manage large-scale protest campaigns. They refer to this as the 'logic of connective action', whose starting point is not that people are persuaded to support a cause but, rather, that what is important 'is the self-motivated (though not necessarily self-centred) sharing of *already internalized or personalized* ideas, plans, images and networks of others' (2012: 753; emphasis added). Earlier, relatively peaceful forms of action in Hong Kong lost efficacy and were superseded by increasingly radical approaches (Lee and Chan 2018). Thus Occupy Central with Love and Peace was originally highly disciplined, but as a consequence of a series of challenges gradually transformed into the more radical Umbrella Movement (UM) that took to the streets in a direct challenge to the police. Other events, some more radical than others, formed the stepping stones to this *relatively* more radical present and future. This included the 'localism' movement, focusing on various forms of local heritage, the student movement, seeking to resist imposed curriculum change, and more challenging events such as the Mong Kok riot (Lo 2016: 195–221), this involving a new group, Hong Kong Indigenous, which fought directly with the police.

Lee (2019: 11) describes the UM as 'a collective self-defense (viz. the slogan "We alone can save our city"), led by the young and educated but with cross-class participation of the local populace, against what many consider Beijing's recolonization of the city after 1997'. However, in broad conclusion, it also appears to represent 'an example that a skeptic about networked social movements and connective actions can refer to' (Lee and Chan 2018: 190), not least as the Hong Kong and Chinese governments made little to nothing in the way of concessions. They stood fast on electoral processes, voted down reform proposals and emerged with a system that critics had feared all along: a chief executive elected by a 1,200-member election committee largely under the control of China (Lee and Chan 2018). And although a minor example, Lee and Chan (2018) compare this with elements of Taiwan's Sunflower Movement, where some negotiation was enabled which, though falling short of the movement's demands, 'was substantive and appealing to the movement leaders' (2018: 191).

The UM was, in part, underpinned by digital and social media, which coordinated participants' actions and provided the basis for the initiation of some movement activity. Despite some criticism alleging 'slacktivism' (Gladwell 2010; Glenn 2015), a low-key form of activity and organization, this was defended as protest that combined online activity with 'real world actions' in line with Castells's (2015) arguments about the interweaving of the space of places with the space of flows. Lee and Chan (2018: 199) describe both the Occupy Central campaign and the later UM as a form of 'radicalization with self-restraint' wherein, when positive outcomes failed to materialize, a more radical approach was adopted, at least among some protesters. Radicalization, as used here, may refer to ideology (the collective identities involved and the claims made), action, or both. Indeed, both were visible in the UM. Where legacy and impact are concerned, in the end it comes down to timescales again. Lee and Chan (2018: 196) say that the UM 'is likely to become another critical event that will have profound implications [for] the pro-democracy movement in the city'. It is certainly too early, however, to make definite and substantive conclusions about the long-term impact, even if the short- and medium-term picture seems settled.

Black Lives Matter and Defund the Police

Having offered a few observations on the policy and political aftermaths of the four main sets of riots, I want to finish with a look at the legacy of the Black Lives Matter movement, the most recent set of events we have considered at length. How might we conclude? Looking back over the history of the movement, Cedric Johnson (2024: 332) has argued that in something a little less than a decade – a short period by any real measure – Black Lives Matter 'evolved from a hashtag slogan into a broad banner for anticarceral and anti-racist forces throughout the United States and around the world'. Prior to its emergence, relatively little was known, for example, about the activities of American police departments where the killing of Black citizens was concerned. National and international bodies started collecting reliable information in 2014, with both the *Guardian*'s 'The Counted'[16] and, centrally, *Mapping Police Violence*,[17] developed by a Black non-profit organization, beginning to offer close to comprehensive monitoring of Black deaths at the hands of the authorities (Francis and Wright-Rigueur 2021). Any initial stocktake therefore would surely conclude that serious consciousness raising was one important product of the emergence of BLM. Even in the fairly early days, the movement's 'narrative capacity', its ability to frame its story in its own terms and to spread this view (Tufekci 2017), appeared strong. Such activity grew through to 2020, and the protests that arose after the murder of George Floyd illustrated that the scale, in America and beyond, of the impact of BLM on public opinion had been huge. A CNN poll in 2020 showed that 84% of Americans believed racism was a 'big problem', and a Pew survey reported that two-thirds of Americans across racial groups expressed support for the Black Lives Matter movement (Francis and Wright-Rigueur 2021). BLM, of course, had by no means sprung up out of the blue. The civil rights movement and the uprisings of the sixties, the emergent armed patrols linked to the formation and growth of the Black Panther Party for Self-Defense in Oakland from 1966 onwards, and more particular pre-hashtag community activities, such as the massive protests after Oscar Grant was killed by BART cops in 2009, were all part of the movement's lengthy history (Francis and Wright-Rigueur 2021; and see Collins 2012).

Yet, despite the scale of the BLM protests, for many observers what initially appeared so promising eventually seemed to dissipate. Certainly, the more radical elements of the movement, coalescing around the demands to 'defund the police', had less impact than many had once imagined and certainly hoped, and much of what is positive has been largely confined to a few jurisdictions. As Cedric Johnson puts it, overall 'reform has not materialized in the manner that many assumed might follow such a massive outpouring of outrage as occurred over Floyd's death'. In the specific case of the Minneapolis Police Department (MPD), as Michelle Phelps (2024: 205) notes, in the end 'it was never "ended", "defunded", or "dismantled", though its size shrank considerably as officers departed and the department struggled to hire new police'. Lengthy battles were fought – legal, political and bureaucratic – each of these slowing change. Once the violence ended, the fires died down and public pressure dissipated, the attention of both the public and journalists turned towards the rise in violent crime in local neighbourhoods and away from violence by police officers. As a consequence, calls for radical change became 'less resonant'. The struggles continued, but often with somewhat mixed strategic goals, ranging from abolition to something less radical and far-reaching, perhaps simply some form of organizational reform.

And, as Phelps concludes, and quite rightly, so much of this is about timescales. As she puts it, change 'is still coming to the City of Lakes. It will take years to build' (Phelps 2024: 206). Just as what happened in 2020 was, in part, a product of the previous 5–15 (or even 50) years of activity, so the future will be the product of more recent mobilizations, with many potentially positive developments, 'some that might be hard to envision from where we sit today' (2024: 206). Unfortunately, by 2020, it was clear that far from being a model of police reform, Minneapolis was more an illumination of the stark limits of such change. And of course Minneapolis is far from alone in being 'unable to resolve the fundamental liberal contradictions in policing. Indeed, in recent years, left-leaning cities across the country, both majority Black and majority white, on the coasts and in the Midlands, have struggled with how to move forward with transforming public safety' (2024: 207) and she highlights New York, Philadelphia and Chicago as key examples here. US policing is far from alone in this either.

Bearing in mind all the provisos about timescales and general realism, it remains possible to conclude moderately positively where BLM is concerned. Radical reform of policing – or even something beyond 'reform' – may currently lie largely out of reach, but in the period since Ferguson, and more so since the murder of George Floyd, there have been some significant enforcement changes. In Minneapolis, in relation to the death of George Floyd, Derek Chauvin was sentenced to serve over 22 years in prison (with credit for time served). In addition, three former Minneapolis Police Department (MPD) officers were found guilty of federal civil rights offences when each failed to intervene to stop Chauvin. Given the general protections extended to police officers historically, this is no small matter. To this, one can add the indictment, though not conviction, of all four officers involved in the 2015 death of Freddie Gray in Baltimore, and the conviction in Chicago of Laquan McDonald's killer on 16 counts of second-degree murder. In addition, there have been institutional developments, such as the announcement by Attorney General Merrick Garland of full Department of Justice investigations into the police departments of Louisville and Minneapolis.

There have been a whole host of reforms that are now relatively mainstream, including 'national use-of-force standards, mandatory and universal body cameras for police units . . . , the so-called Camden model of policing,[18] restrictions on qualified immunity for law enforcement officers' (Johnson 2024: 27), which may have a positive, warming effect on policing and represent progress, albeit within profound limitations. To shifts in the nature of policing and its systems of governance, one might add what Johnson (2024: 332) refers to as the 'tidal wave' of local and state legislation, again including 'laws that created databases for officer misconduct, disciplinary actions and decertifications', revisions to use-of-force policies, 'mandating officers to provide emergency medical aid to suspects, banning the use of chokeholds and restricting the use of deadly force against suspects fleeing on foot or in vehicles' (2024: 332). Johnson's conclusion from all of this is that what he refers to as the 'George Floyd rebellion' illustrates the ways in which identity politics has been and remains a powerful source of mobilization but is, unfortunately, 'a temperamental, unsound means of movement-building and protracted political work' (Johnson 2024: 24). On the positive side, it appears to indicate the emergence of an anti-racist majority with potentially profound implications but, unfortunately, not as yet the local circumstances – the local coalitions, still less the governing majorities – needed 'to achieve concrete policy reforms around police misconduct' (Johnson 2024: 23). Time, though, will tell.

Understanding the aftermath of protest and protest violence

The focus here, once more, has been on the legacies of protest and protest violence, on this occasion looking primarily at policy change, or its absence. In the four main examples, plus the BLM movement, the general picture is largely one of the failure of governments, national/federal and local, to tackle many, or even any, of the myriad issues revealed by the protests. The finding is stark. In LA, for example, long-standing, entrenched problems remain, and the period since the Rodney King riots has been characterized by general inertia or, where ambitions have been outlined and some measures implemented, failures of both design and implementation. In France, little was attempted after the 2005 riots, and the national government was fixated on stiffening its law-and-order agenda. Any gains made were generally small-scale and temporary. The situation in England was broadly similar to that in France with the penal reaction to the violence remaining front and centre of all the government sought to do. A small number of policy developments were undertaken, but in each case it was largely a continuation of pre-existing ideas and commitments. There was nothing new in any of the developments that had alleged ties to the riots. This represented a deliberate and successful attempt not only to gain further purchase for existing priorities but to construct a means of shutting down debate and undermining the legitimacy of alternative claims. In Hong Kong, the protests anyway were a direct challenge to government and, predictably, invited and received a highly and increasingly repressive response from Hong Kong's authorities, with the interests of the Beijing administration clearly in the background.

Does all this represent nothing other than 'failure'? The answer, as suggested above, depends on timescale. From a present-day viewpoint, yes, it very much looks like protest demands, such as they could be discerned, have brought little in the way of progressive change. Over the long term, it is possible the picture may be different. In France and England, it remains possible that further uprisings in the *banlieues* and poor urban neighbourhoods may eventually coincide with an 'open policy window' (Kingdon 1984) and that more progressive outcomes may eventually result. The 2024 riots in England, however, offered little more than further law-and-order reaction, so there are good reasons to temper expectations. In the United States in relation to BLM and change in policing, the longer term may also herald more progressive reform than currently appears possible, especially in the light of the activities of ICE in cities ranging from LA to Minneapolis. Much depends on John Kingdon's three streams – problems, policies and politics – coming together at a propitious moment (Newburn, Jones and Blaustein 2018). In Hong Kong, so far as the Umbrella Movement is concerned, the future appears bleak. The radicalization of the UM will not easily be undone, however steadfast and repressive the response of the state. There remains much that is unpredictable, and certainly enough to make one pause in reaching judgement about 'success' or 'failure'.

Though the overall conclusion here is stark, it is perfectly possible that a somewhat different story would have unfolded had different examples been selected. There is no shortage of major historical examples where we could point to protest that has provoked, in one form or another, significant and positive shifts in governmental policies and practices. Our history is full of them, and runs from the Boston Tea Party – described as 'an act of rebellion that had worldwide significance' (Carp 2011) – to Mahatma Gandhi's 'salt march' of over 200 miles in March 1930, accompanied by 78 followers, to the seaside village of Dandi. In this case, it was the start of a successful non-violent protest campaign, the aim of which was to resist the British government's salt monopoly (Shani 2015). The outcome was a nationwide campaign of civil disobedience and a significant move towards Indian independence. At this point, we might even return to the so-called ghetto riots of the 1960s in America, for, notwithstanding their identification earlier with the United States' experiment in mass incarceration, their role as one element in the growing pressure underpinning the wider civil rights movement in the country surely cannot be doubted (Boskin 1969). Examples in Britain of more positive impact from riot and protest are also available, including the so-called 'poll tax riot' in 1990, which played an important role in the then Conservative government's U-turn where this particular form of taxation was concerned and, indeed, was arguably an important element in the eventual departure from office of the then prime minister, Margaret Thatcher, later that year (Butler, Adonis and Travers 1994). Finally, though there remains a great distance to go, the re-emergence of violence against women and girls as a priority issue within public policy generally and British policing more particularly was itself a consequence of protests that followed on from a series of particularly egregious cases of illegitimate use of police powers (Newburn 2024).

In each of the past three chapters, I have sought to make the case that a focus on the life cycle of riots is important as, among other reasons, it reminds us not to ignore the aftermath of such events. Importantly, as illustrated here, riots have legacies, both positive and negative, and these require analytical attention alongside other features of such disorder. What occurs in the aftermath of protest violence is much influenced by how the disorder is presented and understood or, put differently, which narratives come to dominate public and political understanding. One consistent element of the aftermath is the continuing impact on those individuals caught in systems of punishment. These potentially long-lasting impacts will affect them and the wider communities in which they live. Almost certainly, however, the extent of this impact will be influenced by how punitive the dominant narrative constructions are that are created in the aftermath of the violence. In this chapter, my focus has been on public policy, the wider question of what, if anything, governments are moved to do in response to large-scale public disorder. Once again, my argument is that narrative construction is crucial to this process. In essence, the way that riots are 'read' plays an important constitutive role in any public policy reaction – or, as was the case in at least two of the examples considered here, the absence of constructive policy reaction. Understanding storytelling around protest violence is vital in making sense of its legacies.

13
Reading Riots

It is typical for protest and associated violence to be accompanied by claim and counterclaim. An example occurred in June 2025. The dispute was a consequence of the president of the United States authorizing the use of the National Guard on the streets of Los Angeles, seemingly much against the wishes of the state's governor, who challenged it in court, and very much in contrast with the way in which such forces are ordinarily utilized. Subsequently, President Trump has authorized similar action in Washington, DC, and Chicago. In LA, the protests accompanied the controversial deployment of the Immigration and Customs Enforcement (ICE) agency, which had been rounding up and detaining people prior to formal deportation.[1] The protests, predictably, were accompanied by some violence against people and property, and the president claimed that had it not been for his deployment of marines and the National Guard, this 'once beautiful and great city would be burning to the ground right now'.[2] Many disagreed, including Los Angeles' Mayor, Karen Bass, who suggested Trump's move was a 'deliberate attempt' to 'create disorder and chaos in our city'. In fact, the extent of the violence was limited, and the numbers of arrests of protesters was but a few dozen. Nevertheless, the president referred to the problem as one involving 'riots and looters',[3] as well as 'foreign criminals' and 'paid insurrectionists'.[4] In the event, it was the media – mainstream and social – as much as the streets of LA that became the major front in the battle for narrative dominance.

From the outset, I have been keen to establish that many of the claims made about protest violence – the reading of riots – are based on little that is substantive, often in large part reflecting the values, preconceptions and prejudices of the claimants. It is for this reason that riots can be considered like Rorschach blots. It generally comes as little surprise to be advised to be sceptical about political claims about riots. What is more unusual is being advised to take similar care when assessing what purport to be scholarly claims. What are they actually based on? Is there empirical evidence to support what is being argued? The standpoint of the observer is often revealed through their language – beginning with core terminology. The term 'riot', as illustrated by the case of President Trump and LA, is often deployed as a means of creating a picture of lawlessness. Others will avoid it precisely because of its pejorative implications. Those involved in collective violence are more likely to portray themselves as being involved in 'uprisings' or 'rebellions', as will those sympathetic to them. This diametrically opposed, but equally ideological, portrayal presents such activities as forms of resistance to oppressive authority. The language surrounding protest and protest violence is freighted with political meaning.

Governmental reaction to riots, or more specifically rioters, has long tended to take a number of standard forms. Aspects of the main tropes that are utilized by politicians when making riot-related claims have a long history and can be found all the way back to the bread riots of the eighteenth century (and no doubt beyond). I have argued that these political tropes take three main forms, each in different ways seeking to present a significant element of the body of rioters as 'outsiders'. First and most straightforwardly, rioters are presented as geographical outsiders, not being members of the communities where the violence occurs (on symbolic boundary maintenance, see Douglas 1966). The second views rioters as intrinsically criminal and antisocial, and as separable in their conduct and morality from what is implied are the more 'respectable' members of the community or society more generally. The third, final and linked trope is the one that draws on underclass theory (Wacquant 2022) and presents rioters, as one commentator in England in 2011 put it, as being 'cut off from the mainstream' (Clarke 2011). In this latter case, what begins as a structural observation about the embedded nature of long-term marginality in the labour market transforms into a behavioural and moral critique which focuses on an allegedly antisocial subset of the poor. Alongside the regularity with which such political tropes are deployed is the consistency with which empirical evidence is produced that effectively undermines such arguments. From the social historians of the 1960s, through the Kerner Commission and other official inquiries, to contemporary scholarship, there is now mountainous evidence illustrating precisely the reverse of 'riff-raff' and outsider theory, showing in fact that rioters tend to be drawn from the communities in which the violence is concentrated, even though they are often found among the poorest sections of such communities, as well as among the young and male (DiPasquale and Glaeser 1998; Olzak, Shanahan and McEneaney 1996).

Observations about claims-making are important in helping us navigate the unfolding theoretical and conceptual approaches taken to riots over the past century and earlier. There is no need to rehearse this history at length here. Any sketched outline, however, would contrast the dominant psychological model of the late nineteenth and early twentieth centuries, associated primarily with Gustave Le Bon, which saw crowd conduct as irrational and exceptionally dangerous, with the emergence of a more obviously sociologically influenced approach in the second half of the twentieth century, which emphasized the essential rationality of crowd conduct, finding its logics in the frustrations borne of embedded grievances and unmet expectations. The high points of these two contrasting scholarly approaches also arguably reflected their respective zeitgeists. Le Bon and others were writing in a period in which the fear of revolution remained strong, whereas the sociological critics half a century or more later worked against the backdrop of the US civil rights movement and other campaigns aiming at what was identified as progressive social change. The dominant perspectives reflected their times, and in neither case could they be described as scholarship in the mould of Max Weber's model of 'value neutrality'.

What, then, do we conclude? The tenets of deindividuation theory can be firmly rejected, and with good reason. The broad parameters of contemporary sociological approaches to the crowd, with their emphasis on rational claims-making, appear more of a fit with what we see happening on the streets of cities across America, Europe and beyond. The advantage of this by now standard model of riots is that it entirely distances itself from extant approaches that see individuals as losing themselves within the crowd. It offers an alternative that takes seriously the claims made by rioters, that takes account of their social and economic circumstances, and which sees riots, in part, as ordered and patterned social phenomena. There are, of course, dangers lurking. The one we have encountered most regularly is the danger of over-reading collective violence. As Gary Marx, among others, argued decades ago, there is no necessity for such violence to reflect underlying grievances, and certainly not to have a single meaning. In addition, we should not assume that these are all political events. They are not, as some twentieth-century historians came close to arguing, all proto-rebellions. In fact, it is perfectly possible for riots to be 'issueless'. As Paul Rock (1981) notes in a short but important essay, riots are often invested with more meaning than they can reasonably carry and, indeed, alongside Marx, he suggests it is quite possible for such collective action to be largely 'innocent of meaning'. This is a lesson that remains too regularly ignored or forgotten. Too often, the reaction against Le Bon has been an over-reaction.

When Le Bon's previously remarkably influential view of crowd behaviour fell into disrepute, one of the consequences of the search for rationality in crowd conduct was the relegation of any consideration of the role of emotion in collective conduct. It is only relatively recently that there has been a move to accommodate emotions into accounts of protest and protest violence. Doing so adds richness to our understanding in a number of ways. It draws attention to the excitement to be found in riots, the pleasure derived from involvement, the sense of freedom that pervades such experience, and the carnivalesque elements of such activity. Thus, the emotional constituent also aids our understanding of the occasional attractiveness of such violence, what Jack Katz would call the 'seductions' of such conduct, as well as offering insight into what Randall Collins identified as the barriers that have to be overcome if violence is to be successfully enacted.

I noted above that, to the extent riots carry meaning, It is almost certainly varied or plural. In this connection, and in an all too often overlooked observation, Abudu Stark and colleagues (1974) point to the 'monolithicity' so often found in accounts of riots: the suggestion or implication that the nature and meaning of such collective behaviour is singular or unvarying. Despite some exceptions, they suggest too little attention is generally paid to how riot participants engage in 'interactive, multiple and differentiated behaviors mediated by processes which encourage or inhibit certain behaviors at certain times and places' (1974: 866). Intriguingly, their study, which examined the actions of those involved in the Watts riot of 1965, found relatively little overlap in time and place between two major riot activities: looting and burning. In consequence, they argue that, at least to a degree, these should be seen as complex forms of behaviour engaged in by different groups, with 'varied and shifting motivations, and transmitted or blocked by a variety of formal and informal mechanisms and structures' (1974: 873). Again, it is important not to exaggerate this point, but such an observation serves to remind us that crowds are variegated phenomena, made up of people who are often engaged in very different actions, often underpinned by widely different objectives and motivations. Such internal differentiation may have to diminish in order for violence to ensue but, even so, considerable variation will remain, and those out on the streets during a riot will continue to be far from a monolithic or single group. It is a reminder that a 'psychological crowd' may contain many groupings. In addition, such work also prompts us to remember that riots are patterned social phenomena and that this patterning may be the source of considerable insight. It is redolent of Katz's observation that though from the outside both sex and rioting may look like 'a lot of wild thrashing about', they nevertheless contain coherent interactional meanings. Similarly, Abudu Stark and colleagues (1972: 408) note that rioting 'is not "all hell breaking loose", but a complex socio-political process'. Indeed, and rather more accurately, it is the case that rioting is both at the same time.

In attempting to read riots, we are reminded that within the chaos there is often something remarkably orderly, often quite predictable, about such behaviour. Riots are enacted in particular ways, ways that are often quite unsurprising both to those involved and to the non-combatants who observe what is happening. They are quite heavily scripted social phenomena. There is no requirement to learn anew every time disorder occurs. There are well-established patterns, with initial activity tending to involve a lot of verbal threats, often the throwing of objects, possibly brief attempts at physical attacks also, all, in the main, focused on the police. Much of this will be acted out as a game of cat and mouse,[5] varying according to the landscape in which it all takes place. The most serious violence may occur at any point but, generally speaking, tends to happen in the later stages of a riot. In addition to the cat-and-mouse interactions between rioters and the police, as we have seen, the initial stages of a riot are likely to involve arson. Setting property alight is a key signifier in rioting, signalling that order has broken down and that widespread violence is threatened. Arson, a relatively unusual offence outside the context of a breakdown in order, is generally quite fundamental to a riot. Indeed, it is a core, dramatic component, a staged, spectacular, communicative element of all rioting. In fact, riots are quite difficult to imagine in the absence of burning property. In their analysis of nearly 1,900 actions in the Watts riot, Abudu Stark and colleagues (1974) found that almost half (926, or 49%) involved fire. Far from being an unusual act, as arson is often considered to be at other times, during rioting arson is a common and widespread activity. Looting is a further regular feature in the early stages of rioting and property damage, often facilitated by the destruction wrought by arson, it provides an invitational edge for such theft. Like arson, looting comes close to being a form of ubiquitous riotous activity. It is present at all stages of a riot, though arguably becomes more prominent as rioting develops and as the challenges facing law enforcement become potentially overwhelming. This may also reflect the diminution in power of the original motivating force(s) behind the protest violence, and the growth of criminal opportunities that arise as riots develop.

The patterning of riotous conduct is often revealed in the targets of arson, looting and other property damage. I have just noted that attacks on police and property damage are often the earliest signs of emergent riot, with the targets at this stage rarely random. Usually, at this point the focus is on the state. As we have seen, as riots unfold, further patterning, shaping or predictability is to be found. Again, the police and police property are regularly selected as an obvious target of crowd violence. In part, this stems from their role as the state agency tasked with preventing or limiting the violence. In addition, though, it often reflects deep-seated hostility to the police as an institution. In LA in 1992, Paris in 2005 and Hong Kong in 2018, the police were subjected to regular and sustained attacks. In my research in England in 2011, in every town and city in which rioters were interviewed, significant hostility towards the police was expressed. 'Anti-police' riots may be an exaggeration for what was witnessed,[6] but the description nevertheless contains an important truth. Beyond the police, who are the targets and what does the patterning of violence look like? Though again it can be exaggerated or claimed in the absence of any strong evidence (for example, Allport 1954; Greenberg 1992), selectivity in the choice of targets is far from uncommon where both looting and arson are concerned. Indeed, in the case of looting this is partly a consequence of the fact that such activities are almost always undertaken by members of the local community. It contrasts, therefore, with looting during natural disasters, which is usually undertaken by 'outsiders' (Quarantelli and Dynes 1970). In the case of riots, it is potential 'insider knowledge' about targets that leads to conduct that is often far from indiscriminate, exhibiting patterns in which properties, businesses and so forth differ, sometimes markedly, in terms of their risk. The selectivity often witnessed in connection with riot-related violence reinforces our conclusion that pictures of wild, unconstrained, animalistic 'mobs' are a deeply unrealistic and unhelpful way of understanding collective violence. In fact, such conduct is sometimes underpinned by a set of values or, more broadly, what

E. P. Thompson referred to as a 'moral economy'.[7] Finally, the orderliness of riots can also be seen in their tendency to self-police (Gilje 1999), with emergent normative standards establishing behavioural expectations and limits (Reicher 1984).

Despite the preoccupation of many commentators with the dangers inherent in riots, the literature surrounding protest in general has little to say about the violence itself. Such phenomena are not simply 'riots' without violence. What, then, are the main patterns involved? First, violence against property predominates. It far outstrips violence against the person in almost all riots. Property violence takes three main forms: criminal damage, looting and arson. Arson is intriguing, being thought of ordinarily as a rare and peculiarly individualistic act. In the context of riot, it is a common, almost ubiquitous activity, often involving a sizeable minority, often working collectively. In short, the breakdown in order appears to alter the nature of this particular form of property violence. Looting is another ubiquitous element in rioting – rarely is it absent – and, again, it has been subject to less analytical attention than it arguably deserves. There are aspects of looting which are often spontaneous and opportunistic in character, and yet it is in many respects a collective activity involving, if not organization, then certainly cooperation. Looting displays both patterning and predictability, while also having many emotional, occasionally almost carnivalesque, characteristics. The same can be said of arson. Therefore, looting is neither purely expressive nor a form of straightforwardly rational, if violent, consumerism. It is far more complex than most readings allow. Indeed, I have argued here that theft in the context of riot should be seen as a form of political violence, being conduct that generally requires violent challenges to the rule of law before it can occur on any widespread scale. Indeed, definitionally, this is what makes theft 'looting'.

If we switch our attention to violence against the person, we can once again identify a number of patterns. Where injuries are sustained, these are most likely to be by citizens and to have been inflicted by the police or other law-enforcement personnel. Police officers are at considerable risk and, understandably, are often fearful of what lies before them in a riot. In reality, the number of officers injured is small compared with the number of citizens, and the number of serious injuries much smaller still. In terms of seriousness, fatalities during riots in liberal democracies are rare, particularly outside the United States. Assessing the scale of serious violence against the person during riots is tricky, however. From one perspective, given the large numbers of people out on the streets during a riot, the ferocity with which threats are issued and, on occasion, the numbers of weapons that are found, ranging from bricks to Molotov cocktails, it might seem surprising that injuries are not more, and perhaps far more, extensive. What this reveals is that, despite the often apparently colossal scale of physical injury sustained in riots, it remains the case that there is also likely to be a significant element of symbolic violence involved, by which I mean conduct which superficially threatens severe violence but, in practice, is just that – threatened rather than actual violence. A parallel argument can be found in research on British football hooliganism in the 1970s and 1980s. One group of scholars in particular argued that there was much about this apparently violent conduct that was ritualized, routinized and performative, and that the behaviour on display tended towards symbolic aggression rather than actual physical violence. All too often it was the intervention of law-enforcement agencies, and the disruption to the normative environment that was the consequence of such intervention, that stimulated more serious violent conduct (Marsh, Rosser and Harre 1978). Claims about the symbolic nature of much crowd violence were reinforced by empirical evidence from a study of football-related convictions in the mid-1970s, which found that the majority of arrests were for offences such as using threatening or abusive or insulting words or behaviour – offences of provocation rather than violence per se (Trivizas 1980). Similar arguments can be deployed in connection with riots where, similarly, much violent conduct is ritualized and performative, involving symbolic aggression as much as actual physical violence. The latter is both threatened and often very much present. It ought not, however, to be exaggerated.

In rejecting deindividuation-related theories of crowd behaviour, and pointing to the complex, multiple motivations and meanings characteristic of riots, I remain broadly supportive of approaches that utilize the metaphor of *tinder* (embedded, underlying grievances and strains) and *spark* (incidents that serve to transform relatively peaceful conduct into violence) as the basis for understanding the causes of riots. This model of riot aetiology has been the broadly dominant approach since the late 1960s. Persuasive though it is, there remain two practical reasons for caution. The first, as I have regularly noted, is the danger of over-reading or over-rationalizing protest and violence. The second, notwithstanding the very impressive research that now exists, is that work within the 'tinder and spark' tradition continues to fall down where the notion of 'flashpoint' is concerned. We still await work that convincingly identifies what flashpoints comprise and how, in particular, they operate.

We find ourselves in a situation in which we have a broadly persuasive model of riot development, but one that has at its core a crucial element that is under-specified. That this is so is perhaps unsurprising given the difficulties inherent in the notion of 'flashpoint', all of which emanate from the unpredictable and contingent nature of such phenomena. Though they often lead to very significant and violent consequences, flashpoints are generally minor matters, with little intrinsic to them that sets them apart from other interactions. Given their centrality to our dominant explanatory model, however, it is no longer satisfactory in my view to utilize a notion of a 'flashpoint' without some significant elaboration of what it is about these events that encourages violence, i.e., that makes them act as a 'flashpoint'. The answer, I have argued, lies in combining a number of extant approaches, including the social-psychological social identity model and insights from the micro-sociology of violence, specifically those factors that are conducive to what, following the work of Anne Nassauer, I have referred to as 'situational breakdowns'. Collectively, I suggest, these insights offer us a means of analysing in greater detail, and with greater precision, how crowd violence materializes.

In the 1960s, the historian George Rudé argued that the study of the crowd had been unfairly neglected. The flourishing of work in this field since that time now makes such an argument much more difficult to sustain. Despite this burgeoning activity, a number of limitations remain, of which two are particularly important. First, as I have noted throughout the book, there has been a tendency to privilege the study of the violent crowd. As Harrison (1988: 12) observed, Rudé both played a core role in stimulating the growth of work in this field and was central in reinforcing the scholarly preoccupation with the violent crowd. This concern is linked with the second main limitation in contemporary work: the privileging of questions of aetiology and the consequent underplaying of other questions, not least those relating to the aftermath of riots. What, for example, are the implications of riots for those involved in the violence, whether perpetrators and/or victims, and what is the impact on the localities in which such violence takes place?

I have argued that what is required is a more rounded and extended approach, one that focuses on what I have come to call the *life cycle* of riots. In this case an important element of the investigation into riots involves a concern with the consequences, or what might even be called the legacy, of such disorder. This represents a considerable departure from recent riot studies, widening the gaze from its current preoccupation with the lead-up to violence to include the outcomes and impact of these events. I have argued throughout that riots are highly complex and consequential phenomena, and this requires us to pay attention to the aftermath as much as it does to other, more regularly considered elements. For ease of analysis, I divide the aftermath into three broad areas. The first concerns the political, public and media responses to protest and violence, elements of which we encountered in the primary political frames or tropes utilized in narrativizing riots. Telling stories about protest and associated violence is often a competitive process, a contest to establish and embed a particular version of history. Here, in addition to politicians, the media play a vital role in framing events, establishing diagnostic and prognostic understandings that it is hoped will be both pervasive and durable. As such, they can have a dramatic impact on public understandings of disorder. Focusing on the role of narrative in policy development, Annison (2022) suggests that 'storylines' have three primary functions: connecting policy proposals with broader narratives that are circulating; providing meaning, making proposed developments sound appropriate; and deflecting contestation. Cognate claims can be made in relation to narrative competition around riots and protest violence. Here again, the establishment of a dominant storyline casts other interpretations to the margins or, possibly, silences them entirely. A dominant narrative brings coherence to other developments, providing a rationale for both penal and policy responses to collective violence or, as some of the examples considered earlier suggest, justifying the generalized absence of such constructive responses.

The second of the broad categories is what I refer to as the actions and consequences of the penal state. These include how many people become caught up in the criminal justice and penal systems and with what consequences. Given the scale, and implications, of such responses to collective violence, this is perhaps an especially notable absence in the analytical treatment of riots. Its potential importance is perhaps best illustrated by the argument, developed by the historian Elizabeth Hinton (2021), that the riots that peppered the American landscape between 1964 and 1972 were a significant factor in the development of the law-and-order politics that underpinned what was to become America's experiment in 'mass incarceration'. In what is now a vast literature, explanations for the development of US mass incarceration include changes in crime rates, political culture and political economy, but Hinton is pretty much alone in pointing to the role of the ghetto riots. Nonetheless, here is a potentially persuasive argument that offers an illustration of the significant consequences that can flow from the political and penal response to collective violence.

The third and final area of legacy concerns the public policy response to riot and protest violence. What do governments do in the aftermath of riot? Are any of the issues raised by those involved in protest – issues linked to whatever grievances they harbour – responded to by official bodies? In short, do policies or practices change? There were broadly negative reactions in the four main examples I utilized, though even the cases where positive policy change was largely absent still illustrated the power of narrative in shaping the post-riots response. To take the examples of France in 2005 and England in 2011, governmental arguments, the ones that eventually won the contest for narrative domination, focused on criminality and antisocial conduct, arguing that progressive policy responses were consequently unnecessary. The outcome in both cases was a public arena dominated by strident law-and-order politics against a background of very sizeable numbers of arrests prosecutions and high levels of imprisonment. Added together, these three areas – the narrative, penal and policy responses – illustrate the consequentiality of riot, matters usually ignored.

Academic study of the causes of riots has moved a considerable distance from the traditional, somewhat dismissive, psychology of the late nineteenth and early twentieth centuries. We haven't entirely escaped viewpoints that focus on the alleged irrationality and atavism of the mob but, in the main, they are confined to non-academic circles. Psychological, sociological and historical analysis of riot now coalesces around those broad social, economic and political factors that form the backdrop to local anger and grievance and which are claimed, under certain conditions, to give rise to violence. That they do so is a consequence of particular, localized forms of social interaction. I have argued that in the desire to establish distance from old-fashioned views of crowd conduct, the overreaction, together with the continuing preoccupation with the violent crowd, hampers our understanding of riots in a number of ways. The scholarly reaction against the irrational has created a situation in which those aspects of crowd conduct that are less easy to portray as instrumental can sometimes be lost or underplayed. Ensuring that the emotional element of conduct, for example, is not excluded is vital. In the focus on collective conduct, the rewards of studying the absence of violence are also sometimes underappreciated, both in terms of what peaceful crowds have to teach us and in connection with the more specific question of why riots don't happen (Newburn 2016b). Centrally, the preoccupation with violence has also foreshortened the academic gaze, focusing attention on questions of causation at the expense of wider, equally important questions. In future, I trust that an appreciation of the life cycle of riots will help ensure that the character and consequences of such events are understood to be just as important as their causes.

Notes

Chapter 2 Fear of the Mob

1 See, for example, his obituary in the *Guardian*, 27 January 2009: https://www.theguardian.com/books/2009/jan/27/obituary-christopher-hibbert-historian

2 Malcolm Gladwell is a Canadian writer who takes scholarly ideas and both popularizes them and applies them in sometimes unusual ways. His best-known books include *The Tipping Point* (Little, Brown, 2000), *Blink* (Little, Brown, 2005) and *Outliers* (Little, Brown, 2008).

3 https://www.theguardian.com/uk/2011/aug/15/david-cameron-riots-broken-society

4 Ross was fired from Stanford in 1900 because of his outspoken views on eugenics and immigration, particularly Chinese and Japanese immigration to the United States. On leaving Stanford, he took up a post initially at the University of Nebraska and then, for the bulk of the remainder of his career, at the University of Wisconsin-Madison.

5 https://www.theguardian.com/uk/2011/aug/09/david-cameron-full-statement-uk-riots

6 https://www.gov.uk/government/speeches/pm-statement-4-august-2024

7 https://www.dw.com/en/turkey-erdogan-calls-protests-a-movement-of-violence/live-72017324

Chapter 3 Not So Primitive Rebels

1 A range of forms of protest violence fit at best uneasily into such an approach. The student protests of the mid-twentieth century, for example, can hardly be said to have had such substantive ambitions. See, for example, Thomas (2002).

2 Elizabeth Hinton's (2021) *America on Fire* contains what she suggests is a full list of riots that occurred in the decade from 1964 to 1973, totalling more than two thousand. However, no detail on the scale of the particular events is available, so judging their nature is impossible. Assessing whether, or to what extent, these events might reasonably be described as 'riots' or 'uprisings' requires more information.

3 Again, we must recognize that by no means all forms of protest and protest violence are encompassed by this general rubric and approach. One significant example would be the Kent State shootings in 1970. See, for example, Grace (2016).

4 Despite what some see as an absence of critical assessment of his work (Holton 1978).

5 One must be very careful here, for the treatment of statistics by Rudé, Hobsbawm and others is often shockingly naive, reading from registers and other records data that are treated often as self-evidently meaningful. Naturally, as has been well established by many scholars, they were anything but, being just as much social constructions as the other phenomena studied by the historians. In this particular case, one might reasonably ask whether the bureaucracy that collected statistics relating to 'previous convictions' was efficient enough to allow us to treat such data as reliable in the way Rudé appears content to do.

6 Beloff (1913–1999) was a British historian, Professor of Government and Fellow, All Souls, Oxford. https://www.thebritishacademy.ac.uk/documents/1752/120p021.pdf

7 This is a reference to the famous anthropological work of Bronislaw Malinowski. Living on an island near Papua New Guinea for several years, Malinowski studied the Trobriand Islanders' local customs and practices of gift giving, among much else. What he revealed was a highly complex social system, with elaborate social expectations and a complex social order – all very much in contrast with the views of those who saw only what they took to be a 'primitive', uncivilized set of social arrangements.

8 In fact, it was almost certainly more, as Hinton's (2021) timeline of urban disorder illustrates.

9 Hardly a defensible position in any case, but impossible to sustain, for example, when thinking about the early days of Malcolm X, the Black Muslims and the Black Panthers. See, inter alia, Bloom and Martin (2013).

10 And see also Katz (2019).

11 An investigator for the Kerner Commission who went on to have a distinguished academic career. https://web.mit.edu/gtmarx/www/garyhome.html

12 For example, with the exception of discussion of policing, references to riot or collective violence barely appear in either the *Blackwell Companion to Social Movements* (Snow, Soule and Kriesi 2007) or della Porta and Diani's (1999) *Social Movements: An Introduction*.

Chapter 4 Riots in the Round

1 https://www.theguardian.com/artanddesign/2019/apr/04/photographer-banlieue-monsieur-bonheur-department-93-paris-france-fox-news-no-go-zone
2 See https://www.onpv.fr/uploads/media_items/ra-2015-synthese-uk.original.pdf
3 The police in such situations have, of course, to make decisions both under pressure and without the benefit of time for lengthy consideration. See, for example, Newburn (2022); Gladwell (2006).
4 A form of 'less lethal' weapon used by the police and other law enforcement organizations. In this case, it takes the form of a small fabric pillow filled with lead shot. Such weapons remain controversial as they can cause considerable injury. https://en.wikipedia.org/wiki/Bean_bag_round
5 Readers familiar with David Waddington and colleagues' 'flashpoints model' will see how much I have drawn on elements of his approach in constructing this outline of the riot life cycle, especially its early stages.
6 References taken from McPhail and Wohlstein (1983).
7 In the United States, a distinction is drawn between 'jails' and 'prisons'. Jails tend to refer to local facilities under the jurisdiction of a city, district or county. They hold people on shorter sentences and those awaiting trial or sentencing. By contrast, prisons tend to come under the jurisdiction of the state or federal government and house convicted offenders serving longer sentences.
8 https://files.epi.org/pdf/142084.pdf

Chapter 5 Tinder and Spark

1 And there is no doubt that in some very real respects such long-standing and deeply entrenched grievances do exist and form an absolutely crucial element of the background to violent protest, as has been and will be illustrated throughout the book. However, it is also important to recognize the inevitable element of the *post hoc ergo propter hoc* fallacy here: the assumption that because one event preceded another, there must be some causative relation between them. Such assumptions bring structure and intelligibility to a course of events that is messy, indeed much messier than such explanations would allow. Echoes can be found in the participants' attempts to make sense of their own involvement and their own understanding. Moreover, and once again following W. I. Thomas's dictum that things – in this case rioters' perceptions and assumptions – are likely to be real in their consequences, such assumptions are of very considerable importance. And, in that case, what rioters define as real may be real enough in their consequences.
2 Some publications attach the name of Rodney King directly to the riots as a descriptor. This is understandable but might be considered misleading from the perspective of making sense of the idea of a 'flashpoint'. See, for example, Katz (2016); Matheson and Baade (2004).

3 Wacquant (2008: 1) describes them, and their equivalents in other countries, as places known, 'to outsiders and insiders alike, as the "lawless zones", the "problem estates", the "no-go areas" or the "wild districts" of the city, territories of deprivation and dereliction to be feared, fled from and shunned because they are – or such is their reputation, but in these matters perception contributes powerfully to fabricating reality – hotbeds of violence, vice and social dissolution.' For an extended discussion, see 'The Bitter Taste of Territorial Taint' in Wacquant (2023).

4 Elijah Anderson talks of

> a 'code of the streets', which amounts to a set of informal rules governing interpersonal public behavior, including violence. The rules prescribe both a proper comportment and the proper way to respond if challenged .... At the heart of the code is the issue of respect, loosely defined as being treated 'right' or granted the deference one deserves. However, in the troublesome public environment of the inner city, as people increasingly feel buffeted by forces beyond their control, what one deserves in the way of respect becomes more and more problematic and uncertain. This in turn further opens the issue of respect of sometimes intense, interpersonal negotiation. In the street culture, especially among young people, respect is viewed as almost an external entity that is hard-won but easily lost and so must constantly be guarded. (Anderson 2008: 74)

5 The video material can be viewed at: https://avplayer.lib.berkeley.edu/Video-Public-MRC/b22139628 and on many other sites. It is worth looking for the extended footage, i.e., the footage shown to the jury in the trial of the four officers.

6 Territoriality is discussed in a range of studies, including: Anderson (1999); Brotherton and Barrios (2004); Taylor, Evans and Fraser (1996). Alistair Fraser (2013: 981), in his study of Glasgow's 'Langview Boys', says 'territorial identification is therefore overlaid with the performance of a tough, masculine identity akin to Sandberg's (2008) description of "street capital". In a social environment characterised by limited opportunities, not only territorial space, but also bodily capital, is a resource for attaining distinction.'

7 In this context, see also Bramsen (2018b).

8 Although, as acknowledged earlier in the chapter, violent interaction rituals without obvious domination of one side over another are also possible.

Chapter 6 The Quest for Excitement and Beyond

1 A Los Angeles-based sociologist, Jack Katz has been at the forefront of writing on the subject of emotions and crime for many decades. For further biographical detail, see https://www.encyclopedia.com/arts/educational-magazines/katz-jack-1944#:~:text=SIDELIGHTS%3A%20Jack%20Katz%20is%20a,wrote%20Jeff%20Ferrell%20in%20Social

2 See Matza (1964) on delinquency and excitement.

3 Though see Durkheim (1964 [1912]) on 'collective effervescence'.
4 Much earlier in the century, the Chicago sociologist W. I. Thomas, in seeking to steer a path between determinism and free will, outlined his 'four wishes' (see Colyer 2015). Of most relevance here, arguably, was what Thomas referred to as 'the desire for new experiences', one that 'embodies human curiosity [and] is manifest in hunting, sports, and gambling. Thomas noted that a fight, even a dogfight, never fails to draw a crowd. From this he believed there was an innate human wish or desire to collect new experiences. When this wish is frustrated, "unadjusted" (or delinquent) behaviour follows' (Colyer 2015: 260). Thomas is offering here another example of the way in which emotions penetrate all daily activities.
5 In 'What Pragmatism Means', James suggested: 'In short . . . we have a right ever and anon to take a moral holiday, to let the world wag in its own way, feeling that its issues are in better hands than ours and are none of our business' (James 2000 [1905]). https://www.gutenberg.org/files/5116/5116-h/5116-h.htm#link2H_4_0004
6 Though, as Paul Rock drew to my attention, 'some might point, say, to the licence associated with student rag weeks and Bertie Wooster's Drones Club'.

> The general mayhem seen in the Drones Club onscreen closely reflected its portrayal in the books, with all manner of impromptu indoor games of golf, squash, cricket, and some sort of bizarre game involving piggy-backs and rolled-up papers. While certainly embellished for comic effect, this reflected a long-standing tradition of playing cricket in the bar at Buck's – a club of which Wodehouse himself was an early member, and which provided some of the inspiration for the Drones. (https://clubland.substack.com/p/clubs-in-popular-culture-the-drones)

7 In recent times, criminology, in particular that form that styles itself 'cultural criminology', has shown a particular interest in the notion of carnival. Jeff Ferrell (2010: 313) describes this interest, arguing that a range of activities such as 'drug-taking, gang rituals, arson, and "hotting" or "joyriding" in stolen cars can be understood as free-floating historical residues of carnivalesque excesses that were once contained inside ritualized times and events'. In the absence of such ritualized routines, the argument goes, alternative forms are required.
8 For an extended discussion, see Newburn, Cooper et al. (2015).
9 One of the very few respondents who refused to give their age.
10 Daniel is not his real name. His account is taken from an extended re-interview conducted as part of *Reading the Riots* for broadcast on BBC2's *Newsnight*. The film in which his account appears can be found at: http://news.bbc.co.uk/1/hi/programmes/newsnight/9656166.stm
11 Bramsen (2018b), among others (e.g., Anderson, Nassauer) identifies 'running away' as one of the key situational conditions enabling perpetrators to dominate a situation and engage in violence.
12 A computer game that comes in various formats and which simulates a first-person experience of warfare.

Chapter 7 The Nature of Violence

1 See https://goodallandgoodluck.substack.com/p/trumps-new-age-of-acquiesence?r=4i04j3&utm_campaign=post&utm_medium=web&triedRedirect=true

2 Major disorders tended to last at least two days and were characterized by 'many fires, intensive looting, and reports of sniping' (Kerner Commission 1968: 113). At the other end, minor disorders might not even have been classified as 'riots' had it not been for the national context of widespread disorder and the media attention that went with that.

3 Different sources report different numbers of deaths – generally ranging from 52 to 60. The journalist Lou Cannon (1999: 621), in his definitive retelling of the disorder, suggests that this variance is a consequence of commentators being unsure whether some deaths were a direct consequence of the riots or were simply coincident with it. As a result, he relies on the verdict of the Los Angeles County Coroner's Office, which determined the number of riot-related deaths to be 54.

4 A graphic imagining of being involved in the policing in LA in 1965 can be found in Wambaugh (1971).

5 Gun ownership is far higher in the United States than it is almost everywhere else, particularly in European countries. According to the World Population Review, in 2025 there were 120.5 guns per 100,000 population in the United States, compared with 19.6 in France and 5.1 in the United Kingdom. https://worldpopulationreview.com/country-rankings/gun-ownership-by-country/ . France's gun ownership is high by standards in the West, though it has tightened up its laws in recent times: https://www.rfi.fr/en/france/20220208-france-launches-new-digital-platform-to-tighten-control-on-gun-ownership-hunting

6 Earlier in the chapter, I suggested that there were 43 fatalities. Different sources offer slightly different estimates. In this case, Bergesen relies on sources that identify one fewer, hence the apparent disparity.

7 https://www.bbc.co.uk/news/world-asia-china-42465516

8 https://www.bbc.co.uk/news/world-asia-56636345 See also Schoon (2014).

9 Bramsen (2018b) identifies five such situational conditions: attacking from *afar/above*; from *behind*; *at night*; *from a vehicle*; and *attacking the outnumbered*.

10 And, more popularly, the arguments advanced by Malcolm Gladwell (2006) in *Blink*, his book about 'thinking without thinking'.

11 This may be reflected *positively* in the protection afforded particular properties and *negatively* where particular targets are selected: Korean stores in LA in 1992; libraries in the aftermath of the Southport riot in England in 2024: https://www.bbc.co.uk/news/articles/crk0nk4z25zo

12 See Stephens (2014).

13 Though see Haywood (2013). There are some useful journalistic analyses also: https://www.npr.org/2017/04/26/524744989/when-la-erupted-in-anger-a-look-back-at-the-rodney-king-riots
14 In drawing this contrast, Quarantelli (1994) describes looting during disasters as generally being 'very limited, individual and private'.
15 *Birmingham Mail*, 'From the Archives: Police Parking Ticket Sowed Seeds for Riots'. http://www.birminghammail.co.uk/news/local-news/from-the-archives-police-parking-ticket-sowed-157800. The phrase is remarkably similar to that uttered by one of the *Reading the Riots* respondents, who said, 'It was like Christmas'. http://www.theguardian.com/uk/2011/dec/05/summer-riots-consumerist-feast-looters
16 Katz says:

> Contemporary ethnographers write as if describing the harm poor people do to each other is a hot potato. The guiding fear, increasingly made explicit in anguished reflections, is that descriptions of crime that adhere to the demands of social ontology will lead to blaming the poor, which in turn will elicit support for policies of individual help rather than for government action that could create categorical remedies for inequality. (Katz 2019: 48)

17 Thought of as locations 'where Protestant/unionist and Catholic/nationalist territories meet' (Jarman and O'Halloran 2001: 2).

Chapter 8 Blame the Police?

1 The riot in Baltimore, MD, in the 1960s would be one such example. See Levy (2018).
2 It is more complex than this. Della Porta and Reiter (1998: 214) outline seven different challenges facing the police:

- *Brutal* versus *soft*, referring to the degree of force used
- *Repressive* versus *tolerant*, referring to the number of prohibited behaviors
- *Diffused* versus *selective*, referring to the number of repressed groups
- *Illegal* versus *legal*, referring to police respect of the law
- *Reactive* versus *preventive*, referring to the 'timing' of police intervention
- *Confrontational* versus *consensual*, referring to the degree of communication with the demonstrators
- *Rigid* versus *flexible*, referring to the degree of 'adaptability'

3 https://nationalpost.com/news/no-win-situation-in-wetsuweten-protests-where-police-criticized-for-being-too-aggressive-or-too-lax
4 The legality of this tactic has been challenged not only in the UK courts but all the way up to the European Court of Human Rights in Strasbourg; see Mead (2012).
5 In addition to law enforcement supplies, the program also offered a range of other categories of equipment, such as office furniture, house-

hold goods (e.g., kitchen equipment), exercise equipment, portable electric generators, tents and heavy equipment such as cranes and various types of land vehicles. See Else (2014).

6 https://www.bostonherald.com/2014/08/15/battenfeld-elizabeth-warren-butts-into-ferguson-unrest/

7 The site of very significant rioting in north London in 1985 when a police officer, Keith Blakelock, was stabbed multiple times, later dying from his wounds. See Newburn (2024).

8 A 30-year-old Black British man with mental health issues who died after being restrained by the police. The jury at the inquest returned a verdict of *unlawful killing*, but this was later overturned; see Pemberton (2008).

9 The 29-year-old man shot by the Metropolitan Police prior to the riots in London in 2011.

10 Including Cynthia Jarrett, whose death from a heart attack during a police search of her house was one of the triggers for the 1985 Broadwater Farm riot (see Smith 1991), Roger Sylvester and Joy Gardener, a 40-year-old woman who suffocated while being restrained by police officers; see Scraton (2002).

11 https://www.justice.gov/sites/default/files/opa/press-releases/attachments/2015/03/04/ferguson_police_department_report.pdf at p. 6.

12 George Floyd Protesters Condemn 'Opportunistic' Looting and Violence, *Guardian*, 31 May 2020. https://www.theguardian.com/us-news/2020/may/31/george-floyd-protesters-condemn-opportunistic-looting-violence

13 https://www.theguardian.com/uk/2011/dec/08/victims-voices-confidence-siva-hackney

14 A diagrammatic summary of the College of Policing's approach to command structures in policing in England and Wales can be found at https://www.college.police.uk/app/operations/command-and-control/command-structures

15 And, yet, as I've been clear, a degree of caution is required, for while I in no way doubt the dangers officers face, or the courage shown in the face of such threats, there is a tendency for police representatives to exaggerate these dangers. Indeed, it remains the case that policing is less dangerous than sometimes assumed and may have been becoming less dangerous in recent times (White, Dario and Shjarback 2019).

Chapter 9 Riots, Media and Social Movements

1 There has been much debate about the appositeness of this term. Roberts, for example, says the following:

> What gave a subsequent unity to these situations [in Tunisia, Egypt, Yemen, Libya, etc.] was the overarching construction placed upon them. In so far as talk of the 'Arab Uprising' tended to credit them with a uniform revolutionary potential, it was, if anything, even more of an hallucination than the

> talk of 'the Arab Spring', which is why I have come, reluctantly, to regard the latter as the appropriate term to use, on one condition. This is that the Tunisian case is understood not to belong to the series to which the term refers, because the Tunisian revolution was not only prior to the shock wave that founded this series but also determined by quite other logics. (Roberts 2024: 107)

2 An anti-austerity movement in Spain, sometimes referred to as the 15-M Movement, which began around the time of local and regional elections in 2011 and involved a series of protests, demonstrations and occupations.

3 Oddly, Castells offers no defence of this terminology and no explanation. Indeed, there is no mention of Gilles Deleuze and Félix Guattari, the most obvious sources for such a descriptor.

4 Emmett Louis Till (25 July 1941–28 August 1955), a 14-year-old Black teenager, was lynched after being accused of offending a white woman in her family's grocery store. The brutality of his murder – Till's mother insisted on an open-casket funeral – and the acquittal of his killers focused attention on the continuing violence against African Americans in the South. See, for example, Whitfield (1988).

5 A Ted Talk given by Ghonim, in which he describes the Egyptian revolution, and his role in it, can be found at https://www.ted.com/talks/wael_ghonim_inside_the_egyptian_revolution?language=en

6 By which I mean space that is legally 'public', is perceived, rightly or wrongly, to be public *by* the public, or which, though legally or practically private, has some symbolic claim as an imagined public space.

7 The first such proposal appeared on the Adbusters website on 2 February 2011, under the title 'A Million Man March on Wall Street'.

8 Graeber, for example, made the following observation:

> When we were first putting together the idea for #Occupy Wall Street, there were some who argued that we could make a series of demands that are part of the delegitimation process, by making demands for things that are obviously commonsensical and reasonable, but which they would never in a million years even consider doing. So it would not be an attempt to achieve the demands, but rather it would be a further way to de-structure the authority, which would be shown to be utterly useless when it came to providing what the people need. What we're really talking about here is rhetorical strategies, not strategies of government, because #Occupy Wall Street does not claim to take control of the instruments of power, nor does it intend to. In terms of long-term visions, one of our major objectives has already been achieved to a degree which we never imagined it could have been. Our goal was to spread a certain notion of direct democracy, of how democracy could work. (https://platypus1917.org/2012/01/31/interview-with-david-graeber/)

9 See, for example, https://www.youtube.com/watch?v=qBC2gNRk63s

10 Trayvon Martin, a 17-year-old African American, was shot and killed by Zimmerman on 26 February 2012. Zimmerman was the Neighbourhood

Watch coordinator in his local gated community. Zimmerman fatally shot Martin, who did not possess any weapons, and claimed self-defence. The police chief said that Zimmerman had a right to defend himself with lethal force. See Brodin (2016).

11 https://www.washingtonpost.com/politics/2020/06/06/floyd-protests-are-broadest-us-history-are-spreading-white-small-town-america/

12 On her own webpages, she says: 'I'm an organizer, educator, archivist and curator. My work focuses on ending violence, dismantling the prison industrial complex, transformative justice and supporting youth leadership development. After over 20 years of living and organizing in Chicago, I moved back to my hometown of New York City in May 2016.' https://mariamekaba.com/

13 https://www.nytimes.com/2020/06/12/opinion/sunday/floyd-abolish-defund-police.html

14 All this information and more is available at: https://policeviolencereport.org/

15 Crippen and Lopreato (1989).

16 Mosca' work on elite theory has become particularly pertinent, thanks to a number of contemporary developments. Drochon comments, for example,

> From Occupy Wall Street in 2011 and its slogan of the 99% versus the 1%, to 2016 and the Brexit referendum in the UK, where Leave campaigner and politician Michael Gove declared that the people had had 'enough of experts', and subsequent Prime Minister Theresa May using her Conservative Party Conference speech to attack the 'rootless cosmopolitan elite', to finally the US Presidential Election of the same year and Trump's campaign against the "establishment" and claiming that he will 'drain the swamp', the relationship the 'few' entertain with the 'many' has been forcefully brought back onto the political agenda. (Drochon 2020: 186)

17 This is not to say such phenomena did not exist before 2003. The consensus appears to be that the terminology/nomenclature was established in 2003 (Walker 2013).

18 Of the protesters at such protests, Naomi Klein notes:

> one thing is certain: the protesters in Seattle are not anti-globalization; they have been bitten by the globalization bug as surely as the trade lawyers inside the official meetings. Rather, if this new movement is 'anti' anything, it is anti-corporate, opposing the logic that what's good for business – less regulation, more mobility, more access – will trickle down into good news for everybody else. (Klein 2005: 4)

19 https://www.theguardian.com/world/2008/jul/17/italy.g8

Chapter 10 Reaching Judgement

1 https://committees.parliament.uk/publications/47476/documents/246718/default/

2 Two counter-examples from the United Kingdom can easily be found. The first, concerning an outspoken Black, left-wing London politician, involved considerable condemnation of the police and, especially controversially after the murder of one officer, the claim that the police had 'taken one hell of a beating'; see https://turbulentisles.com/2016/01/14/turbulent-londoners-bernie-grant-1944-2000/ The second occurred in the immediate aftermath of the 2011 riots in England where the police were subject to very considerable criticism from senior Conservative politicians in particular; on both, see Newburn (2024).

3 https://www.theguardian.com/world/2014/aug/19/ferguson-outsiders-protesters-riots-peaceful-unrest

4 http://www.telegraph.co.uk/news/uknews/crime/8713298/London-riots-were-orchestrated-by-outsiders.html

5 Even Martin Luther King Jr had to contend with such portrayal. See King (2018).

6 https://www.theguardian.com/uk/2011/aug/09/david-cameron-full-statement-uk-riots

7 https://www.thenational.scot/news/national/24499315.wes-streeting-condemns-mindless-thuggery-far-right-disorder/

8 https://thelead.uk/mindless-thuggery-comes-blackpool-disorder-breaks-out-talbot-square

9 While most such inquiries will be established during or soon after the events concerned, this is by no means always the case. In relation to the Tulsa riot of 1921, almost three-quarters of a century passed before a commission was formed. In 2001, the report offered a drastically different picture of events and outcomes than many had previously envisioned (Messer and Bell 2010).

10 Members of the Governor's staff say that the reason for the three-month deadline was that the Governor wanted some immediate remedial proposals to take to the state legislature. McCone says he had his own considerations for setting the deadline:

> I set it for several reasons. In the first place I thought it was important to get the study done and get the recommendations in and get something on the rails to improve conditions. And secondly, this is a subject you can study forever and these were busy men; every one of them, including myself, had a full-time job, and we couldn't be expected to set aside a year of our life. And they worked very hard, day and night, seven days a week, to get the study done and the report out and I think it's just as good as if it took a year. (Quoted in Jacobs 1971: 293)

After leaving office in 1979, he resumed his legal practice in Washington, DC, and in 1984 he became chairman of a commercial bank in Boston.

11 Of 'riff-raff' approaches, one of the National Advisory Commission's members, Senator Brooke, had the following to say:

> The people who rioted during the summer of 1967 were, for the most part, neither social misfits nor habitual criminals. They were not alcoholics or drug addicts. They were not Communists, and they were not inspired by Communists. And they were not part of an organized conspiracy designed to bring down the United States by attacking its great urban centers. Rather, they were men and women who were driven by the fear and frustration which accompanies continuing second-class citizenship in a country dedicated to the principle of equality. (Quoted in Gooden and Myers 2018: 5)

12 https://www.amnesty.org/en/latest/news/2020/05/hong-kong-impotent-and-biased-ipcc-report-into-protests-fails-to-bring-justice-any-closer/
13 https://www.fcchk.org/british-policing-expert-who-resigned-from-ipcc-probe-into-hong-kong-protests-wouldnt-feel-safe-returning-to-city/
14 https://www.express.co.uk/news/world/1283245/hong-kong-protests-police-abuse-ipcc-police-complaints-commission-beijing-carrie-lam
15 The third form of framing introduced by Snow and Benford (1988) is 'motivational framing', which, in seeking to deal with the 'free rider' problem, outlines reasons why people should get involved.

Chapter 11 Protest, Violence and the Penal State

1 Garland (2025a: 31) defines this as 'the legal and institutional arrangements, as well as the personnel and physical infrastructure, through which duly constituted government authorities exercise "penal power"'.
2 In England and Wales, judges and magistrates must follow guidelines from the Sentencing Council when deciding what sentences to give. They may also look at decisions made by the Court of Appeal in previous cases – this is called 'case law'. See https://www.gov.uk/how-sentences-are-worked-out and https://www.sentencingcouncil.org.uk/sentencing-and-the-council/about-sentencing-guidelines/
3 According to Martin Duberman (2019: 226–8),

> The Washington Square [bar] was owned by the Joe Gallo family which also controlled Tony Pastor's and the Purple Onion .... The Mob usually provided only a limited amount of money to Family members interested in opening a club; it thereafter became the individual's responsibility to turn a profit .... The Stonewall Inn had, in its varied incarnations during the fifties, been a straight restaurant and a straight nightclub .... In 1966 it was taken over by three Mafia figures who had grown up together. Together they put up $3,500 to reopen the Stonewall as a gay club. [They opened it] as a private 'bottle club'. That was a common ruse for getting around the lack of a liquor licence; bottles would be labeled with fictitious names and the bar would then – contrary to a law forbidding bottle clubs from selling drinks – proceed to do a cash business just like any other bar. (Duberman 2019: 226–8)

4 To the notable historical events one might add, inter alia, the Peterloo Massacre, the fall of the Berlin Wall, the Tiananmen Square protest, the Prague Spring and the events leading up to the end of Soviet hegemony.
5 Described as a 'highly trained, crack riot-control unit that had been set up to respond to the proliferation of protests against the Vietnam War, ... They were a formidable sight' (Duberman 2019: 247).

Chapter 12 Policy Response and Impact

1 In the more confined context of prisons, it is more usually *assumed* that riots will call forth some sort of formal response. This is much less the case for communal rioting. See Adams (1994).
2 Though they are often highly visible in many other aspects of urban life. https://laedc.org/wp-content/uploads/2017/02/Asians_in-LA.pdf
3 Perhaps exacerbated by the extreme geographical divisions within Los Angeles itself, see Clark et al. (2015). https://www.tandfonline.com/doi/abs/10.1080/00045608.2015.1072790
4 Sides 2012.
5 https://placesjournal.org/article/20-years-later-legacies-of-the-los-angeles-riots/?cn-reloaded=1
6 In 2000, make rather than fight a federal civil rights lawsuit alleging a 'pattern-and-practice' of police misconduct, the mayor, the City Council, the Police Commission, and the Police Department signed a 'consent decree' with the US Department of Justice, giving the Federal District Court jurisdiction to oversee the LAPD's adoption of a series of specific management, supervisory and enforcement practices. To monitor the LAPD's compliance with the terms of the consent decree, the Federal Court appointed a monitor on the joint recommendation of the Justice Department and the City (Stone, Foglesong and Cole 2009).
7 Described by Chemerinsky:

> Police officers in the anti-gang CRASH unit in the Rampart Division of the Los Angeles Police Department framed innocent individuals by planting evidence and committing perjury to gain convictions. Innocent men and women pleaded guilty to crimes they did not commit and were convicted by juries because of the fabricated cases against them. Many individuals were subjected to excessive police force and suffered very serious injuries as a result. (Chemerinsky 2000: 2)

8 https://www.thenation.com/article/archive/dismantling-myth-bill-brattons-lapd/
9 *Reading the Riots*, a research project run jointly by the *Guardian* and the London School of Economics (the present author), was widely recognized. The innovative partnership with the *Guardian*, designed to increase public understanding of the 2011 riots, was recognized with the Innovation of the Year award at the British Journalism Awards and the Innovation Award at the European Press awards, and shortlisted for

the THES Research Project of the Year, all in 2012. The research has had substantial reach, with media coverage and engagement in France, Italy, Germany, Sweden, Australia, India, New Zealand, Singapore, the United States, Canada, Russia and Zimbabwe.

10 See, for example, 'Met Police Must "Do Things Differently" after Riots, Says Senior Commissioner': http://www.guardian.co.uk/uk/2011/dec/14/met-police-riots-response-review; 'Rioting is the Choice of Young People with Nothing to Lose': https://www.theguardian.com/commentisfree/2011/dec/05/reading-riots-nothing-to-lose; 'Archbishop of Canterbury Says Riots Will Return unless We Reach Out to Young ': https://www.theguardian.com/uk/2011/dec/05/riots-return-young-archbishop-canterbury (Lewis, Ball and Taylor 2011); 'Riots Report Shows London Needs to Maintain Police Numbers, Says Mayor': http://www.guardian.co.uk/uk/2012/jul/04/riots-report-london-police-numbers; 'Rapid Riot Prosecutions More Important than Long Sentences, Says Keir Starmer': http://www.guardian.co.uk/uk/2012/jul/03/riot-prosecutions-sentences-keir-starmer; 'Reading the Riots – Reaction': http://www.guardian.co.uk/uk/blog/2011/dec/05/reading-the-riots-reaction

11 See https://www.bbc.co.uk/news/uk-england-london-44870768

12 https://insidecroydon.com/wp-content/uploads/2021/08/After-the-Riots-Ten-Years-On.pdf For some of the material and ideas relating to the situation in Tottenham after the riots, and also to Croydon, I am grateful to Dave Hill for pointers in the right direction.

13 Somerset House, in central London, describes itself as

> the home of cultural innovators, . . . a site of origination, with a homegrown, multidisciplinary cultural programme offering alternative perspectives on the biggest issues of our time. We are a place of joy and discovery at the meet point of artistic and social innovation: a centre for ideas where everyone is invited to 'Step Inside and Think Outside,' regardless of age, professional stage or background. Ours is a spirit of constant curiosity and new perspectives, characteristics both integral to our history and key to our future. From our historic site in the heart of London – a storied and celebrated network of neoclassical, Georgian-era buildings – we work globally across arts, creative, business, and non-profit sectors to nurture and foster new talent, methodologies and technologies. Our resident community of in-house innovators – creative startups, arts organisations, artists and makers – all contribute to our unique culture of innovation and invention. (https://www.somersethouse.org.uk/about-us)

14 https://www.somersethouse.org.uk/whats-on/imran-perretta-a-riot-in-three-acts

15 https://www.theartnewspaper.com/2024/09/03/somerset-house-exhibition-legacy-of-protest-Imran-Perretta

16 https://www.theguardian.com/us-news/series/counted-us-police-killings

17 https://mappingpoliceviolence.us/

18 A focus on community engagement, de-escalation tactics, and data-

driven policing. See https://camdencountypd.org/unity-policing-model/#:~:text=Unity%20Policing%20is%20CCPD's%20very,force%20to%20prevent%20crime%2C%20promote

Chapter 13 Reading Riots

1 See, for example, https://www.theguardian.com/us-news/2025/jul/13/los-angeles-ice-raids-terror
2 https://www.ndtv.com/world-news/trump-says-los-angeles-would-burn-to-the-ground-if-he-did-not-send-troops-8634634
3 https://www.independent.co.uk/news/world/americas/la-protests-why-ice-riots-trump-marines-national-guard-b2767122.html
4 https://www.telegraph.co.uk/us/news/2025/06/10/cnn-reporter-arrested-during-la-protests-live-on-air/
5 Bramsen (2023: 93) says, 'A fight can even be said to resemble a good conversation or dance with rhythmic turn-taking'.
6 The headline in the *Guardian* reporting on the newspaper's major research project on the 2011 riots, conducted with the LSE, implied they were anti-police riots, even though the report itself was rather more nuanced: https://www.theguardian.com/uk/2011/dec/05/anger-police-fuelled-riots-study
7 Peter Levy says of Baltimore:

> as in other cities, local residents targeted businesses with which they had grievances. [One reporter] . . . recalled some who rushed into stores exclaiming that they were going to get rid of their 'book', meaning that they owed the merchant of the looted store a debt for previously unpaid goods and they intended to steal the equivalent amount while they had the opportunity to do so. (Levy 2018: 174)

References

Abu-Lughod, J. (2007) *Race, Space and Riots in Chicago, New York and Los Angeles*. New York: Oxford University Press.

Abudu Stark, M. J., Raine, W. J., Burbeck, S. L. and Davison, K. K. (1972) Black Ghetto Violence: A Case Study Inquiry into the Spatial Pattern of Four Los Angeles Riot Event-Types. *Social Problems* 19(3): 408–26.

Abudu Stark, M. J., Raine, W. J., Burbeck, S. L. and Davison, K. K. (1974) Some Empirical Patterns in a Riot Process. *American Sociological Review* 39(6): 865–76.

Adams, R. (1994) *Prison Riots in Britain and the USA*, 2nd edn. Basingstoke: Macmillan.

Aidt, T., Leon-Ablan, G. and Satchell, M. (2022) The Social Dynamics of Collective Action: Evidence from the Diffusion of the Swing Riots, 1830–31. *Journal of Politics* 84(1): 209–25.

Akins, C. (1968) The Riot Commission Report and the Notion of 'Political Truth'. *Social Science Quarterly* 49(3): 469–73.

Alexander, M. (2010) *The New Jim Crow: Mass Incarceration in the Age of Colorblindness*. New York: The New Press.

Ali, S. R. and Fahmy, S. (2013) Gatekeeping and Citizen Journalism: The Use of Social Media during the Recent Uprisings in Iran, Egypt, and Libya. *Media, War and Conflict* 6(1): 55–69.

Allport, F. H. (1933) *Institutional Behavior*. Chapel Hill, NC: University of North Carolina Press.

Allport, G. (1954) *The Nature of Prejudice*. Cambridge, MA: Addison-Wesley.

Anderson, E. (1999) *Code of the Street: Decency, Violence, and the Moral Life of the Inner-City*. New York: W. W. Norton.

Anderson, E. (2008) The Code in the Streets, in M. L. Frampton, I. H. López and J. Simon (eds), *After the War on Crime: Race, Democracy and a New Reconstruction*. New York: New York University Press.

Annison, H. (2022) The Role of Storylines in Penal Policy Change. *Punishment and Society* 24(3): 387–409.

Armstrong, E. A. and Crage, S. M. (2006) Movements and Memory: The Making of the Stonewall Myth. *American Sociological Review* 71(5): 724–51.

Association of British Insurers (2012) £40 Million a Day: Counting the Financial Cost of the August 2011 Riots. London: ABI.

Azzellini, D. (2009) G8 Protests, Genoa, 2001, in I. Ness (ed.), *The International Encyclopedia of Revolution and Protest*, vol. 3. Chichester: Wiley-Blackwell.

Badiou, A. (2012) *The Rebirth of History: Times of Riots and Uprisings*. London: Verso.

Bagguley, P. and Hussain, Y. (2008) *Riotous Citizens: Ethnic Conflict in Multicultural Britain*. Aldershot: Ashgate.

Banfield, E. (1970) *The Unheavenly City*. Boston: Little, Brown.

Barker, A. F. (1994) *Arson: A Review of the Psychiatric Literature*. New York: Oxford University Press.

Baudains, P., Johnson, S. D. and Braithwaite, A. (2013) Geographic Patterns of Diffusion in the 2011 London Riots. *Applied Geography* 45: 211–19.

Bauman, Z. (2007) Collateral Casualties of Consumerism. *Journal of Consumer Culture* 7(1): 25–56.

Bauman, Z. (2011) The London Riots: On Consumerism Coming Home to Roost. *Sociologica Critica*. https://sociologiacritica.es/2011/08/11/the-london-riots-%E2%80%93-on-consumerism-coming-home-to-roost-zygmunt-bauman

Bauman, Z. (2012) Fuels, Sparks and Fires: On Taking to the Streets. *Thesis Eleven* 109: 11–16.

Bawdon, F. and Bowcott, O. (2012) Chaos in the Courts as Justice Systems Rushed to Restore Order. *Guardian*, 3 July.

Bean, J. J. (2000) 'Burn, Baby, Burn': Small Business in the Urban Riots of the 1960s. *Independent Review* 5(2): 165–87.

Becker, H. S. (1967) Whose Side Are We On? *Social Problems* 14(3): 239–47.

Beckett, K. (1997) *Making Crime Pay: Law and Order in Contemporary Politics*. New York: Oxford University Press.

Beckett, K. and Herbert, S. (2008) Dealing with Disorder: Social Control in the Post-Industrial City. *Theoretical Criminology* 12(1): 5–30.

Beckett, K. and Herbert, S. (2010) *Banished: The New Social Control in Urban America*. New York: Oxford University Press.

Bell, B., Jaitman, L. and Machin, S. (2014) Crime Deterrence: Evidence from the 2011 Riots. *Economic Journal* 124(576): 480–506.

Bennett, W. L. and Segerberg, A. (2012) The Logic of Connective Action: Digital Media and the Personalization of Contentious Politics. *Information, Communication and Society* 15(5): 739–68.

Benyon, J. (ed.) (1984) *Scarman and After*. Oxford: Pergamon Press.

Bergesen, A. (1982) Race Riots of 1967: An Analysis of Police Violence in Detroit and Newark. *Journal of Black Studies* 12(3): 261–74.

Bernard-Donals, M. (1994) The Rodney King Verdict, the *New York*

Times, and the 'Normalization' of the Los Angeles Riots; Or, What Antifoundationalism Can't Do. *Cultural Critique* 27: 61–87.

Bittner, E. (1967) Police Discretion in the Emergency Apprehension of Mentally Ill Persons. *Social Problems* 14(3): 278–92.

Blauner, R. (1970) Whitewash over Watts, in P. H. Rossi (ed.), *Ghetto Revolts*. Chicago: Aldine.

Bloom, J. and Martin, W. (2013) *Black against Empire: The History and Politics of the Black Panther Party*. Berkeley and Los Angeles, CA: University of California Press.

Blumer, H. (1951) Social Movements, in A. M. Lee (ed.), *New Outline of the Principles of Sociology*. New York: Barnes and Noble.

Blumer, H. (1969) Outline of Collective Behavior, in R. Evans (ed.), *Readings in Collective Behavior*. Chicago: Rand McNally.

Body-Gendrot, S. (2007) Police, Justice, and Youth Violence in France, in T. Tyler (ed.), *Legitimacy and Criminal Justice: An International Perspective*. New York: Russell Sage Foundation.

Body-Gendrot, S. and Duprez, D. (2002) The Politics of Prevention and Security in France, in D. Duprez and P. Hebberecht (eds), *The Politics of Prevention and Security in Europe*. Brussels: UCV University Press.

Body-Gendrot, S. and Savitch, H. V. (2012) Urban Violence in the United States and France: Comparing Los Angeles (1992) and Paris (2005), in K. Mossberger, S. E. Clarke and P. John (eds), *The Oxford Handbook of Urban Politics*. New York: Oxford University Press.

Bonelli, L. (2010) Policing the Youth: Toward a Redefinition of Discipline and Social Control in French Working-Class Neighborhoods, in S. A. Venkatesh and R. Kassimir (eds), *Youth, Globalization, and the Law*. Stanford: Stanford University Press.

Bonnet, F. and Le Derff, P. (2024) The Consequences of Urban Riots in France and the United States: A Comparative Review. *French Politics* 22: 403–23.

Borch, C. (2006) The Exclusion of the Crowd: The Destiny of a Sociological Figure of the Irrational. *European Journal of Social Theory* 9(1): 83–102.

Borch, C. (2012) *The Politics of Crowds: An Alternative History of Sociology*. Cambridge: Cambridge University Press.

Boskin, J. (1969) The Revolt of the Urban Ghettos, 1964–1967. *Annals of the American Academy of Political and Social Science* 382(1): 1–14.

Bourdieu, P. and Wacquant, L. (1992) *An Invitation to Reflexive Sociology*. Chicago: University of Chicago Press.

Bowling, B. and Phillips, C. (2007) Disproportionate and Discriminatory: Reviewing the Evidence on Police Stop and Search. *Modern Law Review* 70(6): 936–61.

Boyce, M. (2019) From Oral History Interview with Eric Marcus, in New York Public Library (ed.), *The Stonewall Reader*. New York: Penguin.

Bradford, B., Murphy, K. and Jackson, J. (2014) Officers as Mirrors: Policing, Procedural Justice and the (Re)Production of Social Identity. *British Journal of Criminology* 54(4): 527–50.

Bramsen, I. (2017) How Violence Breeds Violence: Micro-Dynamics and Reciprocity of Violent Interaction in the Arab Uprisings. *International Journal of Conflict and Violence* 11: 1–11.

Bramsen, I. (2018a) How Civil Resistance Succeeds (or Not): Micro-Dynamics of Unity, Timing, and Escalatory Actions. *Peace and Change* 43: 61–89.

Bramsen, I. (2018b) How Violence Happens (or Not): Situational Conditions of Violence and Nonviolence in Bahrain, Tunisia, and Syria. *Psychology of Violence* 8(3): 305–15.

Bramsen, I. (2023) *The Micro-sociology of Peace and Conflict*. Cambridge: Cambridge University Press.

Bramsen, I. (2024) Emotional Energy in Conflict, Repression, and Violence, in S. Koschut and A. A. G. Ross (eds), *The Oxford Handbook of Emotions in International Relations*. Oxford: Oxford University Press.

Bramsen, I. and Poder, P. (2018) Emotional Dynamics in Conflict and Conflict Transformation. *Berghof Handbook for Conflict Transformation*. Berlin: Berghof Foundation for Conflict Transformation.

Brantlinger, P. (1983) *Bread and Circuses: Theories of Mass Culture as Social Decay*. Ithaca, NY: Cornell University Press.

Bratton, W. (1998) *Turnaround: How America's Top Cop Reversed the Crime Epidemic*. New York: Random House.

Brodin, M. S. (2016) The Murder of Black Males in a World of Non-Accountability: The Surreal Trial of George Zimmerman for the Killing of Trayvon Martin. *Howard Law Journal* 59(3): 765–85.

Brotherton, D. and Barrios, L. (2004) *The Almighty Latin King and Queen Nation: Street Politics and the Transformation of a New York City Gang*. New York: Columbia University Press.

Brown, R. M. (1975) *Strain of Violence: Historical Studies of American Violence and Vigilantism*. New York: Oxford University Press.

Buchanan, L., Bui, Q. and Patel, J. K. (2020) Black Lives Matter May Be the Largest Movement in US History. *New York Times*, 3 July.

Buckley, A. D. and Kenney, M. C. (1995) *Negotiating Identity: Rhetoric, Metaphor, and Social Drama in Northern Ireland*. Washington, DC: Smithsonian Institution Press.

Budarick, J. (2011) Media Narratives and Social Events: The Story of the Redfern Riot. *Journal of Communication Inquiry* 35(1): 37–52.

Butler, D., Adonis, A. and Travers, T. (1994) *Failure in British Government: The Politics of the Poll Tax*. Oxford: Oxford University Press.

Calhoun, C. (2001) Putting Emotions in Their Place, in J. Goodwin, J. M. Jasper and F. Polletta (eds), *Passionate Politics: Emotions and Social Movements*. Chicago: University of Chicago Press.

Calhoun, C. (2013) Occupy Wall Street in Perspective. *British Journal of Sociology* 64(1): 26–38.

Camp, J. (2016) *Incarcerating the Crisis: Freedom Struggles and the Rise of the Neoliberal State*. Oakland, CA: University of California Press.

Campbell, B. (1993) *Goliath: Britain's Dangerous Places*. London: Methuen.

Campbell, J. S. (1970) The Usefulness of Commission Studies of Collective Violence. *Annals of the American Academy of Political and Social Science* 391(1): 168–76.

Canetti, E. (1962) *Crowds and Power*. London: Gollancz.

Cannon, L. (1999) *Official Negligence: How Rodney King and the Riots Changed Los Angeles and the LAPD*. New York: Times Books.

Caplan, N. S. and Paige, J. M. (1968) A Study of Ghetto Rioters. *Scientific American* 219(2): 15–21.

Carp, B. L. (2011) *Defiance of the Patriots: The Boston Tea Party and the Making of America*. New Haven, CT: Yale University Press.

Casey, M. D. and Hardy, B. L. (2018) The Evolution of Black Neighborhoods since Kerner. *RSF: The Russell Sage Foundation Journal of the Social Sciences* 4(6): 185–205.

Castells, M. (1983) *The City and the Grassroots: A Cross-Cultural Theory of Urban Social Movements*. Berkeley and Los Angeles, CA: University of California Press.

Castells, M. (2009) *Communication Power*. Oxford: Oxford University Press.

Castells, M. (2015) *Networks of Outrage and Hope: Social Movements in the Internet Age*, 2nd edn. Cambridge: Polity.

Cavell, S. (1982) The Fact of Television. *Daedalus* 111(4): 75–96.

Chan, J., Lai, E. Y.-H. and Kellogg, T. E. (2023) The Hong Kong 2019 Protest Movement: A Data Analysis of Arrests and Prosecutions. Center for Asian Law, Georgetown University Law Center, Washington, DC.

Chandra, S. and Foster, A. W. (2005) The 'Revolution of Rising Expectations', Relative Deprivation, and the Urban Social Disorders of the 1960s: Evidence from State-Level Data. *Social Science History* 29(2): 299–332.

Chemerinsky, E. (2000) The Rampart Scandal and the Criminal Justice System in Los Angeles County. *Guild Practitioner* 57(3): 121–33.

Chenoweth, E. (2021) *Civil Resistance: What Everyone Needs to Know*. New York: Oxford University Press.

Cheung, G. Ka-wai (2017) How the 1967 Riots Changed Hong Kong's Political Landscape, with the Repercussions Still Felt Today, in M. H. K. Ng and J. D. Wong (eds), *Civil Unrest and Governance in Hong Kong: Law and Order from Historical and Cultural Perspectives*. London: Routledge.

Christie, N. (2000) *Crime Control as Industry*, 3rd edn. London: Routledge.

Clare, J. (1987) Eyewitness in Brixton, in J. Benyon and J. Solomos (eds), *The Roots of Urban Unrest*. Oxford: Pergamon Press.

Clark, W. A. V., Anderson, E., Östh, J. and Malmberg, B. (2015) A Multiscalar Analysis of Neighborhood Composition in Los Angeles, 2000–2010: A Location-Based Approach to Segregation and Diversity. *Annals of the Association of American Geographers* 105(6): 1260–84.

Clarke, K. (2011) Punish the Feral Rioters, but Address Our Social Deficit

Too. *Guardian,* 5 September. http://www.theguardian.com/commentisfree/2011/sep/05/punishment-rioters-help

Clausewitz, Carl von, 1984 [1832]. *On War*, ed. and trans. Michael Howard and Peter Paret. Princeton, NJ: Princeton University Press.

Clement, M. (2016) *A People's History of Riots, Protest and the Law.* London: Palgrave Macmillan.

Clifton, H. (2011) Rioter Profile: 'The Law Was Obeying Us'. *Guardian,* 9 December. http://www.theguardian.com/uk/2011/dec/09/rioter-profile-law-obeying-us

Clover, J. (2016) *Riot. Strike. Riot: The New Era of Uprisings.* London: Verso.

Colbran, M. (2023) *Crime and Investigative Reporting in the UK.* Bristol: Policy Press.

Collins, R. (1988) The Micro Contribution to Macro Sociology. *Sociological Theory* 6(2): 242–53.

Collins, R. (2004) *Interaction Ritual Chains.* Princeton, NJ: Princeton University Press.

Collins, R. (2008) *Violence: A Micro-Sociological Theory.* Princeton, NJ: Princeton University Press.

Collins, R. (2012) Entering and Leaving the Tunnel of Violence: Micro-Sociological Dynamics of Emotional Entrainment in Violent Interactions. *Current Sociology* 6(2): 132–51.

Collins, W. J. and Margo, R. A. (2007) The Economic Aftermath of the 1960s Riots in American Cities: Evidence from Property Values. *Journal of Economic History* 67(4): 849–83.

Collins, W. J., Margo, R. A., Vigdor, J. and Myers, D. (2004) The Labor Market Effects of the 1960s Riots. NBER Working Paper No. 10243.

Colyer, C. J. (2015) W. I. Thomas and the Forgotten Four Wishes: A Case Study in the Sociology of Ideas. *The American Sociologist* 46(2): 248–68.

Cottle, S. (1990) Television Coverage of the Inner City: An examination of the professional journalist's practices and production domain and their impact upon the public portrayal of the problems and issues of the inner city. PhD thesis, Mass Communications, University of Leicester.

CovertAction Information Bulletin (1993) Uprising and Repression in L.A.: An Interview with Mike Davis, in R. Gooding-Williams (ed.), *Reading Rodney King/Reading Urban Uprising.* New York: Routledge.

Crippen, T. and Lopreato, J. (1989) Pareto's 'The Transformation of Democracy' and Modern Political Theory. *Revue Européenne des Sciences Sociales* 27(83): 47–86.

Cromwell, P., Dunham, R., Akers, R. and Lanza-Kaduce, L. (1995) Routine Activities and Social Control in the Aftermath of a Natural Catastrophe. *European Journal on Criminal Policy and Research* 3(3): 56–69.

Crossley, N. and Krinsky, J. (2015) (eds) *Social Networks and Social Movements: Contentious Connections.* London: Routledge.

Cyr, K., Ricciardelli, R. and Spencer, D. (2020) Militarization of Police: A Comparison of Police Paramilitary Units in Canada and the United States. *International Journal of Police Science & Management* 22(2): 137–47.

Currie, E. and Skolnick, J. H. (1970) A Critical Note on Conceptions of Collective Behavior. *Annals of the American Academy of Political and Social Science* 391: 34–45.

Davis, M. (1992) Burning All Illusions in LA, in D. Hazen (ed.), *Inside the L.A. Riots: What Really Happened – and Why It Will Happen Again*. New York: Institute for Alternative Journalism.

Davis, M. (1993a) Who Killed Los Angeles? A Political Autopsy. *New Left Review* 1(199).

Davis, M. (1993b) Who Killed Los Angeles? Part Two: The Verdict Is Given. *New Left Review* 2(97).

Davis, M. and Wiener, J. (2020) *Set the Night on Fire: L.A. in the Sixties*. New York: Verso.

de Haan, W. (2008) Violence as an Essentially Contested Concept, in S. Body-Gendrot and P. Spierenberg (eds), *Violence in Europe*. New York: Springer.

de Haan, W. and Loader, I. (2002) On the Emotions of Crime, Punishment and Social Control. *Theoretical Criminology* 6(3): 243–53.

Delehanty, C., Mewhirter, J., Welch, R. and Wilks, J. (2017) Militarization and Police Violence: The Case of the 1033 Program. *Research & Politics* 4(2).

della Porta, D. (1995) Social Movements and the State: Thoughts on the Policing of Protest. EUI Working Paper No. 95/13. Florence: European University Institute.

della Porta, D. (2025) Rethinking Social Movements in Intense Times. *Mobilization* 3(1): 1–12.

della Porta, D., Andretta, M., Mosca, L. and Reiter, H. (2006) *Globalization from Below: Transnational Activists and Protest Networks*. Minneapolis, MN: University of Minnesota Press.

della Porta, D. and Diani, M. (1999) *Social Movements: An Introduction*. Oxford: Blackwell.

della Porta, D. and Fillieule, O. (2004) 'Policing Social Protest', in D. A. Snow, S. A. Soule and H. Kriesi (eds), *The Blackwell Companion to Social Movements*. Malden, MA: Blackwell.

della Porta, D., Peterson, A. and Reiter, H. (eds) (2006) *The Policing of Transnational Protest*. London: Routledge.

della Porta, D. and Reiter, H. (eds) (1998) *Policing Protest*. Minneapolis, MN: University of Minnesota Press.

della Porta, D. and Reiter, H. (2006a) The Policing of Global Protest: The G8 at Genoa and Its Aftermath, in D. della Porta, A. Peterson and H. Reiter (eds), *The Policing of Transnational Protest*. London: Routledge.

della Porta, D. and Reiter, H. (2006b) The Policing of Transnational Protest: A Conclusion, in D. della Porta, A. Peterson and H. Reiter (eds), *The Policing of Transnational Protest*. London: Routledge.

Dikec, M. (2017) *Urban Rage: The Revolt of the Excluded*. New Haven, CT: Yale University Press.

Dillon, D. and Fanning, B. (2015) Tottenham after the Riots: The Chimera of Community and the Property-Led Regeneration of 'Broken Britain'. *Critical Social Policy* 35(2): 188–206.

DiPasquale, D. and Glaeser, E. L. (1998) The Los Angeles Riot and the Economics of Urban Unrest. *Journal of Urban Economics* 43(1): 52–78.

Douglas, M. (1966) *Purity and Danger: An Analysis of the Concepts of Pollution and Taboo*. London: Routledge.

Downes, D. (2001) The 'Macho' Penal Economy: Mass Incarceration in the United States – A European Perspective. *Punishment and Society* 3(1): 61–80.

Downes, D. and Newburn, T. (2023) *The Official History of Criminal Justice in England and Wales: Vol. IV, The Politics of Law and Order*. London: Routledge.

Downs, D. (2011) The Evolution of Flash Mobs from Pranks to Crime and Revolution. *San Francisco Examiner*. https://www.sfexaminer.com/news/the-evolution-of-flash-mobs-from-pranks-to-crime-and-revolution/article_80af53fa-a43f-5d1a-ad37-c0ba281a926a.html

Drochon, H. (2020) Robert Michels, the Iron Law of Oligarchy and Dynamic Democracy. *Constellations* 27(2): 185–98.

Drury, J. and Reicher, S. (1999) The Intergroup Dynamics of Collective Empowerment: Substantiating the Social Identity Model of Crowd Behavior. *Group Processes and Intergroup Relations* 2(4): 381–402.

Drury, J., Stott, C., Ball, R. et al. (2019) A Social Identity Model of Riot Diffusion: From Injustice to Empowerment in the 2011 London Riots. *European Journal of Social Psychology* 50(3): 646–61.

Drury, J., Stott, C., Ball, R. et al. (2022) How Riots Spread between Cities: Introducing the Police Pathway. *Political Psychology* 43(4): 651–69.

Duberman, M. (2019) *Stonewall: The Definitive Story of the LGBTQ Rights Uprising that Changed America*. New York: Plume.

Duberman, M. and Kopkind, A. (1993) The Night They Raided Stonewall. *Grand Street* 44: 120–47.

Durkheim, E. (1947 [1893]) *The Division of Labour in Society*. New York: Free Press.

Durkheim, E. (1964 [1912]) *The Elementary Forms of Religious Life*. New York: Free Press.

Dynes, R. and Quarantelli, E. L. (1968) What Looting in Civil Disturbances Really Means. *Trans-action* (May): 9–14.

Eisenberg, A. K. (2023) Policing the Danger Narrative. *Journal of Criminal Law and Criminology* 113(3): 473–540.

Elias, N. (1982) *The Civilizing Process: Vol. 2, State Formation and Civilization*. Oxford: Blackwell.

Elias, N. and Dunning, E. (1986) *Quest for Excitement: Sport and Leisure in the Civilizing Process*. Oxford: Blackwell.

Elias, N. and Scotson, J. L. (1965) *The Established and the Outsiders*. London: Frank Cass.

Ellsworth, S. (1982) *Death in a Promised Land: The Tulsa Race Riot of 1921*. Baton Rouge, LA: Louisiana State University Press.

Else, D. H. (2014) The '1033 Program', Department of Defense Support to Law Enforcement. Congressional Research Service 7-5700 www.crs.gov R43701.

Epstein, R., Guenot, M. and Jobard, F. (2023) Émeutes urbaines, sciences sociales et action publique. Mouvements et stagnations dans la politique de la ville et les politiques de sécurité. *Zilsel* 13(2): 11–22.

Ericson, R. and Haggerty, K. (1997) *Policing the Risk Society*. Oxford: Clarendon Press.

Fassin, D. (2013) *Enforcing Order: An Ethnography of Urban Policing*. Cambridge: Polity.

Feagin, J. R. and Hahn, H. (1973) *Ghetto Revolts: The Politics of Violence in American Cities*. New York: Macmillan.

Fernandes, S. (2017) *Curated Stories: The Uses and Misuses of Storytelling*. New York: Oxford University Press.

Ferrell, J. (2010) Cultural Criminology: The Loose Can[n]on, in E. McLaughlin and T. Newburn (eds), *The Sage Handbook of Criminological Theory*. London: Sage.

Field, D. and Southgate, P. (1982) *Public Disorder: A Review of Research and a Study in One Inner City Area*. London: HMSO.

Fine, S. (1987) Rioters and Judges: The Response of the Criminal Justice System to the Detroit Riot of 1967. *Wayne Law Review* 33(5): 1723–64.

Fine, S. (2007) *Violence in the Model City: The Cavanagh Administration, Race Relations, and the Detroit Riot of 1967*. East Lansing, MI: Michigan State University Press.

Flamm, M. W. (2007) *Law and Order: Street Crime, Civil Unrest, and the Crisis of Liberalism in the 1960s*. New York: Columbia University Press.

Fogelson, R. M. (1967) White on Black: A Critique of the McCone Commission Report on the Los Angeles Riots. *Political Science Quarterly* 82(3): 337–67.

Fogelson, R. M. (1968) From Resentment to Confrontation: The Police, the Negroes, and the Outbreak of the Nineteen-Sixties Riots. *Political Science Quarterly* 83(2): 217–47.

Fogelson, R. M. (1970) Violence and Grievances: Reflections on the 1960s Riots. *Journal of Social Issues* 26(1): 141–63.

Fogelson, R. M., Black, G. S. and Lipsky, M. (1969) Review Symposium on the National Advisory Commission on Civil Disorders. *American Political Science Review* 63(4): 1269–81.

Francis, M. M. and Wright-Rigueur, L. (2021) Black Lives Matter in Historical Perspective. *Annual Review of Law and Social Science* 17: 441–58.

Fraser, A. (2013) Street Habitus: Gangs, Territorialism and Social Change in Glasgow. *Journal of Youth Studies* 16(8): 970–85.

Fraser, I., Billingham, L., Gillon, F., Irwin-Rogers, K., McVie, S. and Newburn, T. (2026) *The Public Health Approach to Violence Reduction: Stories, Movements, and Hope*. Oxford: Clarendon Press.

Fuchs, C. (2013) Critique of the Political Economy of Informational Capitalism and Social Media, in C. Fuchs and M. Sandoval (eds), *Critique, Social Media and the Information Society*. New York: Routledge.

Gaherity, C. and Birch, P. (2022) A Criminologically Informed Examination of Looting Behaviour during Natural Disaster Incidents. *Safer Communities* 21(1): 19–30.

Galtung, J. (1990) Cultural Violence. *Journal of Peace Research* 27(3): 291–305.

Gamson, W. A. (1975) *The Strategy of Social Protest*. Homewood, IL: Dorsey Press.

Garland, D. (2001) Introduction: The Meaning of Mass Imprisonment. *Punishment and Society* 3(1): 5–7.

Garland, D. (2025a) *Law and Order Leviathan: America's Extraordinary Regime of Policing and Punishment*. Princeton, NJ: Princeton University Press.

Garland, D. (2025b) America's Extraordinary Penal State: A Structural Explanation. *Punishment and Society* 27(3): 421–48.

Garrow, D. J. (1978) *Protest at Selma: Martin Luther King, Jr., and the Voting Rights Act of 1965*. New Haven, CT: Yale University Press.

Gerbaudo, P. (2012) *Tweets and the Streets: Social Media and Contemporary Activism*. London: Pluto.

Gerell, M. (2017) Collective Efficacy and Arson: The Case of Malmö. *Journal of Scandinavian Studies in Criminology and Crime Prevention* 18(1): 35–51.

Gilje, P. A. (1999) *Rioting in America*. Bloomington: Indiana University Press.

Gillham, P. F. (2011) Securitizing America: Strategic Incapacitation and the Policing of Protest since the 11 September 2001 Terrorist Attacks. *Sociology Compass* 5(7): 636–52.

Gillham, P. F. and Marx, G. T. (2018) Changes in the Policing of Civil Disorders since the Kerner Report: The Police Response to Ferguson, August 2014, and Some Implications for the Twenty-First Century. *RSF: The Russell Sage Foundation Journal of the Social Sciences* 4(6): 122–43.

Gitlin, T. (2013) Occupy's Predicament: The Moment and the Prospects for the Movement. *British Journal of Sociology* 64(1): 3–25.

Gladwell, M. (2006) *Blink: The Power of Thinking without Thinking*. New York: Little, Brown.

Gladwell, M. (2010) Small Change. *The New Yorker*, 27 September.

Glenn, C. L. (2015) Activism or 'Slacktivism'? Digital Media and Organizing for Social Change. *Communication Teacher* 29(2): 81–5.

Goffman, A. (2014) *On the Run: Fugitive Life in an American City*. Chicago: University of Chicago Press.

Gooden, S. T. and Myers, S. L., Jr (2018) The Kerner Commission Report Fifty Years Later: Revisiting the American Dream. *RSF: The Russell Sage Foundation Journal of the Social Sciences* 4(6): 1–17.

Goodwin, J., Jasper, J. and Polletta, F. (2000) The Return of the Repressed: The Fall and Rise of Emotions in Social Movement Theory. *Mobilization: An International Journal* 5(1): 65–83.

Goodwin, J., Jasper, J. and Polletta, F. (eds) (2001) *Passionate Politics: Emotions and Social Movements*. Chicago: University of Chicago Press.

Goodwin, J., Jasper, J. and Polletta, F. (2004) Emotional Dimensions of Social Movements, in D. A. Snow, S. A. Soule and H. Kriesi (eds), *The Blackwell Companion to Social Movements*. Malden, MA: Blackwell.

Grace, T. M. (2016) *Kent State: Death and Dissent in the Long Sixties*. Amherst and Boston: University of Massachusetts Press.

Graeber, D. (2011) Occupy Wall Street's Anarchist Roots. *Al Jazeera*. https://www.aljazeera.com/opinions/2011/11/30/occupy-wall-streets-anarchist-roots

Graeber, D. and Hui, Y. (2014) From Occupy Wall Street to Occupy Central: The Case of Hong Kong. *Los Angeles Review of Books*, 14 October. http://lareviewofbooks.org/essay/occupy-central-the-case-of-hong-kong

Graham, H. D. (1980) On Riots and Riot Commissions: Civil Disorders in the 1960s. *Public Historian* 2(4): 7–27.

Graham, S. (2010) *Cities under Siege: The New Military Urbanism*. London: Verso.

Greenberg, C. (1992) The Politics of Disorder: Reexamining Harlem's Riots of 1935 and 1943. *Journal of Urban History* 18(4): 395–441.

Greer, C. and McLaughlin, E. (2010) We Predict a Riot? Public Order Policing, New Media Environments and the Rise of the Citizen Journalist. *British Journal of Criminology* 50(6): 1041–59.

Guardian/LSE (2011) *Reading the Riots: Investigating England's Summer of Disorder*. London: Guardian/LSE.

Hagan, J., McCarthy, B. and Herda, D. (2022) *Chicago's Reckoning: Racism, Politics and the Deep History of Policing in an American City*. New York: Oxford University Press.

Hall, S. (1997) The Spectacle of the 'Other', in S. Hall (ed.), *Representation: Cultural Representations and Signifying Practices*. London: Sage in association with the Open University.

Hall, S. (1999) From Scarman to Stephen Lawrence. *History Workshop Journal* 48: 187–97.

Hall, S., Critcher, C., Jefferson, T., Clarke, J. and Roberts, B. (1978) *Policing the Crisis: Mugging, the State and Law and Order*. London: Macmillan.

Halloran, J. D., Elliott, P. and Murdock, G. (1970) *Demonstrations and Communication: A Case Study*. Harmondsworth: Penguin.

Hannerz, U. (1969) *Soulside: Inquiries into Ghetto Culture and Community*. New York: Columbia University Press.

Hansson, U. (2005) *Troubled Youth? Young People, Violence and Disorder in Northern Ireland*. Belfast: Institute for Conflict Research.

Harris, D. A. (2019) How Fear Shapes Policing in the US, in T. R. Lave and E. J. Miller (eds), *The Cambridge Handbook of Policing in the United States*. New York: Cambridge University Press.

Harrison, M. (1988) *Crowds and History: Mass Phenomena in English Towns, 1790–1835*. Cambridge: Cambridge University Press.

Hayton, R. (2012). Fixing Broken Britain, in T. Heppell and D. Seawright (eds), *Cameron and the Conservatives*. Basingstoke: Palgrave: Macmillan.

Haywood, I. (2013) The Gordon Riots of 1780: London in Flames, a Nation in Ruins. https://www.gresham.ac.uk/watch-now/gordon-riots-1780-london-flames-nation-ruins

Heering, S. L., Shobat, T., Lerman, Y. and Danon, Y. L. (1992) The Epidemiology of Injuries Sustained by Israeli Troops during the Unrest in the Territories Administered by Israel, 1987–89. *Israel Journal of Medical Sciences* 28(6): 341–4.

Hibbert, C. (2004 [1958]) *King Mob*. Stroud: Sutton.

Hinds-Aldrich, M. (2009) The Seductions of Arson: Ritualized Political Violence and the Revelry of Arson. *Journal of Criminal Justice and Popular Culture* 16(1): 103–35.

Hinton, E. (2016) *From the War on Poverty to the War on Crime: The Making of Mass Incarceration in America*. Cambridge, MA: Harvard University Press.

Hinton, E. (2021) *America on Fire: The Untold History of Police Violence and Black Rebellion since the 1960s*. London: William Collins.

Ho, L. K.-K. (2020) Rethinking Police Legitimacy in Postcolonial Hong Kong: Paramilitary Policing in Protest Management. *Policing: A Journal of Policy and Practice* 14(4): 1015–33.

Hobsbawm, E. (1971) *Primitive Rebels: Studies in Archaic Forms of Social Movement in the 19th and 20th Centuries*, 3rd edn. Manchester: Manchester University Press.

Hobsbawm, E. (1998) On History from Below, in E. Hobsbawm (ed.), *On History*. London: Abacus.

Hobsbawm, E. and Rudé, G. (1969) *Captain Swing*. London: Lawrence and Wishart.

Hohl, K., Stanko, E. A. and Newburn, T. (2012) The Effect of the 2011 London Disorder on Public Opinion of Police and Attitudes towards Crime, Disorder, and Sentencing. *Policing: A Journal of Policy and Practice* 7(1): 12–20.

Holdaway, S. (1983) *Inside the British Police: A Force at Work*. Oxford: Blackwell.

Holton, R. (1978) The Crowd in History: Some Problems of Theory and Method. *Social History* 3(2): 219–33.

Home Affairs Committee (2011) *Policing Large Scale Disorder: Lessons from the Disturbances of August 2011*. London: The Stationery Office (HC 1456-I).

Home Affairs Committee (2025) *Police Response to the 2024 Summer Disorder*. London: House of Commons (HC 381).

Horley, J. and Bowlby, D. (2011) Theory, Research, and Intervention with Arsonists. *Aggression and Violent Behavior* 16(3): 241–9.

Horne, G. (1997) *Fire This Time: The Watts Uprising and the 1960s*. New York: Da Capo Press.

House of Commons Library (2022) *Police Powers: Stop and Search*. Research Briefing, House of Commons Library.

Huizinga, J. (1949) *Homo Ludens: A Study of the Play-Element in Culture*. London: Routledge and Kegan Paul.

Hunt, D. M. (1997) *Screening the Los Angeles 'Riots': Race, Seeing, and Resistance*. Cambridge: Cambridge University Press.

IPCC (Independent Police Complaints Council) (2020). *A Thematic Study by the IPCC on the Public Order Events Arising from the Fugitive Offenders Bill since June 2019 and the Police Actions in Response*. Hong Kong: IPCC.

Ismail, N. and Ardalan-Raikes, A. (2025) United against Hate: Lessons from the Far-Right Riots in England. *Justice, Power and Resistance* 8(2): 228—36.

Jackson, J., Huq, A. Z., Bradford, B. and Tyler, T. R. (2013) Monopolizing Force? Police Legitimacy and Public Attitudes toward the Acceptability of Violence. *Psychology, Public Policy, and Law* 19(4): 479–97.

Jacobs, P. (1971) The McCone Commission, in A. Platt (ed.), *The Politics of Riot Commissions, 1917–1970: A Collection of Official Reports and Critical Essays*. New York: Macmillan.

James, W. (2000 [1905]) *Pragmatism and Other Writings*. London: Penguin.

Janowitz, M. (1968) *Social Control of Escalated Riots*. Chicago: University of Chicago, Center for Policy Study.

Jarman, N. and O'Halloran, C. (2001) Recreational Rioting: Young People, Interface Areas and Violence. *Child Care in Practice* 7(1): 2–16.

Jasper, J. M. (2018) *The Emotions of Protest*. Chicago: University of Chicago Press.

Jefferson, T. (1987) Beyond Paramilitarism. *British Journal of Criminology* 27(1): 47–53.

Jefferson, T. (1993) Pondering Paramilitarism: A Question of Standpoints? *British Journal of Criminology* 33(3): 374–81.

Jobard, F. (2008) The 2005 French Urban Unrests: Data-Based Interpretations. *Sociology Compass* 2(4): 1287–1302.

Jobard, F. (2009) Rioting as a Political Tool: The 2005 Riots in France. *Howard Journal of Criminal Justice* 48(3): 235–44.

Jobard, F. (2014) Riots in France: Political, Proto-Political and Anti-Political Turmoils?, in D. Pritchard and F. Pakes (eds), *Riot, Unrest and Protest on the Global Stage*. Basingstoke: Palgrave Macmillan.

Johnson, C. G. (2024) *After Black Lives Matter: Policing and Anti-Capitalist Struggle*. London: Verso.

Johnson, P. B., Sears, D. O. and McConahay, J. B. (1971) Black Invisibility, the Press, and the Los Angeles Riot. *American Journal of Sociology* 76(4): 698–721.

Johnson, T. J. (1972) Protest: Tradition and Change. *Economy and Society* 1(2): 164–93.

Joshua, H. and Wallace, T. (1983) *To Ride the Storm: The 1980 Bristol 'Riot' and the State*. London: Heinemann.

Kaminski, M. E. (2013) Incitement to Riot in the Age of Flash Mobs. *University of Cincinnati Law Review* 81(1): art. 1.

Katz, J. (1988). *Seductions of Crime: Moral and Sensual Attractions in Doing Evil*. New York: Basic Books.

Katz, J. (1999) *How Emotions Work*. Chicago: University of Chicago Press.

Katz, J. (2002) Start here: Social Ontology and Research Strategy. *Theoretical Criminology* 6(3): 255–78.

Katz, J. (2016) Culture within and Culture about Crime: The Case of the 'Rodney King Riots'. *Crime, Media, Culture* 12(2): 233–51.

Katz, J. (2019) Hot Potato Criminology: Ethnographers and the Shame of Poor People's Crimes. *Annual Review of Criminology* 2: 21–52.

Kawalerowicz, J. and Biggs, M. (2015) Anarchy in the UK: Economic Deprivation, Social Disorganization, and Political Grievances in the London Riot of 2011. *Social Forces* 94(2): 673–98.

Keith, M. (1993) *Race, Riots and Policing: Lore and Disorder in a Multi-Racist Society*. London: UCL Press.

Kelly, W. R. and Snyder, D. (1980) Racial Violence and Socioeconomic Changes among Blacks in the United States. *Social Forces* 58(3): 739–60.

Kerner Commission (1968) *Report of the National Advisory Commission on Civil Disorders*. New York: Bantam Books.

Khamis, S. and Vaughn, K. (2011) Cyberactivism in the Egyptian Revolution: How Civic Engagement and Citizen Journalism Tilted the Balance. *Arab Media and Society* 14(3).

King, M. (2013) Birmingham Revisited – Causal Differences between the Riots of 2011 and 2005? *Policing and Society* 23(1): 26–45.

King, M. and Waddington, D. (2005) Flashpoints Revisited: A Critical Application to the Policing of Anti-Globalization Protest. *Policing and Society* 15(3): 255–82.

King, M. and Waddington, D. (2006) The Policing of Transnational Protest in Canada, in D. della Porta, A. Peterson and H. Reiter (eds), *The Policing of Transnational Protest*. Aldershot: Ashgate.

King, M. L., Jr (2018) *Why We Can't Wait*. London: Penguin.

Kingdon, J. W. (1984) *Agendas, Alternatives, and Public Policies*. Boston: Little, Brown.

Kirk, D. S. and Wakefield, S. (2018) Collateral Consequences of Punishment: A Critical Review and Path Forward. *Annual Review of Criminology* 1: 171–94.

Klein, N. (2005) *Fences and Windows: Dispatches from the Front Lines of the Globalization Debate*. London: Harper Perennial.

Koff, H. and Duprez, D. (2009) The 2005 Riots in France: The International Impact of Domestic Violence. *Journal of Ethnic and Migration Studies* 35(5): 713–30.

Kohler-Hausmann, I. (2013) Misdemeanor Justice: Control without Conviction. *American Journal of Sociology* 119(2): 351–93.

Kopkind, A. (1971) White on Black: The Riot Commission and the Rhetoric of Reform, in A. Platt (ed.), *The Politics of Riot Commissions, 1917–1970*. New York: Macmillan.

Kusch, F. (2008) *Battleground Chicago: The Police and the 1968 Democratic National Convention*. Chicago: University of Chicago Press.

Lacey, N., Soskice, D. and Hope, D. (2018) Understanding the Determinants of Penal Policy: Crime, Culture, and Comparative Political Economy. *Annual Review of Criminology* 1: 195–217.

Lagrange, H. (2008) Riots, Urban Segregation, and Political Alienation in France. *Revue Française de Science Politique* 58(3): 377–401.

Lagrange, H. (2009) The French Riots and Urban Segregation, in D. Waddington, F. Jobard and M. King (eds), *Rioting in the UK and France: A Comparative Analysis*. Cullompton: Willan.

Lang, G. E. and Lang, K. (1955) The Inferential Structure of Political Communications: A Study in Unwitting Bias. *Public Opinion Quarterly* 19(2): 168–83.

Lapeyronnie, D. (2009) Primitive Rebellion in the French *Banlieues*: On the Fall 2005 Riots, in C. Tshimanga, D. Gondola and P. J. Bloom (eds), *Frenchness and the African Diaspora: Identity and Uprising in Contemporary France*. Bloomington: Indiana University Press.

Le Bon, G. (1952 [1895]) *The Crowd: A Study of the Popular Mind*. London: Ernest Benn.

Le Roy Ladurie, E. (1980) *Carnival: A People's Uprising at Romans, 1579–1580*. London: Scolar Press.

Leach, E. E. (1986) Mastering the Crowd: Collective Behavior and Mass Society in American Social Thought 1917–1939. *American Studies* 27(1): 99–114.

Lee, C. K. (2019) Take Back Our Future: An Eventful Sociology of the Hong Kong Umbrella Movement, in C. K. Lee and M. Sing (eds), *Take Back Our Future: An Eventful Sociology of the Hong Kong Umbrella Movement*. Ithaca, NY: ILR Press.

Lee, C. K. and Sing, M. (2019) *Take Back Our Future: An Eventful Sociology of the Hong Kong Umbrella Movement*. Ithaca, NY: ILR Press.

Lee, F. L. F. and Chan, J. M. (2018) *Media and Protest Logics in the Digital Era: The Umbrella Movement in Hong Kong*. New York: Oxford University Press.

Leitsch, D. (2019) 'The Hairpin Drop Heard around the World', in New York Public Library (ed.), *The Stonewall Reader*. New York: Penguin.

Lerman, A. E. and Weaver, V. M. (2014) *Arresting Citizenship: The Democratic Consequences of American Crime Control*. Chicago: University of Chicago Press.

Levy, P. (2018) *The Great Uprising: Race Riots in Urban America during the 1960s*. New York: Cambridge University Press.

Lewis, P., Ball, J. and Taylor, M. (2011) Archbishop of Canterbury Says Riots Will Return Unless We Reach Out to Young, *Guardian*, 5 December.

Lewis, P., Newburn, T., Taylor, M. and Ball, J. (2011) Rioters Say Anger with Police Fuelled Summer Unrest. *Guardian*. http://www.theguardian.com/uk/2011/dec/05/anger-police-fuelled-riots-study

Lightowlers, C. and Quirk, H. (2015) The 2011 English 'Riots': Prosecutorial Zeal and Judicial Abandon. *British Journal of Criminology* 55(1): 65–85.

Linke, U. (2010) Fortress Europe: Globalization, Militarization and the Policing of Interior Borderlands. *TOPIA: Canadian Journal of Cultural Studies* 23–4: 100–20.

Lo, S. S.-H. (2016). *The Politics of Policing in Greater China*. New York: Palgrave Macmillan.

Los Angeles Times (1992) *Understanding the Riots: Los Angeles Before and After the Rodney King Case*. Los Angeles: Los Angeles Times.

Lowery, W. (2017) *'They Can't Kill Us All': The Story of Black Lives Matter*. London: Penguin.

Lynd, S. (2014) *Doing History from the Bottom Up: On E. P. Thompson, Howard Zinn, and Rebuilding the Labor Movement from Below*. Chicago: Haymarket Books.

Lyng, S. (1990) Edgework: A Social Psychological Analysis of Voluntary Risk Taking. *American Journal of Sociology* 95(4): 851–86.

Ma, S. and Weiss, J. C. (2023) Strong State or Vulnerable Homeland: How Chinese State Media Sought to Combat Democratic Diffusion during the 2019 Hong Kong Protests. *Journal of Contemporary China* 32(139): 106–22.

Mac Ginty, R. (2004) Looting in the Context of Violent Conflict: A Conceptualisation and Typology. *Third World Quarterly* 25(5): 857–70.

Macy, L. (2024) A War on Resistance: Police Repression and Criminalization of Land Defense Movements. *Tapestries: Interwoven Voices of Local and Global Identities* 13(1): art. 8.

Mabrouk, M. (2011) A Revolution for Dignity and Freedom: Preliminary Observations on the Social and Cultural Background to the Tunisian Revolution. *Journal of North African Studies* 16(4): 625–35.

Mailer, N. (1968) *Miami and the Siege of Chicago: An Informal History of the American Political Conventions of 1968*. London: Weidenfeld and Nicolson.

Mann, L. (1974) Simulation of a Protest Demonstration: Its Effect on Attitudes toward Police and Demonstrators. *Australian Psychologist* 9(3): 6–18.

Marks, M. A. (2002) *Los Angeles a Decade after the 1992 Civil Disturbances*. Los Angeles: Loyola Marymount University, Center for the Study of Los Angeles.

Marks, M. A., Barreto, M. A. and Woods, N. D. (2004). Race and Racial Attitudes a Decade after the 1992 Los Angeles Riots. *Urban Affairs Review* 40(1): 3–18.

Marsh, P., Rosser, E. and Harré, R. (1978) *The Rules of Disorder*. London: Routledge & Kegan Paul.

Marx, G. T. (1970) Issueless Riots. *Annals of the American Academy of Political and Social Science* 391(1): 21–33.

Mason, P. (2012) *Why It's Kicking Off Everywhere: The New Global Revolutions*. London: Verso.

Masotti, L. H. and Corsi, J. R. (1969) *Shoot-Out in Cleveland*. New York: Bantam Books.

Matheson, V. A. and Baade, R. A. (2004) Race and Riots: A Note on the Economic Impact of the Rodney King Riots. *Urban Studies* 41(13): 2691–6.

Matza, D. (1964) *Delinquency and Drift*. New York: Wiley.

Mauer, M. and Huling, T. (1995) *Young Black Americans and the Criminal Justice System: Five Years Later*. Washington, DC: The Sentencing Project.

Mayor's Office for London (2012) *It Took Another Riot*. London: Mayor's Office.

McAdam, D. (1983) Tactical Innovation and the Pace of Insurgency. *American Sociological Review* 48(6): 735–54.

McCone Commission (1965) *Violence in the City: An End or a Beginning?* Los Angeles: Governor's Commission on the Los Angeles Riots.

McPhail, C. (1991) *The Myth of the Madding Crowd*. New York: Aldine de Gruyter.

McPhail, C., Schweingruber, D. and McCarthy, J. (1998) Policing Protest in the United States: 1960–1995, in D. della Porta and H. Reiter (eds), *Policing Protest*. Minneapolis, MN: University of Minnesota Press.

McPhail, C. and Wohlstein, R. T. (1983) Individual and Collective Behaviors within Gatherings, Demonstrations, and Riots. *Annual Review of Sociology* 9: 579–600.

McWhirter, L. (1982) Northern Irish Children's Conceptions of Violent Crime. *Howard Journal of Criminal Justice* 21(1–3): 167–77.

Mead, D. (2012) Kettling Comes to the Boil before the Strasbourg Court: Is it a Deprivation of Liberty to Contain Protesters *En Masse*? *Cambridge Law Journal* 71(3): 472–5.

Meares, T. L. (2015) Programming Errors: Understanding the Constitutionality of Stop-and-Frisk as a Program, Not an Incident. *University of Chicago Law Review* 82(1): 159–79.

Messer, C. M. (2021) *The 1921 Tulsa Race Massacre: Crafting a Legacy*. Cham: Palgrave Macmillan.

Messer, C. M. and Bell, P. A. (2010) Mass Media and Governmental Framing of Riots: The Case of Tulsa, 1921. *Journal of Black Studies* 40(5): 851–70.

Metropolitan Police Service (2012) *Four Days in August*. London: Metropolitan Police.

Milkman, R., Luce, S. and Lewis, P. (2012) *Changing the Subject: A Bottom-up Account of Occupy Wall Street in New York City*. New York: City University of New York.

Miller, A. (2001) The Los Angeles Riots: A Study in Crisis Paralysis. *Journal of Contingencies and Crisis Management* 9(4): 179–248.

Miller, R. J. and Stuart, F. (2017) Carceral Citizenship: Race, Rights and Responsibility in the Age of Mass Supervision. *Theoretical Criminology* 21(4): 532–48.

Ministry of Justice (2011) *Statistical Bulletin on the Public Disorder of 6th to 9th August 2011: October Update.* London: Ministry of Justice.

Ministry of Justice (2012) *Statistical Bulletin on the Public Disorder of 6th to 9th August 2011: February 2012 Update.* London: Ministry of Justice.

Moran, M. and Waddington, D. (2016) *Riots: An International Comparison.* London: Palgrave Macmillan.

Moscovici, S. (1985) *The Age of the Crowd.* Cambridge: Cambridge University Press.

Moxon, D. (2011) Consumer Culture and the 2011 'Riots'. *Sociological Research Online* 16(4): 184–7.

Mucchielli, L. (2009) Autumn 2005: A Review of the Most Important Riot in the History of French Contemporary Society. *Journal of Ethnic and Migration Studies* 35(5): 731–51.

Mumford, K. (2007) *Newark: A History of Race, Rights, and Riots in America.* New York: New York University Press.

Murray, D. (2020) *The Madness of Crowds: Gender, Race and Identity.* London: Bloomsbury Continuum.

Murray, G. (2006) France: The Riots and the Republic. *Race and Class* 47(4): 26–45.

Myers, D. J. (1997). Racial Rioting in the 1960s: An Event History Analysis of Local Conditions. *American Sociological Review* 62(1): 94–112.

Nassauer, A. (2016). From Peaceful Marches to Violent Clashes: A Micro-situational Analysis. *Social Movement Studies* 15(5): 515–30.

Nassauer, A. (2019) *Situational Breakdowns: Understanding Protest Violence and Other Surprising Outcomes.* New York: Oxford University Press.

National Advisory Commission on Civil Disorders (1968) *Report of the National Advisory Commission on Civil Disorders.* New York: Bantam Books.

Newburn, T. (2008) 'Tough on Crime: Penal Policy in England and Wales. *Crime and Justice* 36: 425–70.

Newburn, T. (2015) The 2011 England Riots in Recent Historical Perspective. *British Journal of Criminology* 55(1): 39–64.

Newburn, T. (2016a), The 2011 England Riots in European Context: A Framework for Understanding the 'Life-Cycle' of Riots. *European Journal of Criminology* 13(5): 540–55.

Newburn, T. (2016b) Reflections on Why Riots Don't Happen. *Theoretical Criminology* 20(2): 125–44.

Newburn, T. (2020) The 2019 Hong Kong Protests: A Role for Historical Sociology. *Policing: A Journal of Policy and Practice* 14(4): 846–51.

Newburn, T. (2021) The Causes and Consequences of Urban Riot and Unrest. *Annual Review of Criminology* 4: 53–73.

Newburn, T. (2022) The Inevitable Fallibility of Policing. *Policing and Society* 32(3): 434–50.

Newburn, T. (2024) *The Official History of Criminal Justice in England and Wales: Vol. V, Policing Post-War Britain: Plus Ça Change.* London: Routledge.

Newburn, T., Cooper, K., Deacon, R. and Diski, R. (2015) Shopping for Free? Looting, Consumerism and the 2011 Riots. *British Journal of Criminology* 55(5): 987–1004.

Newburn, T., Deacon, R., Diski, B., Cooper, K., Grant, M. and Burch, A. (2018) 'The Best Three Days of My Life': Pleasure, Power and Alienation in the 2011 Riots. *Crime, Media, Culture* 14(1): 41–59.

Newburn, T., Diski, R., Cooper, K., Deacon, R., Burch, A. and Grant, M. (2018) 'The Biggest Gang'? Police and People in the 2011 England Riots. *Policing and Society* 28(2): 205–22.

Newburn, T. and Jones, T. (2007) Symbolizing Crime Control: Reflections on Zero Tolerance. *Theoretical Criminology* 11(2): 221–43.

Newburn, T., Jones, T. and Blaustein, J. (2018) Framing the 2011 England Riots: Understanding the Political and Policy Response. *Howard Journal of Criminal Justice* 57(3): 339–62.

Ng, M. H. K. and Wong, J. D. (eds) (2017) *Civil Unrest and Governance in Hong Kong: Law and Order from Historical and Cultural Perspectives.* London: Routledge.

Oh, S.-K. and Hudson, J. (2017) Framing and Reframing the 1992 LA Riots: A Study of Minority Issues Framing by the *Los Angeles Times* and Its Readers. *Revista de Comunicacion* 16(2): 123–46.

Olzak, S., Shanahan, S. and McEneaney, E. H. (1996) Poverty, Segregation, and Race Riots: 1960 to 1993. *American Sociological Review* 61(4): 590–613.

Paine, T. (1951) *The Rights of Man.* New York: E. P. Dutton.

Pang, L. (2020) *The Appearing Demos: Hong Kong during and after the Umbrella Movement.* Ann Arbor, MI: University of Michigan Press.

Park, R. E. and Burgess, E. W. (1921) *Introduction to the Science of Sociology.* Chicago: University of Chicago Press.

Pemberton, S. (2008) Demystifying Deaths in Police Custody: Challenging State Talk. *Social and Legal Studies* 17(2): 237–62.

Petersilia, J. and Abrahamse, A. (1994) A Profile of Those Arrested, in M. Baldassare (ed.), *The Los Angeles Riots: Lessons for the Urban Future.* Boulder, Co: Westview.

Phelps, M. (2024) *The Minneapolis Reckoning: Race, Violence, and the Politics of Policing in America.* Princeton, NJ: Princeton University Press.

Pina-Sánchez, J., Lightowlers, C. and Roberts. J. (2017) Exploring the Punitive Surge: Crown Court Sentencing Practices before and after the 2011 English Riots. *Criminology and Criminal Justice* 17(3): 319–39.

Piven, F. F. and Cloward, R. A. (1977) *Poor People's Movements.* New York: Pantheon Books.

Pizarro, J. J., Zumeta, L. N., Bouchat, P. et al. (2022) Emotional Processes, Collective Behavior, and Social Movements: A Meta-Analytic Review of Collective Effervescence Outcomes during Collective Gatherings and Demonstrations. *Frontiers in Psychology* 13.

Platt, A. (ed.) (1971) *The Politics of Riot Commissions, 1917–1970: A Collection of Official Reports and Critical Essays.* New York: Macmillan.

Polletta, F. (1998) 'It was Like a Fever . . . ': Narrative and Identity in Social Protest. *Social Problems* 45(2): 137–59.

Poole, R. (2006) 'By the Law or the Sword': Peterloo Revisited. *History* 91(302): 254–76.

Presdee, M. (2000) *Cultural Criminology and the Carnival of Crime.* London: Routledge.

Pressman, J. (2017) Throwing Stones in Social Science: Non-violence, Unarmed Violence, and the First Intifada. *Cooperation and Conflict* 52(4): 519–36.

Pressman, J. and Devin, E. (2024) Profile: The Diffusion of Global Protests after George Floyd's Murder. *Social Movement Studies* 23(4): 558–65.

Prins, H., Tennent, G. and Trick, K. (1985) Motives for Arson (Fire Raising). *Medicine, Science, and the Law* 25(4): 275.

Putnam, R. (2000) *Bowling Alone: The Collapse and Revival of American Community*. New York: Simon and Schuster.

Quarantelli, E. L. (1993) Community Crises: An Exploratory Comparison of the Characteristics and Consequences of Disasters and Riots. *Journal of Contingencies and Crisis Management* 1(2): 67–78.

Quarantelli, E. L. (1994) Looting and Antisocial Behavior in Disasters. University of Delaware Disaster Research Center Preliminary Paper No. 205.

Quarantelli, E. L. and Dynes, R. R. (1968) Looting in Civil Disorders: An Index of Social Change. *American Behavioral Scientist* 11(4): 7–10.

Quarantelli, E. L. and Dynes, R. R. (1970) Property Norms and Looting: Their Patterns in Community Crises. *Phylon* 31(2): 168–82.

Quinton, P. (2011) The Formation of Suspicions: Police Stop and Search Practices in England and Wales. *Policing and Society* 21(4): 357–68.

Ransford, H. E. (1968) Isolation, Powerlessness, and Violence: A Study of Attitudes and Participation in the Watts Riot. *American Journal of Sociology* 73(5): 581–91.

Ratcliffe, J. (2026) *Intelligence-Led Policing*. London: Routledge.

Ray, L. (2014) Shame and the City: 'Looting', Emotions and Social Structure. *Sociological Review* 62: 117–36.

Reicher, S. (1984) The St Pauls' Riot: An Explanation of the Limits of Crowd Action in Terms of a Social Identity Model. *European Journal of Social Psychology* 14: 1–21.

Reicher, S. (1987) Crowd Behaviour as Social Action, in J. C. Turner, M. A. Hogg, P. J. Oakes, S. D. Reicher and M. S. Wetherell (eds), *Rediscovering the Social Group: A Self-Categorization Theory*. Oxford: Blackwell.

Reicher, S. (1996) 'The Battle of Westminster': Developing the Social Identity Model of Crowd Behaviour in Order to Explain the Initiation and Development of Collective Conflict. *European Journal of Social Psychology* 26(1): 115–34.

Reicher, S. (2001) The Psychology of Crowd Dynamics, in M. A. Hogg and R. S. Tindale (eds), *Blackwell Handbook of Social Psychology: Group Processes*. Malden, MA: Blackwell.

Reicher, S., Spears, R. and Postmes, T. (1995) A Social Identity Model of Deindividuation Phenomena. *European Review of Social Psychology* 6(1): 161–98.

Reiner, R. (2000) *The Politics of the Police*, 3rd edn. Oxford: Oxford University Press.

Riots Communities and Victims Panel (2011) *Five Days in August: An Interim Report on the 2011 English Riots*. London: RCVP.

Riots Communities and Victims Panel (2012) *After the Riots: The Final Report of the Riots Communities and Victims Panel*. London: RCVP. http://webarchive.nationalarchives.gov.uk/20121003195935/http:/riotspanel.independent.gov.uk/

Roberts, H. (2024) *Loved Egyptian Night: The Meaning of the Arab Spring*. London: Verso.

Robinson, N. (2022) Rethinking the Crime of Rioting. *Minnesota Law Review* 107(1): 77–138.

Roché, S. (2005) Prevention and Security: A New Governance Model for France through a Contract-Based Territorial Approach. *Canadian Journal of Criminology and Criminal Justice* 47(2): 408–26.

Roché, S. and de Maillard, J. (2009) Crisis in Policing: The French Rioting of 2005. *Policing* 3(1): 34–40.

Rock, P. (1981) Rioting. *London Review of Books*, 17 September. https://www.lrb.co.uk/the-paper/v03/n17/paul-rock/rioting

Rock, P. (2023) The Role of Victim Advocacy in Criminal Justice Reform in England and Wales. *Annual Review of Criminology* 6: 499–527.

Roe, E. (1994) *Narrative Policy Analysis*. Durham, NC: Duke University Press.

Rosenberg, M. (1990) Reflexivity and Emotions. *Social Psychology Quarterly* 53(1): 3–12.

Rosenfeld, M. J. (1997) Celebration, Politics, Selective Looting and Riots: A Micro Level Study of the Bulls Riot of 1992 in Chicago. *Social Problems* 44(4): 483–502.

Rossi, P. H. (1971) The City as Purgatory. *Social Science Quarterly* 51(4): 817–20.

Royall, F. (2019) The *Gilets Jaunes* Protests: Mobilisation without Third-Party Support. *Modern and Contemporary France* 28(1): 99–118.

Rudé, G. (1964) *The Crowd in History: A Study of Popular Disturbances in France and England, 1730–1848*. New York and London: Wiley.

Samuel, R. (1981) People's History, in R. Samuel (ed.), *People's History and Socialist Theory*. London: Routledge and Kegan Paul.

Sandberg, S. (2008) Street Capital: Ethnicity and Violence on the Streets of Oslo. *Theoretical Criminology* 12(2): 153–71.

Sandefur, G. D. (1988) Blacks, Hispanics, American Indians, and Poverty –

And What Worked, in F. R. Harris and R. W. Wilkins (eds), *Quiet Riots: Race and Poverty in the United States*. New York: Pantheon Books.

Scarman, Rt. Hon. The Lord (1981) *The Scarman Report: The Brixton Disorders 10–12 April 1981*. London: HMSO (Cmnd. 8427).

Schlesinger, P. and Tumber, H. (1994) *Reporting Crime: The Media Politics of Criminal Justice*. Oxford: Clarendon Press.

Schneider, C. (2014) *Police Power and Race Riots*. Philadelphia, PA: University of Pennsylvania Press.

Schoon, E. W. (2014) The Asymmetry of Legitimacy: Analyzing the Legitimation of Violence in 30 Cases of Insurgent Revolution. *Social Forces* 93(2): 779–801.

Schuetz, A. (1944) The Stranger: An Essay in Social Psychology. *American Journal of Sociology* 49(6): 499–507.

Scoble, H. M. 1968. The McCone Commission and Social Science. *Phylon* 29(2): 167–81.

Scott, I. (2017) Bridging the Gap: Hong Kong Senior Civil Servants and the 1966 Riots. *Journal of Imperial and Commonwealth History* 45(1): 131–48.

Scraton, P. (2002) Lost Lives, Hidden Voices: 'Truth' and Controversial Deaths. *Race and Class* 44(1): 107–18.

Seeman, M. (1975) Alienation Studies. *Annual Review of Sociology* 1: 91–123.

Sewell, W. H., Jr (1996) Historical Events as Transformations of Structures: Inventing Revolution at the Bastille. *Theory and Society* 25(6): 841–81.

Shani, O. (2015). Gandhi's Salt March: Paradoxes and Tensions in the Memory of Nonviolent Struggle in India, in A. Reading and T. Katriel (eds), *Cultural Memories of Nonviolent Struggles*. Basingstoke: Palgrave Macmillan.

Shek, D. T. L. (2020) Protests in Hong Kong (2019–2020): A Perspective Based on Quality of Life and Well-Being. *Applied Research in Quality of Life* 15(3): 619–35.

Sherman, L. W. (2010) Defiance, Compliance and Consilience: A General Theory of Criminology, in E. McLaughlin and T. Newburn (eds), *The Sage Handbook of Criminological Theory*. London: Sage.

Sherman, L. W. (2020) Targeting American Policing: Rogue Cops or Rogue Cultures? *Cambridge Journal of Evidence-Based Policing* 4(3–4): 77–88.

Shirky, C. (2008) *Here Comes Everybody: The Power of Organizing without Organizations*. New York: Penguin.

Shirky, C. (2011) The Political Power of Social Media: Technology, the Public Sphere, and Political Change. *Foreign Affairs* 90(1): 28–41.

Shoemaker, R. B. (1987) The London 'Mob' in the Early Eighteenth Century. *Journal of British Studies* 26(3): 273–304.

Sides, J. (2012) 20 Years Later: Legacies of the Los Angeles Riots. *Places*. https://placesjournal.org/article/20-years-later-legacies-of-the-los-angeles-riots/?cn-reloaded=1

Sierra-Arévalo, M. (2021) American Policing and the Danger Imperative. *Law and Society Review* 55(1): 70–103.

Silver, A. (1967) The Demand for Order in Civil Society, in D. J. Bordua (ed.), *The Police: Six Sociological Essays*. New York: Wiley.

Silver, A. A. (1968) Official Interpretations of Racial Riots. *Proceedings of the Academy of Political Science* 29(1): 146–58.

Simmel, G. (2008 [1971]) The Stranger, in T. Oakes and P. L. Price (eds), *The Cultural Geography Reader*. London: Routledge.

Simon, J. (2001) Fear and Loathing in Late Modernity: Reflections on the Cultural Sources of Mass Imprisonment in the United States. *Punishment and Society* 3(1): 21–33.

Skolnick, J. H. (1966) *Justice without Trial: Law Enforcement in Democratic Society*. New York: Wiley.

Skolnick, J. H. (1969) *The Politics of Protest: The Skolnick Report to the National Commission on the Causes and Prevention of Violence*. New York: Simon and Schuster.

Slater, T. and Anderson, N. (2012) The Reputational Ghetto: Territorial Stigmatisation in St Paul's, Bristol. *Transactions of the Institute of British Geographers* 37(4): 530–46.

Smelser, N. J. (1963) *Theory of Collective Behavior*. New York: Free Press.

Smelser, N. J. (1970) Two Critics in Search of a Bias: A Response to Currie and Skolnick. *Annals of the American Academy of Political and Social Science* 391(1): 46–55.

Smith, D. J. (1987) Policing and Urban Unrest, in J. Benyon and J. Solomos (eds), *The Roots of Urban Unrest*. Oxford: Pergamon Press.

Smith, D. J. (1991) The Origins of Black Hostility to the Police. *Policing and Society* 2(1): 1–15.

Smith, H. (2019) View from Inside: Full Moon over the Stonewall, in New York Public Library (ed.), *The Stonewall Reader*. New York: Penguin.

SMSEC (Social Movement Studies Editorial Collective) (2015) (eds) *Occupy! A Global Movement*. London: Routledge.

Smucker, J. M. (2011) The Tactic of Occupation and the Movement of the 99%. *AlterNet*. https://www.alternet.org/2011/11/the_tactic_of_occupation_and_the_movement_of_the_99#

Snow, D. A. and Benford, R. D. (1988) Ideology, Frame Resonance, and Participant Mobilization. *International Social Movement Research* 1: 197–217.

Snow, D. A. and Benford, R. D. (1992) Master Frames and Cycles of Protest, in A. D. Morris and C. M. Mueller (eds), *Frontiers in Social Movement Theory*. New Haven, CT: Yale University Press.

Snow, D. A., Soule, S. A. and Kriesi, H. (2007) (eds), *The Blackwell Companion to Social Movements*. Malden, MA: Blackwell.

Snow, D. A., Vliegenthart, R. and Corrigall-Brown, C. (2007) Framing the French Riots: A Comparative Study of Frame Variation. *Social Forces* 86(2): 385–415.

Snow, D. A., Zurcher, L. A. and Peters, R. (1981) Victory Celebrations as Theater: A Dramaturgical Approach to Crowd Behavior. *Symbolic Interaction* 4: 21–2.

Sobol, N. L. (2015) Lessons Learned from Ferguson: Ending Abusive Collection of Criminal Justice Debt. *University of Maryland Law Journal of Race, Religion, Gender and Class* 15: 293–309.

Song, Min Hyoung (2005) *Strange Future: Pessimism and the 1992 Los Angeles Riots*. Durham, NC: Duke University Press.

Soss, J. and Weaver, V. (2017) Police Are Our Government: Politics, Political Science, and the Policing of Race–Class Subjugated Communities. *Annual Review of Political Science* 20: 565–91.

Spengler, O. (1926) *The Decline of the West*. London: George Allen and Unwin.

Spilerman, S. (1976) Structural Characteristics of Cities and the Severity of Racial Disorders. *American Sociological Review* 41(5): 771–93.

Stark, R. (1972) *Police Riots: Collective Violence and Law Enforcement*. Belmont, CA: Wadsworth.

Stein, A. (1955) Adolf Hitler und Gustave Le Bon. *Geschichte in Wissenschaft und Unterricht* 6: 362–8.

Stephens, R., II (2014) In Defense of the Ferguson Riots. *Jacobin*. https://jacobin.com/2014/08/in-defense-of-the-ferguson-riots/

Stevens, A. (2007) Carnival and Comedy: On Bakhtin's Misreading of Boccaccio. *Opticon 1826* 3(1): 1–5.

Stevenson, B. (2015) *The Contested Murder of Latasha Harlins: Justice, Gender, and the Origins of the LA Riots*. New York: Oxford University Press.

Stevenson, J. (1979) *Popular Disturbances in England, 1700–1870*. Harlow: Longman.

Stoesz, D. (1993) Poor Policy: The Legacy of the Kerner Commission for Social Welfare. *North Carolina Law Review* 71(6): 1675–91.

Stone, C., Foglesong, T. and Cole, C. M. (2009) Policing Los Angeles under a Consent Decree: The Dynamics of Change at the LAPD. Program in Criminal Justice Policy and Management Working Paper Series, Harvard: Kennedy School.

Stott, C. and Drury, J. (2000) Crowds, Context and Identity: Dynamic Categorization Processes in the 'Poll Tax Riot'. *Human Relations* 53(2): 247–73.

Stott, C., Drury, J. and Reicher, S. (2017) On the Role of a Social Identity Analysis in Articulating Structure and Collective Action: The 2011 Riots in Tottenham and Hackney. *British Journal of Criminology* 57(4): 964–81.

Stott, C., Ho, L., Radburn, M., Chan, M. T., Kyprianides, A. and Morales, P. S. (2020) Patterns of 'Disorder' during the 2019 Protests in Hong Kong: Policing, Social Identity, Intergroup Dynamics, and Radicalization. *Policing: A Journal of Policy and Practice* 14(4): 814–35.

Stott, C. and Reicher, S. (1998) Crowd Action as Intergroup Process:

Introducing the Police Perspective. *European Journal of Social Psychology* 28(4): 509–29.

Stott, C., Scothern, M. and Gorringe, H. (2013) Advances in Liaison Based Public Order Policing in England: Human Rights and Negotiating the Management of Protest? *Policing* 7(2): 212–26.

Suzuki, M. (1996) The London Apprentice Riots of the 1590s and the Fiction of Thomas Deloney. *Criticism* 38(2): 181–217.

Sykes, G. M. and Matza, D. (1957) Techniques of Neutralization: A Theory of Delinquency. *American Sociological Review* 22(6): 664–70.

Tang, T. Y. (2022) The Evolution of Protest Repertoires in Hong Kong: Violent Tactics in the Anti-Extradition Bill Protests in 2019. *The China Quarterly* 251: 660–82.

Tarrow, S. (1994) *Power in Movement*. Cambridge: Cambridge University Press.

Taylor, I., Evans, K. and Fraser, P. (1996) *A Tale of Two Cities: Global Change, Local Feeling and Everyday Life in the North of England: A Study in Manchester and Sheffield*. New York: Routledge.

Taylor, K.-Y. (2016) *From #BlackLivesMatter to Black Liberation*. Chicago: Haymarket Books.

Tedmanson, S. (2011) Wall Street Protests Turn Global. *The Times*, 15 October.

Thomas, N. (2002) Challenging Myths of the 1960s: The Case of Student Protest in Britain. *Twentieth Century British History* 13(3): 277–97.

Thompson, E. P. (1968) *The Making of the English Working Class*. Harmondsworth: Penguin.

Thompson, E. P. (1971) The Moral Economy of the English Crowd in the Eighteenth Century. *Past and Present* 50(1): 76–136.

Thompson, E. P. (1993) *Customs in Common: Studies in Traditional Popular Culture*. New York: The New Press.

Tilly, C. (1978) *From Mobilization to Revolution*. Reading, MA: Addison-Wesley.

Tilly, C. (1983) Speaking Your Mind without Elections, Surveys, or Social Movements. *Public Opinion Quarterly* 47(4): 461–78.

Tilly, C. (1995) *Popular Contention in Great Britain, 1758–1834*. Cambridge, MA: Harvard University Press.

Tilly, C. (2003) *The Politics of Collective Violence*. Cambridge: Cambridge University Press.

Tilly, C. and Tarrow, S. (2006) *Contentious Politics*. Oxford: Oxford University Press.

Tilly, C. and Wood, L. (2013) *Social Movements, 1768–2012*. London: Routledge.

Tonry, M. (2015) Is Cross-National and Comparative Research on the Criminal Justice System Useful? *European Journal of Criminology* 12(4): 505–16.

Treadwell, J., Briggs, D., Winlow, S. and Hall, S. (2013) Shopocalypse

Now: Consumer Culture and the English Riots of 2011. *British Journal of Criminology* 53(1): 1–17.

Trivizas, E. (1980) Offences and Offenders in Football Crowd Disorders. *British Journal of Criminology* 20(3): 276–88.

Truscott, L., IV (2019) View from Outside: Gay Power Comes to Sheridan Square, in New York Public Library (ed.), *The Stonewall Reader*. New York: Penguin.

Tufekci, Z. (2017) *Twitter and Tear Gas: The Power and Fragility of Networked Protest*. New Haven, CT: Yale University Press.

Tumber, H. (1982) *Television and the Riots*. London: BFI.

Turner, J. C. (1982) Towards a Cognitive Redefinition of the Social Group, in H. Tajfel (ed.), *Social Identity and Intergroup Relations*. Cambridge: Cambridge University Press.

Turner, R. H. (1964) Collective Behavior, in R. E. L. Faris (ed.), *Handbook of Modern Sociology*. Chicago: Rand McNally.

Turner, R. H. (1969) The Public Perception of Protest. *American Sociological Review* 34(6): 815–31.

Turner, R. H. and Killian, L. M. (1957) *Collective Behavior*. Englewood Cliffs, NJ: Prentice-Hall.

Twomey, J. L. (2004) Searching for a Legacy: The *Los Angeles Times*, Collective Memory and the 10th Anniversary of the 1992 LA 'Riots'. *Race, Gender and Class* 11(1): 75–93.

Tyler, T. (1990) *Why People Obey the Law*. New Haven, CT: Yale University Press.

Uggen, C. and Stewart, R. (2015) Piling On: Collateral Consequences and Community Supervision. *Minnesota Law Review* 99: 1871–1910.

Useem, B. (1997) The State and Collective Disorders: The Los Angeles Riot/Protest of April 1992. *Social Forces* 76(2): 357–77.

van Ginneken, J. (1985) The 1895 Debate on the Origins of Crowd Psychology. *Journal of the History of the Behavioral Sciences* 21: 375–82.

van Ginneken, J. (1992) *Crowds, Psychology and Politics, 1871–1899*. Cambridge: Cambridge University Press.

Van Maanen, J. (1973) Observations on the Making of Policemen. *Human Organization* 32(4): 407–18.

Van Maanen, J. (1978) The Asshole, in P. K. Manning and J. Van Maanen (eds), *Policing: A View from the Street*. Santa Monica, CA: Goodyear.

VanDeMark, B. (2024) *Kent State: An American Tragedy*. New York: W. W. Norton.

Vanderbilt, T. (2004) Follow the Crowd. *ArtForum* (Summer).

Vitale, A. (2011) NYPD and OWS: A Clash of Styles, in A. Taylor and K. Gessen et al. (eds), *Occupy! Scenes from Occupied America*. London: Verso.

Vitale, A. (2017) *The End of Policing*. London: Verso.

Vornetti, P., Fauvelle-Aymar, C. and Abel, F. (2009) The 2007 Presidential

Election and the 2005 Urban Violence in French 'Deprived Urban Areas', in D. Waddington, F. Jobard and M. King (eds), *Rioting in the UK and France: A Comparative Analysis*. Cullompton: Willan.

Wacquant, L. (2001) Deadly Symbiosis: When Ghetto and Prison Meet and Mesh. *Punishment and Society* 3(1): 95–133.

Wacquant, L. (2008) *Urban Outcasts: A Comparative Sociology of Advanced Marginality*. Cambridge: Polity.

Wacquant, L. (2022) *The Invention of the 'Underclass': A Study in the Politics of Knowledge*. Cambridge: Polity.

Wacquant, L. (2023) *Bourdieu in the City: Challenging Urban Theory*. Cambridge: Polity.

Waddington, D. (1992) *Contemporary Issues in Public Disorder*. London: Routledge.

Waddington, D. (2008) The Madness of the Mob? Explaining the 'Irrationality' and Destructiveness of Crowd Violence. *Sociological Compass* 2(2): 675–87.

Waddington, D. (2010) Applying the Flashpoints Model of Public Disorder to the 2001 Bradford Riot. *British Journal of Criminology* 50(2): 342–59.

Waddington, D. (2012) The Law of Moments: Understanding the Flashpoint that Ignited the Riots. *Criminal Justice Matters* 87(1): 6–7.

Waddington, D., Jones, K. and Critcher, C. (1989) *Flashpoints: Studies in Public Disorder*. London: Routledge.

Waddington, P. A. J. (1987) Towards Paramilitarism? Dilemmas in Policing Public Order. *British Journal of Criminology* 27(1): 37–46.

Waddington, P. A. J. (1991) *The Strong Arm of the Law*. Oxford: Clarendon Press.

Waddington, P. A. J. (1994) *Liberty and Order: Public Order Policing in a Capital City*. London: UCL Press.

Waddington, P. A. J. (1999) *Policing Citizens*. London: UCL Press.

Waddington, P. A. J. (2000) Orthodoxy and Advocacy in Criminology. *Theoretical Criminology* 4(1): 93–111.

Walker, R. A. (2013) Fill/Flash/Memory: A History of Flash Mobs. *Text and Performance Quarterly* 33(2): 115–32.

Wall, M. (2015). Citizen Journalism: A Retrospective on What We Know, an Agenda for What We Don't. *Digital Journalism* 3(6): 797–813.

Wambaugh, J. (1971) *The New Centurions*. Boston: Little, Brown.

Wanderer, J. J. (1969) An Index of Riot Severity and Some Correlates. *American Journal of Sociology* 74(5): 500–5.

Western, B. and Pettit, B. (2010) Incarceration and Social Inequality. *Daedalus* 139(3): 8–19.

Westley, W. A. (1970) *Violence and the Police: A Sociological Study of Law, Custom, and Morality*. Cambridge, MA: MIT Press.

White, M. D., Dario, L. M. and Shjarback, J. A. (2019) Assessing Dangerousness in Policing: An Analysis of Officer Deaths in the United States, 1970–2016. *Criminology and Public Policy* 18(1): 11–35.

Whitfield, S. J. (1988) *A Death in the Delta: The Story of Emmett Till.* Baltimore, MD: Johns Hopkins University Press.

Whyte, K. (2017) The Dakota Access Pipeline, Environmental Injustice, and US Colonialism. *RED INK: International Journal of Indigenous Literature, Art, and Humanities* 19(1): 154–69.

Wilkinson, S. I. (2009) Riots. *Annual Review of Political Science* 12: 329–43.

Wilson, J. Q. and Kelling, G. (1982) Broken Windows: The Police and Neighborhood Safety. *The Atlantic*, March.

Wilson, W. J. (1978) *The Declining Significance of Race: Blacks and Changing American Institutions.* Chicago: University of Chicago Press.

Wong, J. (2020) *Unfree Speech: The Threat to Global Democracy and Why We Must Act, Now.* London: Penguin.

Wong, J. D. (2017) Between Two Episodes of Social Unrest below Lion Rock: From the 1967 Riots to the 2014 Umbrella Movement, in M. H. K. Ng and J. D. Wong (eds), *Civil Unrest and Governance in Hong Kong.* London: Routledge.

Wong, K. C. (2019) *Public Order Policing in Hong Kong: The Mongkok Riot.* Basingstoke: Palgrave Macmillan.

Woodlawn, H. (2019) *From A Low Life in High Heels*, in New York Public Library (ed.), *The Stonewall Reader.* New York: Penguin.

Zimring, F. (2017) *When Police Kill.* Cambridge, MA: Harvard University Press.

Zimring, F. (2020) *The Insidious Momentum of American Mass Incarceration.* New York: Oxford University Press.

Index